SEARCHING FOR NORMAL

SEARCHING FOR NORMAL

The Story of a
Girl Gone Too Soon

By

KAREN MEADOWS

SHE WRITES PRESS

Published 2016
Printed in the United States of America
ISBN: 978-1-63152-137-9 pbk
ISBN: 978-1-63152-138-6 ebk
Library of Congress Control Number: 2016940083

For information, address:
She Writes Press
1563 Solano Ave #546
Berkeley, CA 94707

Book design by Stacey Aaronson

She Writes Press is a division of SparkPoint Studio, LLC.

In Memory of Sadie
For you, with you, and because of you

Flutes, Bagpipes, Sunflowers, and Édith Piaf

Sadie, if I could compose music for you, it would be an Andean pan flute song that evokes something soulful yet playful. It would be the type of song that mesmerizes you for its solitary beauty and its fragility. Sadie, if I could choreograph a dance for you, it would be an Irish jig —rhythmic, exuberant, and contagious. You'd leap, spread your arms, and invite all of us to follow you to dance with the bagpipes and fiddles. Sadie, if I could paint, I would fill a huge canvas with bright colors. It would have bright van Gogh sunflowers, reclining Matisse women, and a few wild swaths of bold splashes, like Jackson Pollock did with dripping paintbrushes, shovels, and pieces of rope. Sadie, if I could sing for you, it wouldn't be an aria but a tune sung with the deep, raw voice of Édith Piaf: soulful, ancient, and full of poetry. It would capture everyone's attention with its beauty and depth. You did that for me. You inspired me to look at life fully, in all its expressive facets. You embodied a spirit that embraced life in its soaring heights and depths.

—Written and posted on Sadie's memorial website
by Patricia Rengel, a family friend

Introduction

INEVITABLY, WHEN I TALK ABOUT MY DAUGHTER'S ILLNESS AND SUICIDE, people open up to me about their family struggles. People clearly want to talk but usually don't because of the negative stigma associated with mental illness. Baring my soul—opening up about my family's struggles with mental illness—frees others to open up as well. How could I judge others if I lost my daughter to suicide?

After my daughter died, I realized I knew very little of the mental health challenges that many of my friends and colleagues were facing, that so strongly shaped their lives, or of the suffering they and their families were enduring. Unlike some physical illnesses, mental illnesses are often hidden. People dealing with mental health issues do not have the words *mentally ill* stamped on their face. One person told me she doesn't tell others about her mental illness because, in her experience, they will think differently about her, and not in a positive way. She told me that she struggles with the idea of giving up her "privilege of being perceived as normal" to share those experiences and possibly help shift others' perception of mental illness.

Not only do stigmas about mental illness still exist, but it has become equally clear to me that because of these stigmas, people do not talk about their difficulties and therefore cannot help and support one another. Families, friends, and the mentally ill suffer as a result. My daughter and I were no different. Because of these stigmas, we did not talk much about what was going on with her and therefore may not have found the best help for her. That is a source of guilt that I will live with forever.

In this book, my daughter's voice, through her writing, provides insight into the depths of a depressed mind and the impact that seemingly normal adolescent interactions can have on a person suffering from depression. My voice articulates the challenges a mother faces when thrown into the foreign morass of mental health diagnosis and treatment, the difficulty of accepting that your child has and may always have mental health issues, trying to separate "controllable" behavior from behavior caused by mental health issues, and the horror that comes with the realization that you do not know how to help. It demonstrates the recognition that desire, education, money, resources, hard work, and love are sometimes not enough.

Our journey through life took an abrupt and completely unexpected turn when my husband, Dennis, and I watched our precious, precocious, fun-loving daughter slowly sink into the murky waters of mental illness during middle school. Over the years, she was given a variety of ever-changing diagnoses: dysthymia, depression, bipolar disorder, oppositional defiant disorder, anxiety disorder, attention deficit disorder (ADD), and adoption-related abandonment issues. After every diagnosis, we bought books on the illness to try to understand it. We consulted with "experts," but it was clear to us that even they didn't know what was going on in her mind and didn't know how to help her.

Some experts told us she should be on medication; others said she didn't need to be, or that she was too young to be on medication, since her brain was still developing. We tried medication, and we tried to navigate without it. Some of the medications made Sadie feel dull or caused weight gain. Some made her suicidal. We tried therapy, a therapeutic wilderness program, and treatment centers. After a while, we realized that diagnosing her illness and finding the right treatment for Sadie was more trial and error than science, and that the medical profession really didn't know what caused her illness or how to treat or cure it. She valiantly tried to help herself, but the depression and mental illness were stronger than she was.

Our roller coaster ride came to a sudden and horrible end in

August 2008, when Sadie took her life at age eighteen. Our beautiful, bright, talented, and troubled daughter lost her seven-year battle with depression and, likely, bipolar disorder. I know now that we never really understood the depths of her hopelessness and pain. Her death shattered and forever changed us. We lost what brought us meaning, and we lost our future. Society lost what she would have brought to this world. And while we tried to pick up the pieces, we have never found them all. Sadie will always be in our hearts, but she has left a huge hole in our lives. We will never get over her death and will always deeply treasure her, but we are trying to figure out how to go on without her. As the Alliance for Suicide Survivors website fittingly describes:

> Sometimes in life, events occur that fracture the very foundation on which we stand. Our life, as we have known it, is forever changed and we find ourselves in an unexpected struggle, first just to survive and then to move forward.

We tried many strategies to get through the days and months and years after Sadie's death—suicide survivor support groups, counseling, compartmentalizing our minds so we could focus at work and grieve at home, pushing ourselves hard running or biking, writing, sleeping, and crying often. Suicide survivor support groups are helpful to many but they didn't help me; attending allowed me to stay stuck in the past. Rather, it took many coping strategies and years of counseling and time passing for me to realize I needed to make something positive of our tragedy, to leave a legacy on Sadie's behalf. It is so easy to be consumed by grief, but for me, getting stuck in grief would suggest my life had become meaningless, that Sadie's life was meaningless.

So I forged ahead, reading books and scientific reports, searching for answers. I was trying to answer the "why" questions and to figure out what needed to be done to ensure that Sadie's fate would not befall others. I wanted to determine what role I could play to make that happen. I kept coming back to the fact that mental illness affects a significant percent of the population, yet most people do not realize it. According to MentalHealth.gov, one in five American adults has experienced a mental health issue, one in ten young people has experienced a period of major depression, and one in twenty people lives with a serious mental illness, such as schizophrenia, bipolar disorder, or major depression. This means that some of your neighbors, coworkers, friends, and people sitting next to you at the soccer field are likely suffering from mental illness—though you probably don't know which ones.

My reading helped me learn about breakthroughs in genetics, molecular and neuroscientific research, and technology and behavioral science over the last twenty years that have resulted in significant gains in our understanding of the complexities of mental health disorders. This work is allowing earlier diagnoses, uncovering new classes of drugs and therapeutic treatment, and improving our understanding of the link between genetics and mental health. Technology is allowing doctors and scientists to see differences in the brain activity of people with mental illness and to expand their understanding of the complex neural circuits that become disordered in mental illness. These developments are clarifying the interactions between the brain, behavior, and environment. Importantly, all these developments give me hope. While many of my "why" questions still have no answers today, I believe that these advances have set a solid foundation for more accelerated progress toward treatment and cures—*if* sufficient funding is allocated to the necessary research. But how to make that happen?

As I thought about what to do, I wished I were an accomplished orator, someone who could stand up in a crowd or in front of legislators and, with just the power of my words, convince people to contribute billions of dollars to mental health research. But I am not that person. Rather, each of us needs to figure out how to have a positive impact in our own way. I decided I should leverage my analytical and leadership skills in some way that would not only help me through the grief process but also generate awareness about the impact of mental illness on society and influence others to push for and support funding for research. To best accomplish that, I decided to write this book. At least this is a start.

I could write an entire book on my journey through the grief process—the shock, the denial, the guilt, the profound sadness, the attempts to determine how to move on in life without Sadie. But talking about my grief won't help someone else avoid Sadie's fate; it won't change the trajectory of new developments. So, while grief spurred this book and grief was my companion writing this book, the book is not about grief.

Rather, this book will show you what a horrible disease depression is, how depression and other mental illnesses can and do hit normal, happy families, and the devastation it leaves in its wake. The book describes the shortcomings of our nation's mental health services and the shortcomings of the medical and scientific communities' knowledge of how to diagnose and treat mental illness effectively, without dampening or destroying the creative gifts those suffering from it may have. While I highlight the poor state of our mental health knowledge and treatment approaches, I also provide useful resources and strategies for helping yourself or your loved ones today and share some of the recent new initiatives and developments that should give us all hope that the future will bring better diagnosis, treatment, and cures. Most importantly, I end this book with a call to action.

My hope in writing this book is that others dealing with mental illness will decide to open up and talk about what is going on, and that by doing so, we will help break the stigmas and start to realize that people's mental well-being is as important as their physical well-being. That mental illnesses are as real as physical illnesses. That, just as happened with breast cancer and Race for the Cure, we can create grassroots efforts to bring the pain and cost of mental illness to the forefront of our public consciousness—efforts that will result in more funding for research and, ultimately, better treatment and eventual cures.

Writing this book is what I can do. This is my role in helping to achieve the National Institute of Mental Health's (NIMH's) laudable vision of "a world in which mental illnesses are prevented and cured."

That is the genesis of this book and of Sadie's legacy.

1

——

Storybook Beginning

WE FELT THE UNFAIRNESS OF THE SCRUTINY, FELT ANGRY ABOUT HAVING to go through a bureaucratic process when other people could just get pregnant and have a baby. But that was just the way it was. Dennis and I were fortunate; our lives were good. Except we wanted a family. So, in our typical, matter-of-fact, engineering way, we took on the challenge.

If you haven't been in this situation, it is not uncommon to do some soul searching, as we did. *Why do we want children? Do we just love children? Do we want to propagate our genetic line?* Well, we both believed children would enrich our lives. They would keep us young and could give us a sense of purpose. We also felt we had a lot of love to give and decided a child (or two) would make our lives complete. For us, that meant adoption.

You have to really want children to go through the adoption process. Rather than just being able to choose to get pregnant and produce a child, you have to go through a security check to make sure you are not a criminal or child abuser, and a home study to be sure your residence is adequate; you have to provide personal references, and you have to market yourself to prospective birth mothers. In other words, you get put under a microscope and examined to make sure you are "fit" to be a parent, that someone else thinks you are good enough—in fact, the best person—to raise their child.

So Dennis and I put together a photo album of our lives and wrote a letter to potential birth mothers explaining why we would be the best parents for their child. We opened up our lives to public scrutiny, to be sorted through and picked over, and eventually an adoption agency deemed us worthy. Then, within a year, a birth mother chose us to adopt her child and invited us to be part of the birth process. How lucky we felt! We liked her. I went through Lamaze training with her. We were with her during labor and with her in the birth room of a Tacoma, Washington, hospital, when Sadie was born, on July 3, 1990. Three days later, we took her home and the rest of the world faded into the background. Sadie provided constant wonder and joy. Life just got better every day with her.

The next four years, living in Olympia, Washington, we basked in parenthood. My best friend had children about Sadie's age. We both worked three days a week and spent many hours with the kids at the playground, at the beach, going on short hikes in the damp, green, heavily forested Pacific Northwest, searching for salamanders in the creeks and worms under rocks, reading books, and singing kid songs like "Baby Beluga" and "Banana-fana Fo-fana." I had it all: a wonderful daughter, a professional job that I was able to do part-time, a husband, and a good friend to share it all with. We even invited Sadie's birth mother to Sadie's birthday party each year, choosing to stay connected, thinking Sadie would want to meet her someday.

And Sadie—well, she was a unique girl even at a very young age, extremely bright, funny, and passionate about life. If the kids wondered what it would be like to put a piece of pea gravel in your nose, Sadie would try it. If the kids wanted to bury someone in the sand, Sadie would volunteer. She always had to climb to the top of the playground structure. If I asked her to hold on to the handrails on her stroller when were going downhill, she would let go, raise her hands above her head, and shriek, "Yahoo! Faster, Mom!" When she was two and a half, I couldn't skip a word in a book I was reading to her without her saying, "You missed a word, Mom." After some outing with her son and Sadie when the kids were toddlers, my best friend said, "Sadie just marches to the beat of her own drum." Even at age three! She loved who she was. I loved who she was.

Even though we were happy and fulfilled, Dennis and I were always looking for our next adventure and for even greener grass. During the winter of Sadie's fourth year, we had twenty-eight days straight in Olympia with no sun. Twenty-eight days! Maybe I had seasonal affective disorder, or maybe I just wanted more sun. Whatever the reason, that interval sent me over the edge. I applied for and was offered a job in San Francisco, so we decided to move to a small town north of the city, Mill Valley, just before Sadie turned four. We figured it would give her a chance to get to know some of my family—including her grandparents—and, of course, we would have sunshine.

The relocation was a little harder for Sadie than we expected. Perhaps it was because I took a full-time job, or because we put her in a French immersion school, or just because everything was new and different and she had to leave her little friends behind. For the first couple of weeks in our new house, no matter how quiet I tried to be, she would wake up as I was getting ready for work and would hold on to my leg as I tried to leave, begging me to stay home. It was utterly heart-wrenching; each morning, I headed out in tears. Fortunately, rather than working full-time, Dennis decided to go to art school, so he was home before and after preschool for Sadie, and that seemed to ease the transition. Sadie, ever outgoing, eventually recovered from the move and made new friends. She actually recovered more quickly than I. It was hard to have to go to work when I knew Dennis and Sadie were home in the afternoons, playing and enjoying the sun.

When I wasn't at work, we spent much of our time outdoors, biking, hiking, or playing at the beach. The front yard of our small house was surrounded by fragrant honeysuckle and housed a large lemon tree that seemed to constantly produce dozens and dozens of lemons. Sadie and her neighborhood friends loved sitting out there, making lemonade and delivering the extra fruit to all the neighbors. If I close my eyes, I can still smell the gentle sweetness of the honey-suckle and hear the girls laughing on the patio, squeezing one lemon after another, the juice spraying a sticky layer on their clothes and skin. At least some of it made it into the pitcher for lemonade that they could sell at their street stand.

One day when I came home from work, five-year-old Sadie told me that she was going to take me biking up to the top of nearby Mount Tamalpais the upcoming weekend. She knew I had been wanting to bike the dirt trail and decided she would lead the way on her sixteen-inch kids' bike. I didn't really think she could make it, but she was so proud to be "guiding" me up the mountain, I didn't want to discourage her. That hot, sunny Saturday morning, Sadie, Dennis, and I headed out on our bikes. By the time we were halfway up the two-thousand-foot climb, Sadie's face was beet red from the heat and exertion, but she was determined to make it to the top and wouldn't stop. We finally convinced her that we could cut over to the road midway up and head home for some ice-cold water, and could drive back to the halfway point the next day to finish the ride.

After three years in Mill Valley, I wanted more time with Sadie, so it was once again time to roll. I got a great job in Madison, Wisconsin, just two hours from Dennis's hometown, where Sadie's other grandparents and relatives lived. I could work fewer hours each day, reduce my commute time from an hour each way to just ten minutes, and not have to travel so much. The summer before Sadie's second-grade year, we moved to the Village of Shorewood Hills—a small village bound by the University of Wisconsin, Lake Mendota, and the city of Madison. Dennis got a job working just a mile from our new home.

The move went very smoothly, and, once again, Sadie adjusted very rapidly to her new home and made fast friends in the neighborhood. The extra time I had with Sadie and Dennis was spent exploring our new neighborhood, meeting the parents of Sadie's new friends, doing little sewing or cooking projects—just playing together. So much time went by without any problems that we couldn't have imagined what awaited our little girl.

Never a Dull Moment

The seven years we were in Madison turned out to be like living in *Leave It to Beaver* Land. On a typical summer day when she was in elementary school, Sadie would pop out of bed, pull on her team Speedo swimsuit, grab her towel and swim cap, and wheel her bike out of the basement. Sometimes I would get her to eat a banana, but most often she would say, "I'm not hungry, Mom." So, along with a change of clothes, her father or I would put a snack into her daypack for her to eat after swim practice. If she remembered (or if I was vigilant), she would put on her bicycle helmet, then zoom down the driveway on her bike to the pool a few blocks away. Early mornings were usually beautiful in Madison—blue skies, not yet too hot or too humid. The outdoor pool was Olympic size, and it seemed as if every child living in our village was on the swim team starting in second grade. That was one of the great things about Shorewood—all were welcome.

After practice, the girls would sit on the lounge chairs around the edge of the pool, warming up and eating their snacks. Then it was off to drama. Sadie loved theater, because—as she told me years later—she could be anyone other than herself. In her elementary-school days, however, I think she just loved acting and singing. A woman named Lynn ran the Shorewood theater program. She broke the kids into different age groups, and each group put on a performance at the end of the summer, onstage at the local high school. I don't know how Lynn managed so many young, energetic kids, but somehow she was able, year after year, to corral them through daily practice and into creating a pretty good production.

After theater practice, Sadie would hop back on her bike and head home for lunch. During the summers, we hired someone to be around all day while Dennis and I were at work, to make sure Sadie got from one activity to another. Most summers, we hired someone from the French House, a Francophone cultural center and a private residence hall for French-speaking university students, or a French exchange student to help Sadie keep up her language skills. After three years at the Lycée Français in California, Sadie was fluent in French (although she had only a first-grade vocabulary), and we didn't want her to lose that skill.

After lunch, Sadie would get back on her bike and head to the elementary school around the corner for its afternoon recreation program. The kids would play games: dodgeball, softball, tug-of-war. Again, most of the kids in Shorewood participated, and all seemed to love it.

By midafternoon, Sadie would come home, relax, and curl up with a book; she was a voracious reader. One evening a week, she played on one of the many Shorewood Hills children's softball teams. On softball night, parents would gather at the school field, where the kids would don their colored team T-shirts. There were usually four games going on at the same time in different corners of the field. The parents hung out on the sidelines, chatting and cheering on their kids. Everyone enjoyed being outside on those beautiful summer evenings.

On nights when there was no softball, the kids often gathered to play hide-and-seek or kick the can in the streets. Usually one kid (often Sadie) would get the game started; the initiator would run from door to door, saying, "Let's meet in front of Jamie's house!" Soon, kids would start running out of their houses, all heading to Jamie's to play. Eventually, they would get thirsty or hungry and would all descend on one of their parents' houses for a snack. More often than not, we would have to call or head over to Jamie's street to tell the kids it was time for bed.

Once school started, all these summer activities ended and it was time for frolicking in the autumn leaves and playing soccer. When winter came, the Village flooded the school field for ice skating and ice hockey, and the kids spent hours sliding down bumpy tube runs on the snowy hill near there.

A few events that occurred during these years really express who Sadie was and what our lives were like before everything became so complicated. They come to mind whenever I think of those days in Madison, I suppose because they remind me of what an interesting and amazing person Sadie was—and, equally, because they make me sad that mental illness snuffed out someone with such potential.

Otter Lake

Family vacations were always a great time when Sadie was in elementary school—when she was old enough to participate in the same activities as Dennis and me yet still young enough to enjoy spending time with her family. One of the vacations that she absolutely loved was our annual fall trip to Otter Lake, near Stanley, Wisconsin, with Grandma and Grandpa. Sometimes during those trips, I would feel myself standing on the periphery, thinking about how just watching her brought me so much joy. Those weekends had an impact on her, too; by the time she was eight, a typical day on one of these trips was a source of great joy to her. On one such day in 1998, after we settled into our regular campsite by the lake, the grandfather-granddaughter fishing expedition started. I stood at the lakeside and watched Sadie and Grandpa march out on the dock toward his trusty fishing boat. Her flip-flops clicked against her heels as she marched on the old, sun-bleached planks. The breeze stroked my cheek for a moment, and my lungs filled deeply with the menthol aroma that the pines breathed over me. I squinted at the boat—the two fishermen painting a beautiful scene. Sadie turned her head and beamed that dazzling smile at me, chin up. Her arm poked high out of her plump blue-and-yellow life jacket, and she bounced in her seat as she sent me a long, flapping goodbye wave.

When they were a few hundred yards out, about halfway to their lucky spot, I could hear the high hum of the twenty-five-horsepower Mariner motor echoing off the rock faces on the far shoreline. Sadie stood up and arched over the fish finder, toward the stern, her open hand shielding her eyes so she could check the screen. I can imagine the conversation they must have been having: "It's eighteen feet deep here, Grandpa!" The brim of his ball cap bobbed as he nodded to acknowledge her. He eased up on the throttle, and the aluminum boat with the black stripe lowered back into the water, slowing gently to a quiet cruise. Sadie leaped to the bow and peered into the deep water. She always hoped to see a fish below as they glided to a stop at the favorite spot. The magic spot.

Sadie turned around, and Grandpa turned his head forward. They were eye to eye. I bet the excitement pumped in her chest. Grandpa's round face changed for the moment. His no-nonsense mouth curled up just a bit at the edges. His smile lines squeezed into cracks at the edges of his blazing blue eyes. Sadie's eager hands wrestled the slimy worm as she slid the hook into it. Two minutes of struggle, and it was good enough. She swept her pole over her head, and the line whipped out far. The bright orange bobber landed with a splat and turned upright. The trap was set. She stared at it, now sitting motionless, waiting. And waiting. She must have been thinking, *C'mon, c'mon, c'mon, c'mon!* as she gripped the cork handle of her pole more and more tightly, ready for the moment.

The bobber dipped for a tiny instant. Then again. Then again. Then stopped. "Is now the time to jerk, Grandpa?" Sadie was still staring, watching for the tiniest little twitch in the water.

"No, not now," Grandpa said. She frowned, and her body again became motionless with anticipation, her muscles tense and at the ready. "Now!" Grandpa shouted.

She shrieked and gave a sudden yank on the pole. The tip launched skyward, and she felt the pulsation of the tiny fish fighting against her. Sadie reeled it in, and Grandpa helped her remove the hook from the fish's mouth—a bluegill. He clipped it onto the stringer, and it flipped and flapped as he lowered it back into the water for safekeeping.

She grabbed another worm from the bucket, slid it onto the hook, and cast out her line again. This time, she reeled in a small crappie. She pulled in one fish after another—fast enough to keep her attention for a good while. But eventually, when her focus wandered and she started to goof around in the boat, Grandpa signaled that it was time to head back to shore.

The boat glided slowly and bumped against the dock as they returned. Sadie proudly lifted their full stringer of small bluegill and crappie high, to be sure that I could see the catch from a distance. "Mama, Papa, look!"

We shouted, "Wow! Good job," and clapped our hands as I trotted barefoot onto the dock, to the boat. I helped lash it and unload the gear. Sadie still held the fish and would not risk the bundle's being in anyone's hands but hers. We gathered all the stuff, and Sadie led the way, in a hurry to get to the campsite and show Grandma and Papa. As I rushed to keep up with her, she launched into her high-speed babble, telling me all the details of the hundreds of exciting moments out there at her favorite spot and with Grandpa and how she was really good at catching almost all the fish that bit and how she didn't pull too quickly anymore when the bobber went all the way underwater and didn't they get lots of them and it was the best fishing trip ever. Grandpa smiled and winked at me. *She says that every time.*

At our cozy campground, Sadie jumped right into preparing the freshly caught fish. She stood on a stepstool between Grandpa and Grandma, all shoulder to shoulder at the old plank cleaning table, and I watched them from behind. Grandpa, on the left, passed each fish to Sadie as he filleted them. Sadie dunked them in a small rinsing bucket, patted them dry with a paper towel, then passed them to Grandma, who moved artfully in the last phase as she swished each fillet across her soft puff of breading on the wax paper. It was her age-old blend of corn flour and pepper, plus a little something that she called her secret.

Once she had cleaned all the fish, Sadie took a break, heading into the camper to read for a bit. She crawled into the upper bunk and curled up with her book. Just a quick little rest—twenty minutes or so—before she headed back out to the fireside. The fillets sizzled and popped in the cast-iron skillet, sitting on the grate over the fire at the perfect level of very hot. I knew Sadie's mouth would be watering as she breathed in the buttery-fresh aroma against the earthy smell of the wood fire. The sun was setting over the darkening silhouettes of the treetops.

Many years later, I sat in my olive-green armchair by the front window, the late-day sun beaming through the panes. I reached over to a stack of books on the floor to find something to read. There sat one of Sadie's journals. I lifted it and set it gently in my lap, and as I opened it slowly, I saw the title "Otter Lake." As I read her poem, I visualized those camping trips as a sort of slide show that flashed by in a rush of vivid moments. She was almost alive again.

Otter Lake

The dock creaks and sways as I run out on it
and sit down on the edge.
I can hear my mom chopping wood and in the background,
dry pine logs crackle in the fire.
I look out over the turquoise lake,
bordered with the sunlit pines
and blanketed with bright blue skies.
I see fisherman bringing in fish.

The sky is filled with cries of "I got one"
or "that's a big one!"
The boats start motoring in, and then everything is quiet.
Slowly but surely the crickets,
like a chorus of musical instruments,
add their music to the silence.
Then the sounds of dinner add their music to the melody.
The popping of fish is the percussion.
The chatting of the hungry campers
serves as the instruments and the crickets
add their chorus to the background.
I go into Grandma's camper and sit down to a dinner of fried fish,
Caesar salad and strawberry pastries for dessert.
Yum! It has been a long day.

The Dog-Wash Operation

Other memories come to my mind—memories of a girl who was so engaged in life, she was always getting into something. Then my thoughts become about how I never knew what she would be up to next. We never had a dull moment.

One sunny summer day while Sadie was on break after completing fourth grade, I was straightening up the kitchen and enjoying some music on the stereo. The songs drifted through the air as sunshine filled the sky. I was content with my task, and I knew that Sadie was outside, playing close by.

Popping out the front door to check on her, I saw Sadie standing on the lawn with a big, long-haired dog. They were both sopping wet. *A dog? But whose?* I wondered—we were a cat family. One of Sadie's arms reached over the dog's tall shoulders to hold it steady. The other was the arm in action, the hand rubbing in circles through the wavy coat. Then she stooped to grab the garden hose. Soap suds plopped onto the grass as Sadie sprayed down the dog. His ears were drooping, his head held down with concern while he shivered a little, but he stayed still. Sadie tried to control the pressure by squeezing her thumb over the cold, brass end of the hose. The uneven gush hissed and went sideways and then downward, blasting off the dog's back and straight into her face. She was squinting and giggling and laughing through all the commotion.

I let the door shut, hopped down the three porch steps, and took a few steps toward her. Sadie lifted her head and beamed proudly at me. I asked her, "What are you doing?" She stood upright, still with one hand on the dog's collar. Blowing at stray wet hairs that were clinging to her face, she told me that she was running a dog-washing business. "Oh, really?" I asked.

She held open her palm and turned it upward, then swept her arm in front of her like Vanna White revealing a bedroom furniture set. "You see? I have everything I need! Isn't this great?"

Strewn in a circle of puddles at her feet was an array of supplies: a bottle of shampoo, a little, bright blue bottle of perfume (who knew where she had found that?), a hairbrush. I noticed that there was even a blow-dryer on the porch, hooked up to an extension cord she had dug up somewhere in the garage.

A bright cardboard poster was propped up against the tree by the street, facing outward to catch the eye of anyone passing by. The poster was covered with splashes of large, colorful handwriting. I walked closer to the tree and quickly read the headline: "Dog Washing—Regular and Deluxe!" Deluxe was priced higher, of course. I turned back around and saw that Sadie still had her "client," the dog, by the collar and was rubbing a big, damp towel over his thick coat. She dropped the towel and let him shake off, his tags jangling and flinging water droplets into the sunlight like some wild, rotating sprinkler. This operation was clearly the deluxe service. The client dog was due for his blow-dry-and-perfume treatment.

The Palm-Reading and String-Cheese Venture

Another sunny afternoon, after my workday, I drove slowly along the quiet, shady streets that led home. As I neared the entrance sign of our quaint little midwestern village, I caught a moment's glimpse through the trees of some child jumping up and down with flapping arms. One more glimpse, and I wondered, *Is that my nine-year-old daughter?* I squinted and peered more closely, driving more quickly, and could see that, sure enough, the girl in a purple shirt and leggings was Sadie. *What is my child doing now?* I hurried ahead and then quickly parked alongside the curb. By now I could see her running toward me with a big, proud grin on her face. I called out, "Sadie, what *are* you up to?"

"I'm flagging down cars, Mom!"

I got out of the car quickly, a bit surprised. She trotted up to me, pulled my hand, and hurried me over to the spot from which she had chosen to wave down cars. She had obviously selected the place because it was in plain sight, so she could surprise the motorists with her dance. Our green cooler sat on the ground beside her. She bent down and flipped it open, and I saw string cheese inside. "See?" She giggled. "I'm selling palm readings, and if people are hungry, they can buy string cheese for an extra fifty cents. Do you want me to read your palm, Mom?"

I never could have imagined back then that someone so extraordinary and full of life could sink into depression at an early age or be in such internal pain that she would end her life so young. I suppose that is one of my points: that mental illness may strike despite many things—despite decent parenting, despite a happy childhood, despite whatever.

Don't get me wrong—I have asked myself endless times, *What did I do wrong? Was I a bad parent? Did we move too many times? Could I have prevented her mental illness?* And I can easily think of things I did wrong—things I wish I had done differently—but, after a great deal of therapy and reflection, I don't believe we caused Sadie's depression. She had a good life, and mental illness still struck.

The Great Polar Bear Plunge

Exuberant is the word I associate most with Sadie's behavior on our annual winter trip to the Wisconsin Northwoods. There we would join eight or ten neighborhood families at the Afterglow Lake Lodge, a homey and warm and welcoming place that sat right on the edge of a small, forest-rimmed lake.

After the long drive up north, stepping through the lodge's big main doors was a wonderful scene. Next to a blazing fire in a huge stone fireplace, our friends waited to greet us. The knotty pine walls were aglow, bathed in warm lighting. Large, soft couches completed the inviting scene. We took off our winter coats and placed our pot-luck dish on the long wood countertop, eager to join the fun.

Sadie, joking with her friends, seemed to be in her element. They would run up to the counter in little bursts to grab a bit of food, then trot back to the action. The rest of us were scattered all around the room, talking and laughing and enjoying a big meal. Board games, singing, and good conversation carried us for a few hours.

Eventually, Dennis, Sadie, her friend Maggie, and I started yawning, as did others, so we said our goodbyes and found our coats on the crowded hooks. We headed out for the crunchy and crisp walk back to our cabin, our cheeks flushed from the full night of laughing and singing and shouting. Back at the cabin, we tossed our coats and scarves on the couch and headed straight to bed.

I woke up under our thick down comforter after a very deep sleep. Morning light came a bit late this far north, but I could hear

Sadie already shuffling around and whispering to her friend Maggie about the Great Polar Bear Plunge, already playing mentor and providing tips on what to wear and how it all worked. This was one of Sadie's favorite days of the year—she had told me!—but, then again, she had what seemed to be more than 300 favorite days out of the 365.

We finished a big, hot breakfast in the cabin, and the girls pulled on snow pants, heavy winter coats, cold-weather boots, and all the other accessories, excited about the first event of the day: downhill tubing. As families gathered at the lodge, we could see Derek, the owner, on his hefty bright red snowmobile at the edge of the forest, ready to tow kids to the top of the run. Tubing time!

We all heard the whir of Derek's snowmobile carrying the kids up to the top of the hill, two by two, with their tubes lashed to the rear of the machine and a stream of powdery snow in the air behind them and huge, open-mouthed smiles on their faces. Each time Sadie arrived at the top and her tube was unlashed, she would shout a big "thank you!" and instantly run a few steps, slam down her tube in front of her, and dive on top, swishing off at high speed. She never hesitated. I watched her drag her gloves on the snow to steer her route to the biggest bumps while whooping and shouting and prodding the kids at slower speeds to push it to the limit.

A couple of hours later, we walked the path back to our cabins to warm up a bit. After we changed into dry clothes, I quickly heated up some soup and the girls practically inhaled it. The cozy indoor temperature tempted me to try to take a nap, but I knew that wasn't in the cards—Sadie and Maggie were just too excited. In a flurry, they stuffed their swimsuits and towels into our big daypack. Dennis and I did the same. Seconds later, we were hustling up the trail back to the lodge, the kids running ahead and Sadie turning around toward us every few seconds, calling, "Let's go!"

When we got there, families were gathered in the lodge in the big room at ground level. The kids were getting antsy; some had already changed into their swimsuits. The adults reminded them to hold back until everyone had a suit on and was ready to go. The kids' breathing fogged the sliding doors as they pressed their faces against the cold glass to look out at the lake. Twenty feet offshore, a couple of men were working at the edge of a hole in the ice. One was swinging an ice chipper while the other scooped into the water with a shovel and tossed chunks aside into the snow. They were perfecting the work they had done with a chain saw the previous afternoon—the snap of the previous night's subzero air had put a pretty thick layer of fresh ice on the water in the hole. When the ice was clear, they laid down a skinny carpet remnant to create a sort of runway to the hole.

"Okay, ready! Go!" one of the men yelled, and his voice echoed to us as they waved their arms in a big signal. One parent echoed, "Go!" As was typical of Sadie, she had already nudged her way to the front, and before the door was even fully open, she squeezed her way out and bolted toward the lake. One by one, other people followed. She ran to the lake, down the carpet runway, to where two men—the "grips"—each stood on one side of the rectangular hole, ready to grab Sadie's arms (and then the arms of the next brave soul) as she jumped into the ice-cold water and then lift her back onto the ice. Everyone waiting their turn was chanting, "Go! Go! Go!" As Sadie ran across the snow, she shouted, "Dunk me deep!" She sprang off the edge, plunged into the water, and was submerged for more than a few seconds. Then the men lifted her up and swept her to her feet on the carpet and she beamed that big smile at the whistling and cheering crowd.

She took off toward the lodge, running barefoot through the snow. I knew she was headed to the hot tub. But then she paused, laid down, and rolled onto her back to make a snow angel. To Sadie, the icy prickles on her wet skin were a small price to pay; making fine art in the snow was priceless.

By late afternoon, part of the group, including Sadie, was still hanging out in the hot tub, steam rising everywhere, all talking big about their one unbelievable plunge earlier in the day. I could tell from Sadie's flushed cheeks that she was tuckered out. She turned her head toward me, and we locked eyes. I smiled back and winked at her—I knew what she was thinking. I had watched her laps (plunges) throughout the afternoon, from tub to plunge to a new snow angel, and I had counted eight in all. I shook my head in admiration and thought, *That's my girl.* That passion for life was one of the things I loved so much about her. It is people like her who make a difference in this world.

Now, after her death, when I see snow fall, it takes me to that moment. It seems like yesterday, and it seems like forever ago. The tears sting my eyes as a wave of powerful feelings—loss, guilt, and hopelessness—pulls me down. I try to resist losing myself as I spin downward into the blackness once again. I want so very deeply for her to be alive.

2

—

Inklings

I SUPPOSE OUR FIRST INKLING THAT SOMETHING WAS CHANGING IN Sadie came when she was in fifth grade. Something—though we didn't know what—was causing some of her friends to distance themselves a bit from her. Her teacher suggested we test her for attention deficit disorder (ADD), which we did. At the time, she scored high on impulsivity but not high enough on hyperactivity or inattention to be labeled with ADD. Nevertheless, for the shift to middle school, which was sixth through eighth grades in Madison, we thought smaller classes and more structure than was available in the public school might be helpful for Sadie, so we sent her to a private middle school for sixth grade—a school that one of her good friends was also attending.

The social dynamics of sixth-grade girls took us by surprise. The girls' behavior reminded me of that described in the book *Queen Bees and Wannabes*. This was not something Sadie was prepared for. Most of the kids had been at this private school since kindergarten, so many cliques had formed already. Sadie was acutely aware of the social hierarchy, which she described as comprising popular kids, wannabes (those who desperately wanted to be part of the "in" crowd), targets, and nerds/bystanders. She explained that the nerds and bystanders just did their own thing and didn't care about being popular, and also that she vacillated between all the social groups, except the popular group.

Some days she explained this in a matter-of-fact way, but other days she would come home and lie on her bed, crying. Although Sadie seemed to want desperately to be popular, she couldn't (or didn't want to) strip herself of who she was in order to achieve popularity. She seemed to constantly do things that fit who she was but that made her stand apart from the other girls, whether it was cutting her hair short when the popular look was long hair in a ponytail, or dressing in some unconventional way. Her poem "Gossip" showed how aware she was of the cattiness.

Gossip

Who am I?
I am Gossip.
I whisper and slither and slide,
I murmur lies and mumble secrets,
and watch them spread like wildfire.
I am the pathway from
the mouth of the betrayer
to the crumbling of the betrayed.
I tarnish reputation
and rust friendship,
I am vicious and unrelenting,
I am hard to find
and even harder to escape.
Who am I?
I am Gossip.

I hated to see how hard it was for her to navigate the social dynamics but was proud that she was her own person. Sadie had always been such an independent girl that I thought she was strong enough to find her way. But as the year progressed, she came home from school and cried on her bed more and more frequently. We considered switching her back to public school but decided we were not quitters; plus, I thought she would feel better about herself if she successfully found her place there, rather than withdrawing and changing schools. I was concerned enough to talk to the teachers and the principal, even though Sadie would have been mortified if she had known, but they said only, "We don't see the girls doing anything."

One teacher said she could see mean behavior in the boys because they were verbally loud or hit each other, but that the girls operated more subtly, so it was difficult to catch them being cruel. I can't help but feel as if that year had a significant and lasting negative impact on Sadie's self-esteem. Even today, as I write this, I feel anger boiling up in me; I think, *Who taught those girls to be so cruel?* But I suspect that most parents were unaware that their daughters were participating in such harmful behaviors. Today, we call this behavior bullying, and we know how persistently damaging it can be to fragile self-esteem. This "queen bee" dynamic needs to stop. Parents and teachers all need to talk about the impact that bullying and other subtle but mean behavior has on others and to emphasize to children the importance of valuing differences and treating one another respectfully.

Sadie retreated into her writing—journals, poems in notebooks and on crumbled scraps of paper—as a way to deal with the difficult social scene at school. I didn't read what she wrote unless she offered it, because I thought she deserved her privacy. Years after her death, I found a volume of private journal entries and poems that she had written and that reflected her inner pain and turmoil. Now I know the extent of her unhappiness, which wasn't just a normal part of growing up, and how very alone she felt in her private mind and heart. And now I wonder whether I would have done something different if I had invaded her privacy and read what she was writing when it was happening. Would I have been better able to help her? I will never know, because these questions are unanswerable, and I have to try to stop my guilty thinking because it won't change anything.

Sadie's poem "On the Outskirts" describes her struggles with the social scene in sixth grade. I found it interesting that she wrote about changing her clothes and looks, as that is not something I remember her doing. Rather, I remember her dressing unconventionally. Perhaps this really shows how conflicted she was—how what she said she wanted was often inconsistent with her actions.

On the Outskirts

I'm always on the outskirts,
never fitting in.
Always so close to the popular crowd,
but never getting in.

People whisper about me,
spreading rumors and vicious lies,
and they never really seem to care
when tears fill up my eyes.

But still I always feel so close
to being popular and cool.
I never seem to understand
how these kids can be so cruel.

I change my clothes, I change my look,
I make a whole new me,
then I lock my personality up,
and I throw away the key.
And still they won't accept me.
I'm always pushed away.

But I keep on trying, because I hope
I'll be popular someday.

As the school year progressed, the other students' cruelty and Sadie's misery increased. The fact that she was overweight at the time made her even more of a target. One day she came home in tears from a pool party at one of her classmates' houses, saying the girls had yelled, "Tidal wave!" whenever she jumped into the pool. We knew something had to change, so we agreed to Sadie's request to transfer back to public school for seventh grade. And at the start of the school year, she indeed seemed much happier and was making and enjoying new friends. *Good move*, we thought.

Late that fall, we received a letter in the mail from the school. At a glance, it looked like all the others that we received every few weeks or so, with announcements and such. It was probably no big deal, so I slid it into the "read on weekend" slot in my old roll-top desk.

Saturday morning, I opened the letter, and the heading "Student Depression Screening" caught my eye. It was a notice from the vice principal to parents saying that the school would be hosting a depression screening for seventh-grade students. It was to be a fairly quick and easy questionnaire, and, the vice principal assured us, the results would be kept confidential; this assessment was "recommended for schools that strive for highest-quality health services for their students."

I was relieved that the school was conducting the screening and hoped that Sadie's results might reassure us that her mood swings were "normal" for a girl her age, due, perhaps, simply to adolescent hormonal changes.

3

The Screening Results

WEEKS AND WEEKS PASSED, AND I ALMOST FORGOT ABOUT THE school's depression screening. Then one day when I was at work, the phone rang and a woman introduced herself pleasantly as the school nurse. She then spoke to me mechanically, her voice sounding pre-programmed, to inform me that Sadie had scored very high for depression, based on the screening. She made a follow-on comment, almost like an afterthought and as though she were reading from a script: "Of course, you might want to think about getting her some kind of help." She thanked me and added, "Have a nice day, and thank you for participating." We said goodbye, and I set down the receiver.

I paused, eyes wide, and realized that I hadn't even been given a moment to ask a question like "What does 'getting her help' mean?" My face flushed, and I felt frozen. I stared out the window of my office for quite some time, thoughts chasing themselves around in my head. Later, when I was driving home from work, my heart started to pound. I was eager to talk to Dennis about the call and screening results.

"So, where are we supposed to go from here?" That was where Dennis and I ended up in our conversation, sitting in the living room, speaking quietly, after Sadie had gone to bed. The school nurse had left us in the dark. We wondered how many other kids might have scored high on the screening. We wondered if we should call the nurse back. We wondered if we needed to talk to someone else. We wondered if we should tell Sadie. We wondered.

Dennis and I decided to sleep on it. It was late and time to try to rest before we got up early for our workday. I lay down in bed and realized I had forgotten to brush my teeth, so I got up. I lay back down but minutes later spun out of bed once again to shut off my phone. I turned off my bedside lamp, kissed Dennis, and rolled onto my back. My eyes twitched and twitched as I tried to close them. Half an hour passed. I heard wind blowing and turned to look outside for a moment. I heard a dog's bark echoing from way down the street. I heard the ticking of the grandfather clock from downstairs in the living room. My ears started to ring; I was hearing little things way too loudly. Everything seemed loud. I could even hear my heart pulsing in my head.

I gave up. I wouldn't get to sleep. The news about Sadie had brought an endless tumble of questions and concerns and problems to try to solve in my head. I questioned whether the news from the nurse could have resulted from a paperwork error, or maybe just from a problem with how the school had graded the assessments. Sadie had probably just been in a sad mood when she'd taken the survey. Of *course* she had normal ups and downs, like every child experiences, especially through adolescence and puberty and all that change.

Oh, what a tangled web we weave when we try to deceive ourselves by viewing reality through the distorted lens of self-protection and denial. Now, though, when I'm honest with myself, I do remember more than a rumble of concern. I did have a bad hunch about Sadie's mood changes and had indeed wondered whether something was a little "off" for her; I was afraid about the times she seemed so sad when she came home from school and lay on her bed, either silent or crying. I had hoped privately that the depression screening might reveal to us something that would give us insight about our daughter.

It is so perplexing, so tormenting, so unthinkable now. How could I not have allowed myself to accept the possibility that Sadie had a serious problem? One of her poems, entitled "So Why Bother?" (which I believe she wrote in seventh grade but which I found only after her death), reflects how much she was struggling. In retrospect, her pain was far deeper than what would have been normal for a person her age.

So Why Bother?

So much blood in the world.
So much pain to live through.
Why bother?
Too much darkness to live through.
The light at the end of the tunnel
has shorted out.
So why bother?
There's no love in the world,
nobody to care,
evil has taken over.
So why bother?
Happiness is a thing of the past,
no reason to live.
So why bother?

Over the few days after we got the screening results, we moved quickly through the surprise and the denial and then looked hard at the risk of not acting. Even without the benefit of seeing that poem, we knew deep down that Sadie was unhappy. Dennis and I continued to cling to the school nurse's statement "you might want to get her some help." We could not just let it lie, so we made the decision to seek medical attention as quickly as possible.

I was eager to get on the phone with a friend, a psychiatrist who I thought might be able to help. First thing the next morning, I dialed her number. I told her about our situation with Sadie and asked her if she had any ideas for us. She said that she could put us in touch with a Dr. Angel, who was the best adolescent psychiatrist in town and could probably help. She said that she would call her office right away. "Be a bit patient, until you can actually speak with her directly," my friend added.

The term "psychiatrist" had already intimidated me. *Is Sadie that sick that she needs a psychiatrist?* I thought. This was all so foreign to me. I went to work but had a tough time concentrating on my tasks. I was eager for the phone call and at the same time anxious, thinking, *What if Dr. Angel is not taking new patients and I can't get an appointment?* I tried to keep my "script" well practiced in my mind.

The phone rang, my chest tightened, and I answered. A kind-sounding woman introduced herself as Dr. Angel's assistant, Catherine. "I'm calling you, Karen, because Dr. Angel asked me to set an appointment for her to see you and your daughter, Sadie." She mentioned a few available time slots, and my heart sagged when I realized every opportunity was two or more weeks in the future. As I looked at my calendar, the dates and times seemed to spin in front of me, but I finally jumped to a slot that we could book, and then we said goodbye. The instant I set down the phone, I realized that I couldn't remember the date and time we had set. Panic set in. *Oh no—now I have to call her back. I feel so stupid.* I was relieved when, about sixty seconds later, I received an e-mail confirming the appointment details.

At work I felt entirely competent, but at home we were embarking on a journey into a very different world. It was a world of therapy, possibly even psychiatric medications—a world in which I had no experience. I felt inept—a feeling that would stay with both Dennis and me for many years.

Two weeks was a long time to wait. At times, we looked forward to the doctor visit, in hopes of some immediate breakthrough. Other times, Dennis and I asked each other, "What if the whole psychiatrist thing ends up being a dead end? What then?"

4

The Couch

WE WALKED INTO THE RECEPTION ROOM OF DR. ANGEL'S OFFICE. IT had nice chairs and art on the wall and more than ample seating for the six or seven other patients who were waiting. When we stepped forward to the receptionist's window, we were greeted with a tepid "How can I help you?" For a moment I didn't quite know what to say, as the other people lifted their heads from their magazines.

"We're here for an eleven-thirty appointment with Dr. Angel," I said in a hushed voice. The receptionist glanced down through her bifocals, raised an eyebrow, and said, "Since your daughter is a new patient, you'll need to fill out these forms. Here. Please pay attention to everything on both sides of the clipboard and just bring the forms back to me when you're finished." We went back to our chairs, and I was halfway through the form when I heard, "Mrs. Ladick [although I kept my maiden name, Meadows, I often get called Mrs. Ladick, which is Sadie and Dennis's last name], Dr. Angel is ready to see you and Sadie now." We stood up quickly, and I placed the clipboard on the receptionist's counter, apologizing for not having finished. She said, "That's okay, as long as you signed the release form." I thanked her, and my heart fluttered a bit as an unfamiliar but nice woman ushered us down the hallway. Most of the doors along the way were closed, and there was a hushed tone to it all. As we passed them, I saw a little Persian rug sticking out from one office door, a plush beige one from another, and unique placards that made each private office distinctive. One door was open all the way at the end, sending soft, filtered light whispering into the hallway.

We stepped through the doorway, and I was struck by the chapel-like quiet and the dark paneling and the couch. The couch. *Oh no—we really are in a psychiatrist's office*, I thought.

Dr. Angel was a well-dressed, middle-aged woman. Her glasses somehow made her look kind but professional. I felt comforted by her appearance and the framed credentials on her walls. As she stepped around her desk, she held out her hand to greet us. We traded pleasantries, and she gestured for us to take a seat in two big chairs. The empty couch sat to the side, some looming hint of the depth of the sessions to come. *Will Sadie have to lie there every time? This is all so unreal.*

5

The Dysthmia Diagnosis
and Hope of Zoloft

THUS BEGAN OUR WEEKLY APPOINTMENTS FOR SADIE AND HER DIAG-
nosis. Sadie willingly went to her sessions, and Dr. Angel said Sadie
did open up to her. The process lasted several weeks and eventually
led to an assessment of Sadie's "condition." Dr. Angel rendered a diagnosis of chronic dysthymia and explained its implications in detail
to Sadie and me. Fundamentally, the disorder meant that Sadie's
normal, basic level of happiness was lower than that of most people.
In general, over Sadie's lifetime, she could and would have happy
times and sad times. The risk with dysthymia was that when something happened that made Sadie sad, upset, worried, anxious, or despondent, she could sink lower than people without dysthymia, and
perhaps into a deeply depressive state. We listened carefully as Dr.
Angel also described the medical community's theory and knowledge about what physically goes on in the sufferer's brain.

Giving a name to what Sadie was dealing with made it much
more real. My already-shallow breathing paused as Dr. Angel recommended that Sadie start taking the antidepressant Zoloft. She
described in layman's terms, as best she could, how the drug worked,
talked about its potential benefits, and gave us a bit of hope by telling
us that it had achieved positive results in many patients with chronic

dysthymia. My throat tightened as she then gave us quite a laundry list of Zoloft's potential side effects. She handed us a leaflet and mentioned that it would be best if we read it thoroughly before Sadie started on the medication. I couldn't resist flipping it open immediately; I stopped on the page with the heading "Potential Side Effects," skimming over the first three or four items on the list, and then my eyes dropped right to the last item.

COMMON SIDE EFFECTS	RARE SIDE EFFECTS
Dry Mouth	Serotonin Syndrome–Adverse Drug Interaction
Drowsiness	
Dizzy	Hemorrhage
Chronic Trouble Sleeping	Hepatitis Caused by Drugs
Low Energy	Fever
Excessive Sweating	A Feeling of Restlessness with Inability to Sit Still
Involuntary Quivering	
Loss of Appetite	Rash
Weight Loss	Nosebleed
Head Pain	Heart Throbbing or Pounding
Feel Like Throwing Up	Abnormal Liver Function Tests
Gas	Reaction Due to an Allergy
Diarrhea	Low Amount of Sodium in the Blood
Stomach Cramps	
	Behaving with Excessive Cheerfulness and Activity
	Mild Degree of Mania
	Having Thoughts of Suicide

My lips parted and my jaw opened instinctively when I saw the phrase "having thoughts of suicide." Speechless. I folded the leaflet and leaned over to tuck it right into my purse on the floor, trying to show no reaction to Sadie or the doctor, but my face flushed and my hands started shaking as I sat back up and brushed my hair away from my face. Dr. Angel asked if we had any questions, and she glanced toward the clock on the wall. She paused briefly, as though inviting a question from us, but all I could do was look at her with my eyes open wide, slowly shaking my head.

"I'm afraid we're out of time for today," she said gently. "But please don't hesitate to call me if questions come to mind." She looked down, quickly jotted on the top slip of her prescription pad, tore off the little sheet, and handed it to me. "You can fill this at the pharmacy downstairs or at your preferred drugstore. We should also continue our weekly therapy sessions. The combination of medication and therapy works better than either treatment alone."

Dennis and I were not medicine people; we were believers in the idea of managing one's health primarily though diet, exercise, and stress management. I certainly did not want my daughter put on powerful medications that might affect her developing brain and was terrified about all the potential side effects.

At home that evening, Dennis and I sat at the dining table before dinner, talking about the visit to the doctor. Sadie was upstairs in her room, although I had asked her if she wanted to sit down with us a little bit. I spoke in a low tone with Dennis, trying to fill him in, and I found myself looking down at the table as I spoke. The idea of our daughter starting on a drug for mental health reasons still had me stunned, and as I brought it up to Dennis, I could see that he did not know what to say.

Our faces fell flat as together we read through the whole list of potential side effects. We both raised our chins and looked eye to eye in silence, speechless for a long while. "I really do want a quick fix," I whispered to him.

"I do, too," he replied, "but I'm afraid to even get my hopes up."

My mind raced in search of some fast solution, some big hammer, something I might have missed that could bring it all to a halt. I wanted to freeze that moment and just stop. I told myself, *This isn't really happening.* I wanted to shut my eyes, shut out my hearing, shut off my speaking, and just pretend the whole thing didn't exist. But the truth kept pushing and pushing its way deeper into my head. Fear washed over me like some ooze of cold black ink, and my head pounded.

We were out of our element, struggling for knowledge to guide our choices. The stakes were so high—it was our daughter's well-being. So, with tepid thoughts of inadequacy laced with anxiety, we set our sights on figuring this out and getting our daughter back to her normal, beautiful self. *Oh, can we do this?* we wondered. We just wanted Sadie to be happy. Our hopes would need to win out over our fears.

We were vaguely aware at that time that there was no right or wrong or surefire answer in this whole world of mental illness drug treatment, but I don't think we realized just how much the medical and psychiatric community did not know. I don't think we really understood how much trial and error was required to find medications that would help Sadie. Today, I don't even know whether her dysthymia diagnosis was correct, or perhaps it was correct but changed as she grew older.

Our psychiatrist friend had told us that children's brains are still changing at Sadie's age, and that, as a result, psychiatric drugs might have negative long-term effects for her. So we wondered, *Might some cobweb of side effects change how she would think and feel forever? Does the medical industry really know? Could we be causing irreparable damage?* She had recently sunk into a hopeless, despondent, dark mood. *Will she feel "branded" now that others can judge her and label her "mentally ill"?* Surely, the truth would leak out, and we knew about the enormous stigma.

The blow to her self-esteem could also be irreparable. We knew about the power of peers and friends and social structures at her age. *Might this labeling cause others to avoid her, bring her only more unhappiness, and send her into some self-fulfilling downslide? Would we have to blame ourselves for this decision?* Amid all the negatives, all the fears, we knew that we couldn't sit by and do nothing.

6

Zoloft at Work

THE WEEK WE FINALLY COMMITTED TO THE IDEA AND STARTED SADIE on Zoloft, it was late March, spring break of her seventh-grade year. I am not sure Sadie really understood the implications of taking medication, but she was hopeful that it might make her happier.

The three of us were soon to depart on a family backpacking vacation in southwestern Utah. Dennis and I debated whether to start Sadie on medication before our trip, in case she had a negative reaction, but the psychiatrist said it could take up to four weeks to see the full impact of the medication and encouraged us to start it.

We filled the prescription on a Thursday. When we arrived home from the pharmacy, Sadie and I set our groceries on the counter, and alongside them the little red-and-white paper sack, in unusual silence. I reached into the cupboard and then filled a glass with water. Sadie stood on the other side of the counter, alert, in a sort of preparedness for the event. She took the bottle of tablets out of the bag, opened it, and pinched one little tablet between her thumb and her forefinger. I did have a hint of hope for her at that moment, in that little pill. Yet I also shuddered at the thought that it might be too potent. *It could also be the start of something bad*, I said to myself. She popped the little blue, oval pill into her mouth, took a swallow of water, glanced into my eyes, and headed off to her room to read. The process had begun.

By Monday, four days later, we were in Utah, having spent a couple of days visiting Four Corners and Mesa Verde and looking forward to the hike that we thought would be the highlight of the trip. We pulled into the parking lot at the start of the trail and got out of the car. The red gravel crunched under our hiking boots in the silence of the high desert. We opened the hatch of our vehicle to reach for what we would need. We rooted around in our loose piles of equipment and supplies and then tucked them all carefully into nooks and crannies in our three backpacks. We locked the car, slung on our packs, and made final adjustments, and then we were off into Grand Gulch Primitive Area for the next several days.

After just a few steps on the trail, I felt my senses opening. It was a beautiful spring day with brilliant blue skies as the backdrop to the stark red-rock cliffs, still air, and warblers' bursts of happy song coming from within the sagebrush. The magnificent Southwest was putting on a show for us.

Dennis and I were both expecting the usual whining from Sadie as we started out hiking—*it's hot; my pack is too heavy; how much farther; I'm tired*—but just half an hour into it, having glanced at each other curiously several times, we were stunned by Sadie's attitude. She was the happiest we had seen her in months. She moved along at a good pace, commenting on the beauty everywhere, rattled on about the geology of the area, and floated airy questions about the hieroglyphics on the rock walls and what they might mean. She was bouncy, with a free and pleasant smile, walking briskly toward the next fascination. "Oh, I know how this rock developed!" she'd say with surprise. My heart warmed and I felt lifted; I drew deep and relieved breaths. It was the old Sadie coming back into the picture again, full of life and curiosity.

I was struck that she was in a good mood the entire trip, though backpacking was never without its challenges, even as soon as the first night out. We had set up camp and pulled out the food we planned to cook for dinner. I grabbed the stuff sack that I thought contained our trusty backpacking stove and its nested cookware, and my eyes bugged out when I reached in and found only a lantern. Big packing error. There we were in the wild, freeze-dried food spread on the ground in front of us and no way to boil the necessary water. We tried to heat the water over our little backpacking lantern, but lukewarm was the best it got. We had very little to eat that night, but Sadie just laughed about it, all the way through, as though it were some fun adventure. *Yes, she really is on the way back*, I thought. *The happy and resilient girl is still inside her.*

It was an amazing trip, and Sadie's rebound played the biggest part in it. As most any parent would agree, if your kids are happy, life is good. We just had to believe that Zoloft was playing a major role. Sadie was lucky that it had such a positive impact so quickly, given how long it can take for the drug to take effect.

For the next six months, her good mood and happiness and lightness of heart continued. One of many anecdotes from that time, the fall of eighth grade, sticks in my mind as a memory of Sadie's reawakened self. She was not a strong athlete and was especially weak in tennis. So it went for most sports, but she participated gamely. This particular fall afternoon at tennis practice, she was playing doubles against her extremely athletic friend and another girl, who was also quite good. They were making fun of Sadie when she missed shots or swung clumsily or whacked the ball out of bounds. The teammates didn't let any of that go by. Their bursts of laughter grew louder and more frequent, and their overdone scoffs and dramatic face making gained momentum with each of Sadie's flubs.

The coach told me later that she had overheard the comments and thought she might need to intervene. But when she listened more carefully, she was surprised—Sadie was just laughing along, with a big smile on her face. Eventually, the other girls must have thought, *Well, this is no fun*, because they just plain backed off.

Had Sadie still been depressed, they might have kept coming after her. She might have starting weeping inside or even just left the court. She might have been crushed for days and withdrawn to her room, feeling like an outsider once again. Not this time. Not with the wonder drug—or at least that's what we thought it was at the time. She was focused and bouncy and delighting in the game.

Darkness Falls

As the fall of her eighth-grade year progressed, Sadie's happier self began a downward pitch, like a small plane weakening and slowly losing altitude. After six months on the Zoloft, she was regressing. There were plenty of little signs, but no one thing stood out, though Dennis and I grew increasingly watchful, ever cautious because of our initial learnings about Zoloft.

But Sadie still had enough "good days" to make us hope that this was just a phase: Sadie and her friends chatting and laughing as I drove them to the local ski hill; Sadie and her best friend pretending they were different characters in a Shakespeare play, speaking with Shakespearean accents, sometimes for hours; Sadie making Niçoise salad for dinner while singing show tunes at the top of her lungs. Our fortunate life contrasted starkly with Sadie's depression in a way that was difficult to accept.

After each good time, our relief, our hope, our optimism grew, and for a little while, we suspended our concerns. But increasingly Sadie spent more time in her room. She sang less frequently, and when she did sing, it was not in her normal, boisterous voice.

Then the sad mood began to grow. The occasional good days ebbed to good hours (and even those occurred less and less frequently), then to flickers of a few good minutes that showed up a couple of times a day. By early winter, full darkness fell. Sadie's face moved to flat and fallen all day. She said very little; she was mostly withdrawn, silent. Her shoulders slumped further every day, until her arms fell limp at her side, and she moved with a sad and weak shuffle. She started eating huge quantities of food—seemingly in a desperate attempt to get some comfort or pleasure out of life. Eventually, she had chronic puffy eyes from weeping and losing sleep. We tried and tried to reactivate her "happy" self, sometimes wanting to shake her, awaken her somehow.

Our hopes finally succumbed to reality. Sadie had plunged into a deep clinical depression. The demons had invaded her head. A poem that I found later but that she wrote around June 2003 shows the depth of her despair; in fact, she even titled it "Despair."

Despair

Broken,
cobwebbed hearts
litter the ground.
I crumble under the weight
of the world on my shoulders,
punished for uncommitted sins,
hoping,
praying,
wishing,
for that moment
of relief,
so long in arriving,
know now
that I am weak.
For all those who enter
the misery of my mind,
let no hope survive.
For I have let
DESPAIR
take over the bleak outlook of my twisted mind.

Dennis and I, in perfect sync in our constant vigilance over Sadie, both concluded on exactly the same evening that it was time for urgent and strong action. We didn't know exactly what action to take, but it started with my calling and leaving a voice mail for Dr. Angel, asking that she call us back first thing in the morning.

Too Much of a Good Thing

The doctor responded and said that she could see Sadie just two days later. It took only that appointment for Dr. Angel to strongly recommend that Sadie's dosage of Zoloft be doubled. She wrote that prescription and added one for the drug Concerta, for the purpose of hopefully restoring some of Sadie's focus at school. Concerta is a drug that helps some people with attention deficit disorder. I immediately thought, *Focus at school? An attention disorder? Why add another drug, when of* course *she is losing focus at school? She is smart and often bored, and now she's deeply depressed!*

We had big concerns about tampering with the dosage of a drug—Zoloft—that we had once witnessed as so effective. And as far as Concerta was concerned, its potential side effects raised new alarms: "Tell your health care professional if you or your child has had depression, abnormal thoughts or visions, bipolar disorder, or seizure." Why would we add a drug that could potentially contribute more issues to our situation, only adding to a cat's-cradle equation that was already tough enough to understand?

Dennis and I went back and forth, each looking for leadership from the other. Could the "old Sadie" appear once again with more drugs, as we had witnessed on our backpacking trip in the Southwest? I couldn't help but hope. After all, Dr. Angel was the one caring and competent professional who had brought us to that miracle drug in the first place. So we eventually, uncomfortably, decided to accept her recommendation. We didn't question the diagnosis at the time and didn't know what else to do, and we couldn't just let Sadie continue to be so very unhappy without our taking action.

While Zoloft had resulted in a dramatic improvement in Sadie's happiness, it had really worked for only six months or so, and now it was not working at all. I can still feel the anxiety and fear we experienced at that time. We had so many questions rumbling through our minds: Why had Zoloft stopped working? Was Sadie developing a tolerance for the drug and thus would require increasing dosages for them to have any positive effect? Was her brain itself adjusting to the medication so that, even on an increased dose, it would no longer work? Would she develop a dependency on the medications? Should we really add another drug to the mix? Shouldn't we make only one change at a time to see how she would react? How would all these drugs affect her developing brain? What were we doing? Was our lust for hope just blinding us to all the wreckage we might be inviting?

Despite all these reservations, we decided to follow the doctor's recommendation, because Sadie was so desperately unhappy. However, rather than helping, the increased dosage of Zoloft seemed only to cause her to become more severely depressed. We of course wondered what role Concerta was playing in the equation, too. Along with her increased depressive symptoms, Sadie continued binge eating, and beyond the blatant behaviors we could see at home, she started gaining a visible five to ten pounds per month—no small change to a girl's frame. Her weight gain also made her an easy target for teasing at school, which, of course, resulted in increased blows to her self-esteem.

Her poetry from that time makes it clear that she hoped for our help—that she was trying to reach out to us. She even dedicated the following poem to us.

Loving Pain

A mockingbird sheds a silent tear
beneath a turbulent blue sky,
dust gathers on my broken heart.
A fallen angel,
shivering in the cold,
a scar from a knife,
stabbed in the back.
Fear and pain from a hurt long ago
prevent me from living again.
Through the fog
of my emotions,
my hand reaches out.
Will you take it?

We were weathering depression—the diagnosis, the successes and failures of one medication, the downside of mixing it with another—and now binge eating. We were tired, beaten. What next force, what unknown, could possibly add to the storm? Its howl would soon rise to a roar.

7

Blood Chases Away the Betrayal

IT WAS AFTERNOON, AND I WAS UPRIGHT IN MY OFFICE CHAIR, STAR-ing intently at my monitor and clacking away on a report for an up-coming team meeting, when the phone rang. The middle school vice principal, as she introduced herself, was on the line, speaking in a somber tone but at a hurried clip. She told me, "You need to come and pick Sadie up from school." My throat tightened, and my breath stopped. I pressed the receiver hard against my ear and asked, "What is it?"

"Sadie has been found in the restroom. She has been cutting herself. Evidently, she took a razor blade from her eighth-grade art class and—"

"*And?*" roared out of my mouth, with the power a mother uses when her child is in danger.

"She used the blade to cut her forearm," the vice principal mut-tered quickly, as though bracing herself for what I might say next.

"*What?* Is she okay? *Where* is she?"

"She's in the office. Please come straight here and ask for me."

I didn't even take the time to shut down my computer or say a word to anyone. I grabbed my car keys and sprinted to the stairwell door, barely touching the steps while flying down toward the ground level. The steel door above slammed in my ears just as I hit the land-ing. I lunged for the door, pounded the heels of my hands on the safety bar, and shoved the door open, nearly falling on the concrete sidewalk outside.

In my car, heart pounding, I drove faster than ever to Sadie's school. I parked, pushed the door open, and ran to the front desk. I shouted something as I pushed through the waist-high swinging door, five feet from the vice principal's office. I pushed through the barely open office door and scanned the room in an instant. No Sadie. "*Where* is my daughter!"

"Come with me," said the vice principal, as she clutched my elbow and spun me around. We rushed down a long hallway, heels clacking and echoing down the tile-and-steel tunnel of endless lockers. I squinted ahead through the sunlight glaring off the shiny floor, trying to see any gap along a wall that could mean a doorway or the next turn.

We stopped abruptly, and I almost tripped as we spun to face an entryway on the right, where a woman stood waiting. She pushed down the lever on the door, barely opening it as she paused and whispered, "Sadie has locked herself in a stall. Please come in, but be careful—she's already frightened." My vision zoomed straight ahead, and I could see Sadie's ankles and black shoes in the gap below the stall walls. My heart jolted and my head pounded instantly, adrenaline surging through my body. I stepped forward slowly, knees shaking, trying hard to stuff down my fear.

I paused and said softly, with a tight throat, "Sadie?" Another woman standing at the stall door moved silently out of my way. No response. I could hear Sadie's feet shuffle a bit, and I caught a quick breath, knowing she was at least conscious.

"Mom? Oh . . . . . . Mom," I heard her mumble in a shaky voice, sounding like a lost and frightened little girl.

"Sadie, I'm here. Are you okay?" I asked.

Silence lingered. The restroom went quiet for too long; then Sadie let out one quick burst of a sob and stopped it short. "Sadie, you're safe now. Let's go home." A sob once again, a pause. Then she broke loose into an uncontrollable flurry of weeping and gasping for breath. She was trying to say something amid it all, but I couldn't make out the words. I glanced to the space under the door and saw the blood-spotted paper towel, the bright red color against the whiteness of the paper blazing into my vision.

"Sadie, unlock the door!" I said, my voice overpowering hers. The weeping stopped. "*Please*," I begged. "Come out to me!"

Frantic, I raised my fist to the steel door and knocked, then jumped back, hearing the rattle of the door latch as she struggled with the lock. I froze, holding myself back from pulling or pushing or doing anything else that might add to the struggle. The door popped open, pinching its way into the stall, and thumped as it hit her body. Her fingers appeared now, gripping the edge of the door, and she struggled to move back and get out. It swung in farther, and I wanted to push through it, but I kept myself frozen.

Sadie wedged her way around the door, I saw her face, and in an instant I pulled her into my arms. We both burst into tears of relief. I shut my eyes and wrapped her against my body as close as I could. Our chests were heaving, and we melted together and nearly became one person.

My eyes flashed open, and I stepped back quickly, my hands now holding her shoulders as I glanced quickly over her body. I saw a wide, faint smear of blood on her forearm, and I reached for her wrist and pulled it up quickly to where I could see it. No gushing blood—just rows of tiny beads of red, showing as dots traced along thin lines of surface cuts. My eyes closed again, and I sighed.

From behind me, I felt a tap on my shoulder. One of the women edged her way in to us and handed me a bottle of alcohol and some white pads. I stretched out Sadie's arm, swabbed it in quick strokes, and dabbed it dry quickly, gently. The woman handed me scissors and a roll of gauze, and I unrolled it around and around Sadie's arm in sweeping circles, then snipped the gauze and tucked the end in. Sadie was clean and bundled and safe. Once again, we melted into a warm embrace. We held that embrace for a long, long time.

I remember very little after that, until the point when Sadie and I were seated across a big gray desk in a school office. We were light-headed, with flushed cheeks, and we leaned close together, next to each other in two separate chairs. I so wanted just to get Sadie home, but the vice principal was talking to me and trying to follow some makeshift "procedure" before we could leave the school.

I could sense that she was trying to do her best at her job, but this part of the conversation felt like a lecture. She said things like, "Sadie shouldn't have taken the blade from art class" and, "That's stealing. It's against the rules to take something from the art room, and you need to take her home." Sadie's head was bowed; she was gazing at the floor and silent, with tears rolling down her cheeks.

The blood rushed even harder to my face. I wrapped Sadie in my arms, pulled her up, and said in her ear, "C'mon, honey, let's go home."

The car felt somehow warm to me as we climbed in, even though it was only ten degrees, and comfortable, away from what had become a cold interrogation room. We drove home slowly, in silence. I didn't know what to say except things like, "Honey, it's okay now," and, "It'll be better when we get home." *Such tiny things*, I thought, with my daughter having just been pounded by that tidal wave of pain and incrimination. Sadie was shivering. Her tears had stopped, and now she sat dejected, head down, staring at the floor, brow wrinkled. I will never forget the sadness of those few hours.

We arrived at home and walked through the door to silence. Sadie turned slowly and shuffled toward her bedroom. I followed, hugging her whenever she paused, but she kept pulling away in shame after just a few seconds. When she got to her bed, she plopped down, spun around to face the wall, and drew her knees up toward her chest.

I couldn't help but say something, anything. I asked in the gentlest way, in a whisper, about why she thought she needed to cut herself. No matter how I asked, she either stayed quiet or tried to speak but could not get out the words to explain why she had done it. She would close her eyes, her lower lip would start quivering, and she would shake her chin slowly from side to side, as if to say, *Mom, please quit asking me, because I don't know.* I was ashamed that I had no approach, no solution to bring. My heart wrenched. I myself wanted just to weep.

I started saying anything that came to my head. I somehow brought up positive coping mechanisms—unbelievable to me now. I remember blithering about how Sadie could go outside for a run and that that would make her feel better. While exercise can be beneficial, I didn't realize at the time just how hard it is for people who are depressed to get up and make themselves be active, to summon the motivation to do something that might actually help. I realize now how I thought rationally about what might work, but I did so from my perspective—from the perspective of someone not suffering from debilitating depression. Eventually I got up from her bed. As I headed out of her room, I said, "Sadie, why don't you do your homework?"

My pitiful comments went unanswered. Sadie remained in a ball in her bed, and I remained helpless. Years later, she described the impact my response had on her: it made her think that I would never understand what she was feeling and why she cut herself. She severed herself then from the anchor—from me, from her father—and retreated into herself. She felt alone, totally alone.

It is now very strange to me that, upon discovering her cuts, I would have suggested that she do her homework. I suppose I just wanted to move us back to some sort of normalcy. But that mistake of mine still brings tears in an instant. I wish I could take back that afternoon, rewind the whole day, and put myself in that bed alongside her.

It was months after the incident before Sadie could try to express to me why she cut. Eventually she explained that when she felt sad or hopeless, she ate. When she ate, the shame of knowing that she was gaining more and more weight built inside her and she had to somehow relieve the power of the pain. Although drastic, cutting herself seemed to her to be the way to do that.

Years later, sometime around 2004, I found a poem she had written that described what she could not verbalize. It showed how cutting made her feel better in some unimaginable way, even if only for a couple of minutes, during the act.

Cut

I'm in pain,
but not from the blood,
I revel in it.
It chases away the betrayal
and washes away my fear.
It cleanses my body of anger
and hurt.
Drip, drip, I watch it fall,
as I realize
it's not enough.
It comes back
like a dark cloud,
so I do it again,
a long, red trail.
I sigh in relief
and wait for the dark
to claim me.

My failure to connect with Sadie's hidden emotional side was only the start of my shameful cover-up. I remember not wanting others to know what she had done. I hesitated in social settings, feeling sure that at least one person in any group would have heard of Sadie's big shocker at school. What was I supposed to say when one mom gleamed about how well her boy was doing on the basketball team or another was so pleased about her girl's great test scores in math? *Well, as for my daughter, she has been cutting herself?*

The more I withdrew, the more I continued my own spiral, convincing myself that I was an inept and undeserving mother. I neither knew nor had even heard of one parent who had experienced their child's cutting. Aside from Dennis, my pillar, I had nowhere to turn. If I talked to him about my shame, I felt as though I might impose that deep burden on him, too.

That miserable event, which I turned into something about me, was only the start of what would become years of silent suffering. Years of hiding what was really going on. Years of not having anyone to talk to about it, of not admitting to others that my child was suffering from very deep-seated unhappiness, and of feeling lost as to how I might somehow help.

Later, I discovered that a lot more people deal with similar kinds of issues than I had thought. Data on just how many youth cut or self-harm are scarce, but a 2012 study on rates of nonsuicidal self-injury in youth, published in the American Academy of Pediatrics' journal, *Pediatrics*, found that 8 percent of youth self-injured and that ninth-grade girls were at the greatest risk of doing so. Whatever the statistics, the point is that there most certainly were other youth cutting at the time Sadie was, but they were invisible to me.

I now understand that youth often cut to cope with or relieve emotional pain, hard-to-express feelings, or frustration. Cutting and other self-harming behaviors are a sign of deep suffering and, if left untreated, can lead to even more serious actions, such as suicide. But there is such power behind the social stigmas around mental disorders and illnesses that, in conjunction with my not realizing others were dealing with similar issues, it kept me from reaching out, from expressing myself, from seeking help from others in the secret community of strugglers. We, the parents and families of sufferers, missed the opportunity to learn from each other.

A number of resources described in the back of this book provide information on cutting, such as the article entitled "Self Injury, Self Harm Statistics and Facts," on www.healthyplace.com.[1] Some are designed to help young people who are cutting, such as the Butterfly Project (http://insteadofcutting.tumblr.com/thebutterflyproject) and To Write Love on Her Arms (www.twloha.com). You can also read more about self-harm on the Mayo Clinic's website (www.mayo clinic.org).

Years later, I empathize with the vice principal and her having strained and grasped for anything to say to us. Perhaps she had not had any training to help her deal with Sadie's kind of situation. While we don't know exactly how prevalent self-harming behaviors are, clearly, enough youth engage in them that school counselors, teachers, and other medical professionals need to receive training on how to effectively handle such situations, as well as on how to provide guidance to the parents of these youth. I certainly would have benefited from some guidance beyond "take her home."

8

I Swallowed Every Last One

THAT PARTICULAR MARCH EVENING FELT ESPECIALLY COLD AND DARK. Dennis and I were reading in the living room, and Sadie had been in her bedroom, also reading, I assumed. My attention turned from my book as it dawned on me that the water in the upstairs bathroom sink had been running a long time. *Why is Sadie letting the water continue to run? Has she left the faucet on and forgotten?*

I set my book down and went to check on her. I reached the landing at the top of the stairs and saw that the bathroom door was open a bit. I peered in and could see just the heels of her shoes, raised slightly off the floor. Sadie had stood in front of the mirror on tiptoes when she was in grade school, and now, even though she was in seventh grade and tall enough, she did it out of habit.

Projecting my voice a bit over the faucet noise, I said, "Hi, honey, how're you doing?" No response. I said, "Sadie," and still heard only the hiss of the faucet. I eased the door open, saying, "Hey."

What I saw stunned me. Sadie's face was covered with dark green makeup. In a whirling flurry, both hands pressed hard against her face, she was smearing and smearing the ghoulish paste. I moved toward her, and my eyes flashed on the chaos all around her—hairbrushes and toothbrushes and tweezers thrown on the floor, and green handprints swept across the wall. The toilet was open, with Q-tips and tissue inside it, and other objects were scattered everywhere.

I reached for her forearm and asked loudly, "What is going on?" She dropped her hands and turned to me, staring me down for a second with red eyes blazing wide open and a clenched jaw. Her hands were trembling, and she whipped her head back to the mirror, smearing and smearing in a mad spasm, stretching and slapping her cheeks. "*What is going on?*" I repeated, as panic set in and adrenaline blasted through my body.

She turned to me, looked at me blankly, and said, "Nothing. Everything's fine, Mom." She turned away, slowly bent down, and started picking up the items on the floor.

"Really, Sadie? You don't look okay," I countered.

I spun and rushed down the stairs to Dennis, out of breath, my chest heaving. "Something is wrong—really wrong—with Sadie!"

He leaped from his chair and rushed up the stairs ahead of me. He took one glance at her and said, "What's going on, Sadie? Talk to us!"

She looked at the floor, trembling, then raised her chin. "I took my bottles of pills, okay? I mean, I took them and swallowed every one of them."

"Hospital!" Dennis shouted. We both knew instinctively that we could beat any ambulance if we drove there on our own, so I ripped one thick wool coat out of Sadie's closet, then another, and Dennis threw them over her shoulders. The three of us ran down the stairs, moving forward and downward and almost falling. We eased Sadie, still trembling, onto the entryway bench, and I jammed boots onto her feet, struggling between moving fast and trying to be gentle, and ran to the car.

At the wheel, Dennis snapped his head around to look back, slammed the car in reverse, and swung down the driveway and into the street. He popped the car in drive, and the tires whirred on the slick snow and ice. *Go, go!* I shouted in my head, knowing that every minute counted, keeping my arms wrapped tightly around Sadie in the backseat. The windshield was fogging over, and Dennis was swiping it frantically with one gloved hand, trying to keep control of the wheel with the other.

We approached the front drive of the hospital, and our headlights flashed on the EMERGENCY sign. Our stop came with a bit of a screech under the awning. We quickly jumped out of the car, pulling Sadie along, and ran to the emergency entrance, where the doors whooshed open. We ran to the registration desk, and I blurted, "Help! My daughter has overdosed!"

Two nurses from the entry desk scrambled to roll a wheelchair toward us, and Sadie collapsed into it. One nurse spun to grab the handles of the chair and wheeled Sadie briskly down a shiny, wide hallway toward big double doors. The other trotted alongside the chair and focused on Sadie's dark green face and blazing red eyes; her eyelids had begun twitching, and her head was bobbing forward and down as she moved quickly into a dizzy state. I started to follow, but another attendant waved urgently at me to return to the desk. I complied, not wanting to stand in the way of my daughter's care.

My hands were shaking as I fumbled through my bag to find my health insurance card. "What? Where is my wallet? I'm so sorry—I think I left it behind! What can I do?" I pleaded.

I turned to Dennis and saw that he was already reaching out his hand, holding his card; he was more poised than I, and right there with the right move at the perfect time. "What else?" he asked the attendant. "And how soon can we see our daughter?"

"In just a few minutes," she assured us. She slid a clipboard across the counter toward us, and I forget what she said—all I heard was "forms." I guess I scratched down everything that I could think of, as Dennis stood over my shoulder, giving me answers whenever he sensed my memory blanking. "What is the name of that second prescription?" I was shaking and squinting at the form and then glancing every other second down the hall at the closed double doors. Amid the chaos of people in crisis, the emergency room, with its professional look and competent staff, provided some relief that they would help Sadie, but only time would tell us if we had made it in time.

"Now, let's get you to your daughter," said the attendant, after glancing to confirm that there was just enough information there in my shaky handwriting. She picked up the phone and asked the staff whether they were ready for us to come in. She nodded to her co-worker, who escorted us down the hallway toward those big double doors. "Is she all right?" I asked, breathing hard and walking quickly alongside the woman.

"The doctor is with her right now," she replied.

She pushed open one of the doors and revealed a disorienting scene: beeps and machines and blinking little blue screens and hot spotlights with gowned staff leaning over unknown patients with their bare feet sticking out from bright white sheets, and blankets thrown over them. Some people with surgical masks, others without—it was a beehive of workers in their blue pajama-like uniforms, nudging past each other and signaling to each other in brief and technical phrases. We passed by several rooms with glass panels that separated them from the hallway. One gesture from our escort, then one turn to the left, and we went into a small room filled with blinding lights and instruments on wheels and bags of liquid hanging from stands.

I turned and saw Sadie, her face under a bright operating lamp, framed by the backs and shoulders of doctors hunched over her. My breathing stopped. Her eyes were shut, but her mouth was open around a clear tube and, within it, another tube, which snaked into the back of her mouth and farther.

I wanted to rush to her but waited for a moment as one doctor stepped aside to make room for us to slide by. Upon a nod from him, I placed my palm on Sadie's heart and turned and said to her, "I'm here and Papa's here, honey. You're okay."

She looked to be anything but okay. Her face was now pale green under the fluorescent lights, still with some dark green makeup spots that had escaped cleaning off in the commotion. Her

hair was greasy and sweaty and strewn every which way on the pil-
low that propped her up. She blinked slowly and looked at me with
vacant, enlarged pupils almost blacking out her brown eyes. I
thought she might be trying to smile, but maybe she was wincing, or
maybe someone was pulling on a tube that was moving her lip.

I glanced down along her body, her palms face-up and even
more tubes in her arms, with needle nozzles making bumps under
patches of surgical tape. Needles and tubes surrounded by the thin
scars from when she had cut herself. Tape on top of needles on top
of slices and scars. Urgency on top of tragedy. My daughter looked
like some sweet and innocent and helpless and motionless voodoo
doll, flat on her back.

They had pumped her stomach. They monitored her for several
hours, until the staff and the supervising doctor deemed her recovered and in safe health. Although she was out of the woods, the
doctor made sure to emphasize the severity of what had happened
and how destructive the effects could have been.

Once she was resting comfortably, a new person from the hospital
staff came from around the curtain and introduced herself as Sara.
She said that she'd like to have Sadie lie back a bit and asked that
we step out with her to cover some release details. I nodded and
stood up slowly, kissed Sadie on the forehead, and whispered to her,
"*Breathe deep.* We'll be right back." Sara opened a different door for
us, smiled, and said, "This way, please."

It was quiet and soothing in the hallway, almost silent compared
with the noise and the chaos of the emergency room. Sara invited us
into a small, private room to talk and introduced herself as a psychiatric nurse at the hospital.

She asked us broad and exploratory questions about what we
thought had happened, what we thought had caused the incident,
and about Sadie's life in general. I sensed that she was also trying to
detect whether Sadie might have been subject to any abuse or neglect. I thought, *I don't believe this is happening. I was afraid for my*

daughter's life, and now I have to defend my parenting? My face grew
flushed; my answers became blunt. I wanted to get out of there, get
back to my daughter's side. I was sure Sara could sense that I was
frustrated and eager to leave; she picked up the pace of her questioning, and we soon finished.

We burst through the doors and once again joined Sadie. She
looked so relieved to see our faces. Her mouth was now free of
tubes, and someone had brushed her hair, but her eyes were sad,
plaintive, remorseful. I looked over her body—no more needles, no
more tubes, no more sensor clipped on her finger. My heart gushed,
and I wanted to weep. I laid my head softly on her chest, and we
both breathed deeply, suspended in a couple of minutes of safety,
relief, and exhaustion.

Then another new face summoned us: a tall man in a white coat
with a gentle smile and a calm, smooth manner. He asked if Dennis
and I could join him for a moment in private while the staff helped
Sadie gather her things and got her ready to go home soon. "We just
need to chat for a bit," he said.

We followed the doctor in the white coat, once again down a
hallway, and soon were seated in a much bigger office, in two comfortable chairs across from his large desk. He sat down, smiled, and
put on his reading glasses, flipping through charts and papers that I
thought must have included the narrative from our questioning by
the psychiatric nurse. Sure enough, Sara soon appeared in the doorway and stood leaning against the threshold, her arms crossed over a
clipboard she held to her chest. The doctor started speaking, and my
ears began ringing loudly when I heard his first words: "I want to err
on the safe side, for Sadie's well-being. I am recommending that we
admit her to the adolescent psychiatric hospital for ten days, for ob-
servation and counseling." I don't remember clearly what happened
after that—just the ringing in my ears and Dennis's strong arm
around me as we walked out of the office.

An untitled poem I found several years later, written by Sadie

around 2004, clearly shows the depth of her despair and her suicidal
impulses at that time.

Untitled

I'm hopeless,
I'm drowning,
in a pool of my tears.
In just one short month,
I've gained 20 long years.
You don't understand
and you don't want to know
that no matter what happens,
I'm gonna blow!
You don't seem to notice
all the cuts on my arms,
all the blood on my sheets,
and all the signs of self-harm.
You don't seem to care,
and now neither do I,
so I am taking my life!
and deciding to die,
and the bottles have opened,
all the pills have spilled out,
the note's on the table,
and my letters are written out.
But the clock has ticked on,
and the pills have been popped,
it's all turning black,
and my heart has just stopped.

A high percentage of youth give signals to somebody about their suicidal feelings before an attempt. Those signals are often a cry for help. Perhaps this poem was Sadie's way of signaling, but, if so—if she did want help—why didn't she share it with us? And given how depressed she was and how concerned Dennis and I were about her well-being, why didn't we violate her confidence and read her private journals so we better understood what was going through her mind? Would we have been able to stop her suicide attempt if we had?

She was a young girl battling demons she didn't know how to control. She knew we loved her and were there for her, but she still felt alone and clearly didn't think she could share her feelings with us. We could not fathom what could have driven her to try to end her life. Could she even understand the magnitude of that? Was it the only way she knew to deal with the pain? Was it the only way she knew how to reveal her agony to us? Or was it the depression medication itself that, rather than helping her, caused her suicidal thoughts and action? Remember, the warning on the Zoloft literature stated that one of the rare side effects of the medication was "having thoughts of suicide." If a drug prescribed to eliminate or reduce depression actually has the opposite effect, it seems clear to me that there is something the medical industry does not understand about the medication. Perhaps we actually made Sadie worse by putting her on Zoloft, but what was the alternative? Getting her on medication was the right approach, from a statistical standpoint, only my daughter was not a statistic—she was a real, innocent, and frightened young girl.

While we were frightened, Dennis and I also felt some sense of relief that our daughter was going to be in a safe place and in skilled hands. Little did I know that this was just the beginning of what I now can describe only as medical professionals' trial-and-error experiment with my daughter's life.

9

A Psych Hospital? Really?

THE THREE OF US LEFT THE EMERGENCY ROOM AND GOT IN THE CAR. Dennis took the wheel and drove slowly and carefully, turning on unfamiliar roads and glancing at a map. Sadie sat quietly in the backseat next to me—shoulders sloped, staring at the floor of the car. Other than my hugging her, I don't remember any of us interacting during the drive. I think we all felt as if we had somehow lost control of our lives in a matter of hours and didn't understand or really believe what was happening.

After we had been on a country road for a few miles, Dennis clicked on the brights, hunching forward and squinting so that he wouldn't miss a turnoff we were approaching. He slowed almost to a stop and then swung the car smoothly onto a long, well-kept driveway that headed perfectly straight up a gradual hill ahead. Thick-trunked trees lined the shoulder of the drive, and their bare branches arched overhead to create a tunnel, a dense gateway stretching toward post lamps I glimpsed in the distance. Once we emerged into open space from the tunnel of trees, I saw, across the moonlit, snow-covered lawns, a large, two-story brick building, almost like a personal residence yet too stately to be out there in the country. The big, circular drive brought us toward the front entry, and now it felt like a church. Soft inset lighting from the arch above the entryway glowed welcoming and warm against the cold winter night. We slowed to a stop, and I could see farther back, into the entrance. Set deep within were clean, classic doors and lots of windowpanes. For that moment, I felt eased, comforted.

Then I snapped back to reality. My breathing stopped, and my stomach knotted in a powerful ball, twisting wretchedly. *We are here because Sadie is going to be locked in a psych ward. They think my daughter is mentally ill.* My mind filled with images of *One Flew Over the Cuckoo's Nest*: crazies shuffling about, living a drug-induced nonlife, while characters like the mean Nurse Ratched keep watch. The thought *this can't be happening to my family* kept entering my mind.

We walked through the front doors, holding hands. The admitting nurse, whom the hospital had notified, said, "It's late, so let's get Sadie settled in, and then we can chat for a few minutes." A staff person said hello to Sadie and asked her to follow. We said goodbye, telling her that everything was going to be okay and that we would see her soon. I forced a smile to comfort her, but her lip quivered. She looked five years old and frightened. I slid my hand from hers, kissed her on the cheek.

It took every ounce of strength for me to turn away, as Dennis guided me gently by my elbow. As we took our first few steps, I closed my eyes and tried to shut out the pain. Then I opened them and looked over my shoulder at my daughter. She was already shuffling slowly away down the hallway, a nurse at her side, head down and shoulders fallen.

The admitting nurse led Dennis and me to a private alcove, where she told us that because it was late, she would ask us only a few questions and have us complete some paperwork, then would send us home. We would return in the morning for a more thorough explanation of the next ten days and to meet with Sadie's psychiatrist.

We drove away down the tree-lined driveway, even more slowly than we had when we'd arrived. The tires crackled over a thin layer of fresh snow, and the car felt empty. Dennis and I breathed deeply and slowly and started into low conversation, reassuring each other with any positive thoughts we could share. *At least the staff are kind and gentle and the place looks warm. At least she's in the hands of professionals who can hopefully make her feel better. Maybe they can tell us what to do to make things return to normal. Maybe this is all the start of a new beginning. Maybe we can regather some of our happiness and bring some peace back to our family's life.*

After we ran out of optimistic words, we drove in silence the rest of the way home, each lost in our own thoughts. I realized that I was shivering, still in shock from the trauma that had begun just hours earlier. *Was it only hours ago? It seems like weeks since I found her in the bathroom. How did we end up here?* Our beautiful, bright, fun-loving daughter was now alone, without us, and locked in a psych ward. *This really isn't happening. This is really happening. I want it to go away. I need to be strong. I want to cry. I want to rewind the clock.*

Neither of us slept that night. We were out of bed at six o'clock the next morning—three hours before we could visit Sadie. Dennis headed out the door to fill the car with gas. I stood at the front door and watched. He stood in the gray light outside, his breath puffing clouds of vapor in the subzero temperature, scraping the windshield with vigor in an obvious attempt to direct his mind away from his racing thoughts and aching heart.

We sat in the lobby of the hospital, having arrived thirty minutes before visiting hours. I had checked in at the front desk, and the attendant had let me know that we would be seeing a managing psychiatrist before we saw Sadie, to get an introduction to the program that they would put in place for her during her stay. Just a few minutes afterward, a middle-aged man came to where we were seated, greeted us, and welcomed us to the Meriter Child and Adolescent Psychiatric Hospital. "Please join me in my office," he said, "and I will walk you through my plans for Sadie."

At the start of our conversation, I was somewhat comforted to hear that he would spend part of the day overseeing an evaluation of Sadie. He continued to assure us that he would then develop a treatment plan to meet Sadie's individual needs, and that we would be welcomed as part of the process. He also shared that we would be asked to come to the facility during the week for family therapy sessions. At first, that idea was encouraging. Then my mind jumped to how we would need to put everything else in our lives on hold. *Just logistics*, I thought. *Easy logistics. And nothing is more important than figuring out what happened and how to help Sadie.*

Nothing. This blend of family therapy, one-on-one therapy, and group therapy that the psychiatrist mentioned was foreign but gave me hope—and was scary at the same time. There were no guarantees.

I distinctly remember the kind words and hope the psychiatrist shared with us during one of our sessions later that week. He told us, "Don't worry—she will get through this. She's so bright, by the time she's twenty-five I predict she'll have two PhDs and will be making more money than you were at that age."

I know now that we were naive and way too optimistic, thinking that love and science would just fix it all. At the time, we didn't realize that was just the start of our long, mysterious, and bizarre quest to uncover the secret to stop the torment brewing inside Sadie. I did not learn until later that while close to 80 percent of depressed patients are responsive to medication, only 50 percent are responsive to their first medication or to any particular medication.

I learned that there were four classes of antidepressant medications available at that time: serotonin reuptake inhibitors (SSRIs), such as Zoloft, which bring about higher brain levels of serotonin; tricyclics, such as Elavil and Norpramin, which affect serotonin and dopamine; monoamine oxidase inhibitors (MAOIs), such as Nardil, which inhibit the breakdown of serotonin, dopamine, and norepinephrine; and atypical antidepressants, such as Wellbutrin and Effexor, a category of drugs that operate on multiple neurotransmitter systems. Determining which antidepressant, if any, will work on any particular individual is more of an art than science. Trial and error is what it takes, starting with the drug that has the least unpleasant and least dangerous side effects. In Sadie's case, we were told that once someone has a bad reaction to one class, the norm is to switch the person to a different class.

Over the ten days Sadie was at Meriter, the doctors got her stabilized and she, Dennis and I attended therapy sessions. I don't remember much about the sessions—we were in such a fog. The Meriter psychiatrist took Sadie off Zoloft immediately and told us it was too risky to try another SSRI. Rather, he recommended that we put her on Wellbutrin. At the end of her ten-day stay, they released Sadie with a prescription for it.

10

Back Home—but Not for Long

WE BOUGHT A SMALL LOCKING CASE TO STORE SADIE'S MEDICATION in, just to be on the safe side, and hid the key. We felt cautious but hopeful, and the week started out okay. Sadie was glad to be home. We wanted to envelop her in a cocoon, but she wanted to return to school and get back to her normal activities, so off she went. Wednesday night was karate class. She had achieved her first-degree black belt the prior fall. It was something she had worked toward over the last several years and was quite proud to have accomplished. On the day of her seventh-grade year when she tested for and was awarded her black belt, her grin was ear to ear. She seemed so happy, depressive thoughts gone, or perhaps just pushed aside. And we were so proud of her!

After her time at Meriter, we thought her wanting to go back to school and to karate was a good sign. As I recall, even though she was put on Wellbutrin, we didn't understand that Sadie's depression might have been what is called "atypical" depression—depression that lifts temporarily when good news or positive events cheer you up but that returns later. So when she enjoyed some activity, we would think, *She is better!* We didn't realize her happiness was only temporary.

School seemed to go well, so, at Sadie's request, we agreed to drop her at karate practice that Wednesday evening. Although we were nervous about leaving her, and even though she had been home from the psychiatric hospital for only four or five days, she seemed excited to be returning to practice and her karate friends.

Then déjà vu—we received a call from the Madison police less than an hour later, saying that Sadie had apparently left practice, called a suicide crisis hotline, and told them she had taken an overdose of her depression medication.

Frantic, we rushed to the hospital. *No, no, no, no—not again.* By the time the police got her to the emergency room, she had started having seizures. The doctors told us she had taken a deadly dose— that had she gotten to the hospital much later, she would not have survived. As I recall through my foggy memory of that time, doctors used charcoal to absorb the medication in her stomach, and by the time Dennis and I got to the emergency room, we could see the black residue from it in her mouth.

I can think only that her calling the suicide hotline was a call for help—her way of telling us she was desperately unhappy and didn't know how to talk to us about it or how to deal with her deepening depression. Anyone dealing with depression should have the twenty-four-seven national suicide lifeline phone number handy (1-800-273-TALK (8255)) or know where to get it quickly. In Sadie's case, calling that number was literally a lifesaving action.

A second suicide attempt, again while she was under the supervision of a psychiatrist and while taking prescribed depression medication, and only five days after she had been released from inpatient treatment! In our desperate attempts to help Sadie, we seemed to have only made her worse. But what were we supposed to do? Why did the medication cause her to be suicidal, rather than helping her? What had we done? And how had she gotten her medication in the first place? We had locked it in the lockbox! But somehow she had found the key we had hid.

The warnings in the Wellbutrin literature about the medication's causing suicidal thoughts were embedded in my mind. I didn't understand how yet another drug that was supposed to help could have the opposite effect. Why did the medication help some people but not others? The shortcomings of treatment options were abundantly clear: understanding what was going on in Sadie's brain and how best to help her was, or seemed to be, guesswork. I didn't want the "experts" to experiment on my daughter!

Sadie went back to Meriter for two more weeks of inpatient treatment. While she was there, the doctor switched her to a third depression medication: Prozac. I felt as if we were running in a maze shrouded in tulle fog. Everywhere we turned we hit a dead end, and our time was running out. We were the parents; we were supposed to keep our daughter safe, but instead had made decisions that had almost resulted in her death.

As I think back on those events, I just remember how lost we were—where do you turn when you don't know what to do and when even the experts aren't helping? Even today, these feelings of inadequacy and the resultant guilt appear to be seared into my self-definition.

When Sadie was released a second time from intense inpatient treatment, we tried again to establish some semblance of normal life—school, after-school activities, and play with friends. But really, we didn't want to let her out of our sight. How do you balance protecting your child while giving her freedom to stand up on her own two feet? How in the world do you parent a child who is depressed and suicidal? If your depressed child doesn't do her homework, doesn't do her chores, skips a class, what do you do? We tried not to say or do anything that might make her feel criticized or worse. It felt like walking on broken glass. We struggled with holding her accountable. Above all, we didn't want her to become more sad, more depressed.

I have no idea how we functioned in our jobs during that time. I was still working part-time out of the house, and Dennis's office was only a ten-minute walk from home. I do know that sometimes, having something else to focus on provided a needed respite from the intense, stressful emotions we were experiencing. Work was a place where we felt competent and capable—unlike how we felt about being parents.

The nightmare was not over, either. Just a few weeks after she had returned, in the late afternoon of a beautiful spring day, Sadie told me she was going to go for a short bike ride. I thought the fresh air and exercise would do her good. I watched as she put some things in her bike basket: a ball of twine, some sticks. At first it seemed normal for Sadie—she was always experimenting with things—but after she took off, I started wondering, *What is she doing with the twine? Why did she take that?* I busied myself with dinner preparations but kept looking out the window, expecting her to roll up the driveway.

Dennis arrived home and asked, "Where's Sadie?"

"She went on a bike ride but should get back soon," I said. "Dinner is ready." But no Sadie. I could feel the butterflies starting to flutter in my stomach: *She should be back by now. What's keeping her? And what was she doing with that twine?* Dennis drove off to search for her, checking her normal haunts. No luck. I started to panic. *She knows to be home for dinner. What if . . .*

I decided to call the police. I told them she had left on a bike ride and had been suicidal, and that I was worried she might again try to take her life. I cried uncontrollably as I pleaded with the police, "Please help us find her. She's just a little girl!" The police jumped into action—I was so grateful. They checked all the local hospitals and sent a patrol car out to interview us and to search for her.

Shortly after that, the police called me. They had received a call from a hospital. Sadie was there. She had tied the twine around her neck, climbed up a tree, tied the twine to a tree branch, and jumped. Fortunately, the twine broke and she walked half a mile to a phone, called 911, and told the operator what she had done. The 911 operator called the police, who picked her up and took her to the hospital. She had rope burns around her neck but otherwise was okay.

Tears of relief ran down my face, but the relief was only temporary. What was going to stop this cycle? How were we going to stop it before she succeeded in her attempts to die?

Per protocol, she was again sent to inpatient care back at Meriter Child and Adolescent Psychiatry Hospital, during which time we looked for a longer-term treatment program. Ten days was just not sufficient; it was just too risky to let her come home. Dennis had planned a weeklong fishing trip in a remote fly-in lake in Canada with Sadie, her two cousins, and their fathers (my brothers). They were supposed to leave as soon as school was out, just a couple of weeks away. It was a tradition in Dennis's family to take the kids, when they got old enough, to a remote lake in Canada for fishing. Instead, he was going without Sadie and she was headed to a longer-term treatment center. Life can turn out so differently than planned.

11

—

The Stigma Rears Its Head

WORKING WITH THE HOSPITAL, WE IDENTIFIED WHAT SEEMED TO BE AN ideal longer-term treatment center for Sadie: Rogers Memorial Hospital, only an hour's drive from Madison. Although I hate to admit it, I felt a sense of relief, in some ways, sending her off for two months of treatment over the summer. Now someone else would be responsible for keeping her safe. We no longer knew how to help her; we didn't even know how to keep her alive.

Rogers sounded like the kind of place that could help Sadie. It specialized in children and adolescents and was a nationally recognized treatment center. The psychiatrists there believed in strong family involvement and parent education, and that no medication should be used without therapy. They provided a comprehensive treatment approach that included helping each child understand their personal strengths, talents, and mental health challenges and effective ways of dealing with them. Rogers claimed to help patients understand and manage the triggers that contribute to their behaviors. Treatment plans included some combination of components such as cognitive behavioral therapy, family education and therapy, group and individual therapy, pharmacology, and experiential therapy. At the time, the center also combined the intensity of inpatient treatment with an adventure-based therapy program.

The cost? In 2003, the estimate was $34,800 for sixty days. That was roughly equivalent to a year of college. We were both lucky and unlucky: lucky that we had the resources (Sadie's college fund) to cover such necessary care, unlucky that Sadie needed it in order keep her alive. I can only imagine the guilt and anguish we would have felt had we not had the savings for this type of intense treatment.

Yet, as became increasingly apparent to us over the coming years, parents had little to go on in terms of assessing treatment programs' effectiveness, beyond the programs' own descriptions of their approach and assurances that their psychiatrists were accredited and that their facilities were clean and well-staffed. These treatment centers did not have statistically based program-effectiveness data or data on outcomes correlated with specific types of challenges facing a child. Still, when you are desperate, you will grab at the best thing you can find.

About that time, a family with young children moved into the house across the street from us. During the few weeks when Sadie was home, waiting until Rogers had space for her, the kids came over to play in the yard with her. She was so good with them. She would sit them down in a circle and tell them stories or play tag in our wooded yard with them. Their mother was delighted to have Sadie across the street. I remember her saying to me that her kids really liked Sadie, and Sadie would be a great babysitter. I also remember my big lie. "Oh, too bad, but Sadie is going off to camp for the summer, so she won't be around." The woman tilted her head and gave me an inquisitive look that seemed to ask, *Why would you send your daughter away for the whole summer?*

I was oh, so aware of the stigmas associated with mental illness. I felt terribly guilty telling a lie, but I couldn't bring myself to tell the truth—that my daughter was so depressed, she was cutting herself, binge eating, and trying to end her life. What was I afraid of? I suppose I thought the mother would turn, grab her kids, and run away from Sadie. That even when Sadie was better, people would still shy away from her; I was sure that they would think she was "mentally ill" and not want their kids to be around her, that she would never be viewed as normal, that her peers would ostracize her. In truth, I was afraid of all those things. Even today, I tend to think that people would have those thoughts. I wanted to protect her, and maybe even myself, from that loss of the perception that we were normal.

If she had had cancer or leukemia, I believe I would have shared that. I would have asked if people knew anyone else struggling with the illness, if people knew any exceptionally good doctors or treatments. But I didn't share and I didn't have the benefit of learning from others. I will never know whether sharing would have changed the outcome of our story, but I do feel angry that mental illness is thought of so differently than physical illness is. Even today, even though it is prevalent, many parents and youth don't talk about their mental health challenges because of the stigma.

It was at Rogers that Sadie was first diagnosed with bipolar disorder. Originally known as manic-depressive illness, it's a brain disorder that causes unusual shifts in mood, energy, activity levels, and the ability to carry out day-to-day tasks. We learned that depression medication for someone who is bipolar can cause more harm than good. According to Andrew Solomon, author of *The Noonday Demon: An Atlas of Depression*, antidepressant medications may launch mania in people who are bipolar. And the greatest danger with manic-depressive illness is that it sometimes bursts into what are called mixed states, in which one is manically depressed—full of negative feelings and grandiose about them. That is a prime condition for suicide, and it, too, can be brought on by the use of antidepressant medications without the mood stabilizers that are necessary parts of bipolar medication. So I began to wonder whether Sadie's suicide attempts happened because her depression medication caused suicidal thoughts, or because she was actually bipolar and on the wrong medication.

At Rogers, diagnosed with bipolar illness, she was put on a bipolar medication, Lamictal, in addition to Prozac. After about a month, the doctors at Rogers added Concerta to help with her ADD (in particular to help reduce her impulsive behaviors). It was hard to keep track of the cocktail of medications, but while she was at Rogers, we did start to see a huge improvement in Sadie's attitude, happiness, and ability to have normal conversations and work out problems without blowups. Even Sadie felt better, albeit briefly, as evidenced by a journal entry she wrote a few years later:

> During that summer, I truly thought I had changed. I felt happier and even acted like I hadn't in years. Unfortunately, I was wrong. The following fall was probably the worst time of my entire life. Once again, I had lied so convincingly and repeatedly I believed myself.

12

A New Start, Cold Turkey

THAT SUMMER OF 2004, WE HAD BEEN IN MADISON FOR SEVEN YEARS. We had always planned to return to the West Coast. I especially was eager to return to the mountains, oceans, and wilderness of the Pacific Northwest. When a great job opportunity for me opened up in Portland, Oregon, the spring of Sadie's eighth-grade year, when she was in and out of psychiatric treatment centers, we figured if we were going to move, that summer, right before the start of high school, would be the best time. We certainly didn't want to move her in the middle of high school, so it was now or not for at least another four years.

I thought that because I was getting older, if I waited another four years, I might not be as marketable and might not find a job out West, so I applied for and was offered the Portland job during the summer Sadie was at Rogers. We thought a new start for her when she left Rogers might be good. We were also aware that she had started to alienate her friends in Madison; it is hard for youth to be around someone so depressed, even though she hid her depression as much as she could. When we asked her psychiatrist about the move, he told us it wasn't ideal for Sadie but she would probably do fine. So we made the decision to relocate.

To this day, I wonder why I would have done anything that wasn't ideal for Sadie. Was I just being selfish at the time? I wonder whether things would have turned out differently if we hadn't moved from Madison when we did. Of course, we will never know.

I suppose I thought that we had figured out what was wrong with Sadie and had identified the medication that would allow her to stabilize and move on with her life. I thought that we would be giving her that new start. But fate intervened. Two days before she was to be discharged from Rogers, her skin started to bubble. Her psychiatrist said she was having a very rare but potentially deadly reaction to the Lamictal she was taking, so they had to take her off it—which they did, cold turkey, the day before her discharge.

Even today, I feel as if fate was against us. You hear stories of people down on their luck, who get hit again and again with tragedy—a parent whose firstborn child is diagnosed with, then successfully treated for cancer, only to be killed a year later by a stray bullet—and you wonder, *Haven't they already had more than their fair share of problems?* and, *Why them? How much can a person take?* I felt like we were in a similar situation. Every time we found an answer and thought things were going better, we got hit again with another problem. It just didn't seem fair. *Can't we get a break?*

The move was already in motion—the house was sold and my new job accepted—so we just kept moving onward. Dennis stayed in Madison for a few weeks to finish his work commitments, and Sadie and I loaded up our truck and headed out West, touring the great American sites (Custer State Park, the Badlands of South Dakota, Mount Rushmore, and Yellowstone) on the way. Those were some good times—the music cranked up, singing at the top of our lungs as we rolled along the miles.

But Sadie started to show signs of anxiety. She just wanted to get to Portland and make new friends. She was often very difficult to be around on the trip. "Slow down, Sadie—just enjoy today," I would say, but internally she was racing. Now, I do not understand why the doctor would have discharged Sadie when he had just taken her off her medication, cold turkey. Why wouldn't he have kept her there until she got stabilized on a replacement medication? And why wouldn't we have insisted that happen before discharge? Had the hospital already promised her "bed" to a new patient and therefore no longer had room for her? I don't remember. But it seems almost unbelievable to me now that we didn't insist she stay longer, until she was stabilized. Were we in denial? Did we not understand the implications of removing her cold turkey from the Lamictal?

Whatever the case, after that happened, she entered what I can describe only as a manic phase. When we arrived in Portland, Sadie was desperate to establish herself and to make friends in our new town. She connected with the high school drama-club kids and started hanging out with them; she tried out for and was accepted into the Portland Symphonic Girlchoir; she had me drive her to numerous martial-arts studios offering karate, tae kwon do, aikido, judo, and others, so she could figure out what kind she wanted to pursue next. She met with the drama teacher and told him she was so good that he should move her to an advanced program.

One day before school started, we biked downtown to check out the waterfront. At one point, I turned around to make sure she was still behind me and I saw her, bike dropped on the ground, bike helmet turned upside down to accept donations, people standing around her while she sang for money.

Some of her behavior was just so Sadie. But mostly she was frenzied, impatient, and demanding, and I, exhausted trying to keep up, was just attempting to slow her down. She reminded me of a souped-up car with the tachometer spiked at eight thousand rpm from morning to night, running everywhere, trying to do everything. Sadie had always been active and extroverted and involved in many activities—only now, she wasn't balancing all that with quiet reading time. In fact, she virtually stopped reading during that period, after having been an avid book lover until that point. It was as if something had taken control of her and injected her with massive quantities of caffeine.

13

Into the Dark Pit

As the psychiatrist at Rogers instructed, I embarked on a search both for a good adolescent psychiatrist for Sadie in Portland and for a medication that would help her. What a nightmare. How do you find a top-notch psychiatrist in a town that's new to you? Start with the Internet, identify referral hotlines, and start calling them. Ask everyone you call for referrals, and try to hone in on names that keep coming up. Make dozens and dozens and dozens of calls—then hit one dead end after another. Panic and tears set in as the "best" told me, "I'm not taking new patients," or "I work for a hospital and only see patients there," or "I don't have a private practice," or "I'm only doing research for now," or "I don't take your insurance."

What was I supposed to do? Dennis was still working in Madison, Sadie was out of control, and I couldn't find someone to help her. Little did I know that this would become my mantra for years to come: "I don't know what to do; somebody please tell me what to do!"

As I learned much later, my experience trying to find a good adolescent psychiatrist was a common one. A shortage of them exists today, as it did then, even in a large metropolitan area. I can only imagine that there are many smaller communities where the problem is even worse. This needs to change—addressing mental health issues when they first surface, which is often in adolescence or young adulthood, can result in better outcomes than waiting until someone is older.

Finally, one psychiatrist who was referred to me (and not taking new patients) recommended one of her colleagues. He didn't specialize in adolescents, but I was desperate, so I took Sadie to meet him right before school started. He prescribed Abilify, which he added to the Prozac Sadie was still taking, and sent us on our way. Although I didn't know it yet, this psychiatrist would turn out to be a big mistake. I should have trusted my instinct that he was more the type to quickly write prescriptions than one who would take the time to understand Sadie. I should have trusted Sadie's saying she didn't like him. But, again, I was desperate. So we took his advice.

Sadie's first weeks of school as an incoming freshman at Lincoln High School seemed to go well. She was engaged, doing her homework, connecting with kids through the drama club, and involved in tae kwon do. But she was very obsessed with making new friends and was somewhat volatile at home. As her new medication took effect, her behavior started to change. She struggled to stay in class; she kept going to the school nurse, saying she didn't feel right. Then one of those fateful, life-changing events happened. She met a girl at school whom she liked and started hanging out with her.

Years later, I found the following journal entry, describing how desperate she was to make friends. Her statement about what she called her "acceptance complex" and the influence this girl had on Sadie really stunned me.

My acceptance complex was in full swing. I was desperate for anybody who would let me be his or her friend. On my first few days of school, I found someone. Her name was Kate, and she would end up leading me into my dark pit again.

I knew transitioning to a new school in a new town and making new friends would be hard, but I always thought of Sadie as someone who was so outgoing that she of all people would adapt quickly. Now, I realize that she was in a manic phase and that she was so anxious about making friends that she threw caution and values to the wind and wound up jumping into the wrong crowd.

One day, a few weeks into school, I got a call at work. Sadie had been picked up across the street from school by campus security with her new friend Kate and a few other kids, who were smoking pot. The other kids fessed up that Sadie did not actually smoke, so she was released. The story the kids told school officials was that of an innocent midwestern girl exposed to big-city life. Apparently, they asked Sadie if she wanted some Mary Jane, then thought it was very funny that she didn't know what that was.

Sadie started to spend more time with this girl, Kate, along with her older brother and his friends, some of who hung out with Portland street kids. For the first time, Sadie started deliberately disobeying Dennis's and my rules. Between her bike and Portland's good public transit system, she was able to get around on her own and often headed over to a friend's house and not call to tell me where she was. She also started blowing off her martial arts classes and girlchoir and skipping school.

I did not know the parents of Sadie's so-called friends, or where they lived. Of course we told her that before she could go to a friend's house, we needed their name, address, and phone number, but she would not give us that information and would simply take off without telling us.

14

—

Portland Street Life

THINGS SOON WENT FROM BAD TO DESPERATELY WRONG, BUT WE didn't really know what was happening or how to fix it. Sadie started hanging out with more street kids and at some of the local homeless youth centers, and continued not to abide by house rules—if she didn't like the consequences we tried to enforce, she would just walk out the door. Why didn't you just put her on restriction, you might ask? Well, that works only if your child is afraid of the consequences of disobedience. Sadie was fearless and was willing to be out on the streets. Other than tying her down, we couldn't keep her at home. Rewards, punishment—nothing worked. We didn't know how to parent her.

Her descent was so rapid that in less than a month she transformed from an innocent thirteen-year-old starting her first year of high school to someone we didn't even recognize as our own. She deliberately disobeyed virtually every rule we established; she blew off everything that society accepted as normal. I suppose we had entered child rearing thinking that if we provided unconditional love, opportunities, structure, and support and we modeled the behavior we wanted to see, our child would grow up to be a happy, productive individual. Nothing we had learned in life prepared us for what was happening to Sadie. Clearly, her desperation for friendship overrode her values and perhaps everything else she had grown up believing in.

The following spring, after months at a treatment center, Sadie wrote in reflection about this time:

> *Over the next couple of months, I slowly started to fall apart. By mid-October I had been hospitalized. Despite all of the negative actions that Kate and all my other "friends" were doing, I was still convinced that my parents were the ones that were the cause of my pain. I had pushed away all of my other support systems. Since my acceptance complex was worse than ever, I was terrified of cutting ties with the only people who let me into their lives. To me, life being abused and being misled was better than life alone. I continued to cling to them until several months of my stay here.*

We thought the medication she was taking was causing her behavior, so we kept going back to the psychiatrist in attempts to get it "right." In late September 2004, the psychiatrist prescribed Topomax. Sadie's outbursts declined, but her lying increased, her school performance declined dramatically, and she became even more obsessive about seeing her "friends." She hated the Topomax. "The medicine makes me dull, Mom," she told me. Was the dullness because the medication brought her down from a manic phase? Was it an unpleasant side effect? Or was the medication just wrong for Sadie overall? We didn't know. We just knew she didn't do well either off or on medication.

Although we didn't understand it at the time, Sadie had jumped headfirst into Portland street culture, replete with its own "families"—a culture we knew nothing about. What we observed at the time was a sector of the population that lived and operated by its own rules, in many ways, outside society. The youth all went by street names—names like Necro, Paradoxx, and Siren—and only by first name. We couldn't figure out where their real families were or whether or not their parents were involved with their lives. Perhaps they were also struggling with mental health issues. I suspect some came from abusive families or had parents who were drug addicts. It seemed clear to us that while Sadie chose to hang out with these people, they had some sort of control over her that we didn't understand. These street families had a risky, dangerous lifestyle. They were alienated from the rest of society because of their behavior and attitudes. People living "normal" lives were afraid of these youth—possibly because they seemed to purposely look and act like deviants.

Was Sadie lured? Brainwashed? How could a bright, educated, independent girl from a loving family have fallen into this life? The street kids seemed to operate like a cult, but I had never imagined Sadie would succumb to that kind of thing. She was never one to sit back and let things happen to her. As far back as elementary school, she used to tell me which kids were leaders and which were followers, and she had never been a follower. But now she had become one. She seemed to embrace street life—the life of kids free from "controlling" parents.

We did meet some of these young people; Sadie occasionally invited one of them over for dinner. We *wanted* to meet them. We were trying to understand who they were, where they came from, why they lived the life they did. For the most part, the ones we met seemed polite and respectful—at least in front of us. But there were others we never met; we heard only their names.

What attracted Sadie to these youth? Sadie's exposure to what I assumed were more opportunities than many of these kids had made them an unlikely fit as friends, in my mind. Maybe living outside society's rules appealed to her? Maybe she felt more kinship with these kids because they struggled, like she did, with a variety of difficult life challenges and therefore were more accepting of differences? Did she think we held unachievable expectations of her?

One of her journal entries, which I found much later, shows the kind of hold these kids had on Sadie:

*One time Paradoxx (my street mom aka Kate) was carrying pot at
school. She was afraid there was going to be a drug search and asked
me to carry the drugs for her. I refused. She went on to tell me that the
role of a good daughter is to take care of the mother. "You have a
clean record, I'm swamped with charges, just carry them, and we'll go
see Necro and Siren after school like we always do," she said. I felt
guilty for not carrying them for her, but still said no. "Do you want to
get DISOWNED?" she asked. She went on to tell me that I was a
newbie and so I had to do whatever she told me to do. I was scared of
losing her, and so I agreed to carry the drugs.*

Years later, on Sadie's memorial website, Paradoxx wrote this
story in reflection about Sadie and their friendship:

My Sadie Story/Name Withheld (Old Friend)

*When I met Sadie, we were both 14 years of age and freshmen
at Lincoln High School. We didn't have much in common yet,
but we found ourselves gravitating towards each other
nonetheless. I was a really messed up kid at the time, and she
was, in many ways, quite the contrary: I remember my friends
and I making fun of her for being so innocent. Her parents
thought I was a terrible influence, which, in retrospect, was a
very reasonable perception. That never stopped Sadie, of course;
she always followed her own path, even in the face of harsh
consequences. We had a very, very close friendship after my short
career at Lincoln ended. To an outside observer, it may have
looked like a big game of "who can get in more trouble," but I
tried my hardest to encourage her not to get into the same kind
of trouble as me. But she kept to her own fascinating, winding
path and ended up finding her own ways to get into trouble.
But her motives were so strong: she was going to be her own*

person, rules and parents and disapproving friends be damned! That tenacious individuality endeared her to me all the more. And, well, she did find her trouble. And it got her taken away from me. I missed her so terribly.

Sadie's own writing from this time illustrates poignantly just how frustrated, angry, and hopeless she felt inside. The language shows the intensity of her thoughts and feelings. I know we did not realize she was in this much pain. The lesson, I suppose, was that the behavior someone is showing on the outside may be very different from how the person feels on the inside. Clearly, that was the case with Sadie.

What am I doing? Why won't these people shut up? Crawl into a corner and hide from the world, from yourself, from your friend, screaming at you till your heart feels like it's going to burst. You wish for a gun, not to shoot her but to kill yourself, to finally know that this pain will no longer endure, to feel the sweet bliss of nothing. I don't want people to lay into me anymore. I want everyone to SHUT THE FUCK UP!

SHUT UP!

SHUT UP! SHUT UP! SHUT UP! SHUT UP! SHUT UP! SHUT UP! SHUT UP! SHUT UP! SHUT UP! SHUT UP! SHUT UP! SHUT UP! SHUT UP! SHUT UP! SHUT UP!

I need to see blood. Need to really fucking see blood. I hate everyone. I need to die. I just don't want to HURT anymore. I hate the world. I hate myself. I hate everything. I just want to feel nothing. I want to lock myself in somewhere, and take all the fucking chemicals, pills, anything that'll kill me. I want a gun so I can pull the trigger. I want a knife so I can watch the blood run down. I need a hug so badly. I just

need someone to show that they care. I want someone to just tell me
how important I am to them. But that will never happen. I'm not
important, people don't love me. When someone says they love you, all
they're waiting for is for a chance to hurt you. That's all everyone
wants from you, drugs, sex, power, or money. My god I hate my life. I
just want to die.

Why didn't she tell us how desperate she was feeling? She never exhibited any violence toward others; rather, she was in so much internal pain she just wished she herself would die. But why, when she so desperately needed our love, did she instead do everything she could to push us away? She made it so hard for us to help her. While I didn't consider it then, I now think that she felt a deep sense of rejection because she was given up for adoption, and that feeling of rejection impacted her self-esteem, which in turn made her susceptible to the influences of others who didn't judge and lived outside life's normal boundaries. But at that time, she did not talk to us about how her adoption impacted her or why she was pushing us away.

By mid-October, Sadie had stopped going to school and many nights did not return home until very late. Each night, frightened, bewildered, and desperate, we would search the streets and homeless youth centers for her. What was happening to our beautiful, smart, funny daughter? How could this happen to someone raised in a loving home? Sadie's behavior just didn't make sense—she seemed bent on destroying herself. Thoughts of her consumed us day and night. *Why is she doing this? What should we do? How do we help her?* I just couldn't believe she would behave this way unless she simply didn't know how to control her feelings. It was so like Sadie, though, to try to take action herself, rather than asking us for help.

Sadie describes this period in an online journal I later found:

I moved from Madison, WI to Portland, OR during the late summer of my 9th grade year. When I first began attending Lincoln High I was committed, motivated, and in a very good position to move up in my class schedule. Unfortunately, it was too good to be true. I met a girl named Kate, who was involved in the "street culture" or basically used drugs and ran away. I became very close to her and also to a man named Adam who went by Billy for reasons once told to me but erased by time. Some even thought I was in love with him. I very certainly thought myself in love. I began to defy my parents more openly than I ever had before. By mid-October, my obsession with my friends had not diminished. In my mind I saw them as my only escape. These people never judged.

Yet in a different journal, she talked about her "street father." Even though she thought the street kids were "family," she did see how they were draining her of hope.

I can feel him in the room with me. His eyes burn a path to my broken heart, F . . . you! they say. Those black pits of hell are merciless. They care not about pain or hurt, all that matters to him is to fulfill his own twisted desire. I can see him now, face laughing at my terror, but those soulless holes can't show emotion, you can get lost in eyes like that, forget your hopes, dreams, and loves, fall into the pools of despair, and drown in sorrow. Why did that happen? What did I ever do?

Despite what observers would have called deviant behavior, Sadie tried in her own way to get help—not from us but from crisis lines and hospital emergency room staff. From late September through October, Sadie called 911 or the crisis hotline five times, saying something was wrong with her. Each time, the police came to our house to talk to us. We explained again and again that she was suffering from depression and that we were getting professional help to find the right medication for her. Each time, we had to convince the police that we were not abusing her, that we were not neglectful parents. Of course, we felt like we were terrible parents—we were the accused. The police visits were humiliating and humbling and just hard. I would cry after they left, and would ask Dennis, "What are we doing wrong? Why is this happening?"

During this time, Sadie also admitted herself to the local emergency room four times (with help from her street friends). Rather than helping her, the ER staff always told us, "She's fine. We've seen this behavior of repeatedly showing up in the emergency room before. You need to stop this. It's becoming a bad habit with Sadie." I was confused—were the hospital professionals right? But it didn't make sense—why would Sadie have taken herself to the hospital if nothing was wrong? There are lots more fun ways to spend your time than going to the ER, so she must have known something was wrong but didn't know how to fix things, and she must have felt as if the attention we were giving her wasn't helping.

As I look back on that time, I feel mostly angry. How could medical professionals have just blown us off like that? Did they not have any training in mental health issues? Did they think Sadie was just a bad apple who didn't deserve help? Did they actually think she might be struggling with mental health issues but they didn't want to have to deal with them? Did they just not know how to help? Really, it doesn't matter why they told us what they did—it is clear to me now that their statements and their behavior (just sending us away) was and is unconscionable. Sadie needed help, was asking for help, and got turned away.

Given the prevalence of mental health issues, medical professionals who may interact with young people need to be trained to identify symptoms and behaviors that mental health disorders might cause, as well as trained in how to help these young people. After years of reading and researching, I don't believe these youth choose to struggle. I believe the vast majority of them want to have good lives. They want to be respected and successful, but something gets in their way. Rather than being shunned, they need understanding, respect, and help.

In addition to the fact that the medical professionals we saw did not help us, Sadie continued not to talk to us about her behavior. We kept returning to the psychiatrist, telling him something was wrong, and he kept changing her medications. By mid-October, he had dropped the Prozac and added Cymbalta. We kept asking him, "How do you know what will happen when you are mixing medicines?" It didn't seem right to have an adolescent on so many meds. I wanted her to just stop taking all of them, but these are not the types of medications you can just discontinue all of a sudden—not to mention that she hadn't been doing well without them, either. I was beyond scared—scared not only that I was not finding the right help for Sadie but also that maybe the help I had found was doing far more harm than good.

Throughout the fall, we kept searching for a different psychiatrist. Dennis and I spent nearly every evening talking, researching, trying to figure out what to do, while Sadie was spinning out of control right in front of our eyes. Then a psychologist friend of mine recommended we try dialectical behavior therapy (DBT)—a cognitive behavioral treatment that was originally developed to help people diagnosed with borderline personality disorder and chronically suicidal people struggling with an inability to regulate their emotions. When I researched it online, I thought it would be a good fit for Sadie. There was a DBT center right in Portland, and the treatment seemed to work on the kinds of issues that had been affecting her: cutting, depression, suicide attempts. So we took her there for an assessment and scheduled her first appointment. Unfortunately, while perhaps it was the right approach, by then she was just too wigged out and too defiant, and she would not go to her appointments. Our lives were unraveling so fast.

Certainly, the lack of available, qualified professionals and the difficulty I had in finding someone with the right expertise and capability contributed to Sadie's decline. Sadly, our experience is not unique. I have friends today who are facing the same challenges in finding the right help for their struggling kids—and someone whom their health insurance also happens to cover. Why aren't there more professionals with the proper training and approach to help young people dealing with the onset of mental illness? There has to be a more effective way to accomplish this goal, but I honestly don't think the medical and psychiatric industries know what that is. And after everything we went through with Sadie, after all the reading and research I have done, I still feel at a loss for how to best help others—parents or youth who are struggling. What I do feel sure of is that as a society we need to fund necessary research efforts more robustly, in order to find better solutions.

Late one Friday night in October, we received a call from one of Sadie's "street friends" saying Sadie had collapsed in the park, and they were scared. We called the police and asked them to meet us at the park; we were worried that she would run when we showed up. We zoomed to the park and headed toward a group of street youth hanging out there. As we approached, our eyes straining to see her in the dimly lit area, they slowly parted, leaving Sadie standing wobbly in front of us. Fortunately, she willingly went with us (with the stipulation that two of her "friends" come, too) to the hospital. I never thought we would feel the need to have police support to get our daughter to leave with us, but we did that night. The hospital staff, after taking some tests, said she was okay—no drugs or alcohol in her system—and just needed to go home and rest. Once again, we took her home with her unwilling or unable to explain her behavior.

Shortly after that, following Sadie's fourth self-admittance to the ER, we told the staff there that we did not accept their telling us once again just to take her home; she needed more help. Finally, they agreed to admit her for diagnosis at the Providence Child and Adolescent Psychiatry unit, then located in the Providence Portland Medical Center. The psychiatrist at the hospital said Sadie was on the wrong cocktail of medicines—that in fact it was a terrible one—and immediately took her off all but the Topomax. Our heads were spinning, and Sadie's brain was probably scrambled by the start and stop of so many medicines.

As I write this, so long after that experience, I cannot believe we would have allowed her to take so many different medications. It seems as if we blindly followed psychiatrists' recommendations, even though it didn't feel right, even though we were worried about the impact all these medicines were having—not only on her behavior but on her developing brain. But what was our alternative? I can describe this time only as life in a house of horror—at every turn, some other horrible thing popped up or we reached a dead end. We couldn't find a path out. We hadn't realized how much trial and error was involved in identifying medication that would effectively treat mental health issues. We were in such a state of panic, and were so desperate, that we just weren't thinking clearly.

15

—

A Scary Place

THE PSYCHIATRIST AT THE PROVIDENCE CHILD AND ADOLESCENT
Psychiatric unit agreed that Sadie needed more help. Once again, we
began researching—where to send her? Providence staff made some
suggestions, and we made the calls, as we had only a few days to find
someplace before she was discharged from the psych unit. Northwest Behavioral Healthcare Services was the only lockdown, inpatient treatment center in Portland that our insurance covered, and
they had a bed open. The description made it seem like a place that
could help Sadie, and the fact that it was a secure facility meant she
would not be able to run. Northwest Behavioral describes its services
on its website today as follows:

The Finest Adolescent Residential Treatment

Northwest Behavioral Healthcare Services provides help to
families and residential treatment for adolescents (ages 12
to 17) with emotional, behavioral, or substance abuse
problems. The staff of Northwest has shown itself to be
successful with those more "difficult to treat—especially
those with a dual diagnosis who require a secure setting for
their care."

We combine keen insight, kind guidance, and caring consistency with a positive peer group under the watchful eye of dedicated, competent professionals and counselors. The young person is led down a path of self-discovery and introspection that will enable them to understand and deal effectively with problems. New habits and attitudes that grow out of healthier choices build self-esteem and confidence. This common-sense system has resulted in solid outcomes, unmatched in the adolescent treatment industry.

It sounded like just what we needed. We made the arrangements and drove her there straight from the hospital. We read and signed a bunch of papers, then said goodbye to Sadie. She looked so innocent and scared. I just hugged her and said, "Sadie, we love you and hate to leave you, but you're not safe on the streets. Let the professionals here help you." Internally, I couldn't hold back my own tears. *Please make this nightmare end. Oh, my baby—what has become of us? How can I turn over my daughter to strangers yet again? She needs me, and really, I need her.* If this was tough love, it was heart-wrenching. When Dennis and I got back into our car without our daughter, a flood of tears fell. I just sobbed and heaved.

Yet another hard-earned lesson: the place turned out to be a nightmare, at least from Sadie's perspective. She told us the center was a scary place—full of screaming, violent teens. "Mom, they put kids here in restraints to control them." I cried when we visited and she told us what was going on, but center staff, with whom we had regular sessions while Sadie was there, told us a very different story, so we weren't sure whom to believe. As of the writing of this book, Northwest Behavioral is not accredited by the Better Business Bureau but has a BBB A-plus rating, due in part to the lack of complaints it received between 2012 and 2015. So perhaps both the center and Sadie were telling the truth. The kids who were there were out of control, and Sadie was in a different league—still young and relatively innocent. I now think perhaps part of the problem is that these type of treatment centers lump together violent youth, those who have been abused or neglected, those with mental health issues, and those with drug and alcohol addictions. How can they possibly deal effectively with young people who have such a wide range of challenges? Does the medical industry know so little about how to distinguish between and treat these youth that the only solution is to group them all in one place and treat them all the same?

After a month at Northwest, she was discharged. The center wrote that her reason for discharge was that "Sadie successfully completed her treatment goals and objectives. She demonstrated a consistent pattern of behavior marked by improved problem-solving skills, improved parental relationships, and an increased ability to relate with individuals in her peer group. She presents as a generally euthymic adolescent female." This summary was accompanied by a recommendation that she receive wraparound services—the concept of which is to collaboratively develop and manage holistic, individualized, and coordinated support and services designed specifically to meet the needs of the patient and his or her entire family. The problem with wraparound services, as we quickly found out, was that they did not really exist, besides ideologically. At the time and even today, that coordination doesn't often occur between treatment providers, schools, families, and community services.

We were both hopeful about and fearful of how Sadie would behave when she got home, and we quickly realized she would tell us what she thought we wanted to hear—so much so that we would not be able to separate truth from fiction. It became clear to us very rapidly that the monthlong treatment program hadn't resulted in any concrete improvements in her.

After she was released, we flew from Portland to San Francisco and drove to Pacifica, a small town just south of San Francisco, to have Thanksgiving at my brother's house, thinking it might help Sadie to get out of town and spend some time with her cousins at the beach. She was very irritable and antsy but hung in there, visiting with her cousins and at times talking on her cell phone. Friday afternoon, she told me she just needed to go for a walk to clear her head. "Okay," I said, still always encouraging her to exercise, to get outside.

But when she didn't return after an hour, we started getting nervous. Where was she? More time passed, and we couldn't eat dinner. Déjà vu. Dennis got in the car and drove through the neighborhoods, trying to find her, checking the beach and the streets and parks around my brother's house. No sign of her.

The evening dragged on as we kept looking. Late that night, the phone rang. It was Sadie, saying, in a very timid voice, "Would you come pick me up?" She was scared—apparently, she had taken a bus to San Francisco, then hitchhiked in an attempt to get a ride back to Portland. She had been obsessed with returning to her "street family" there. Some man picked her up, but by the time they had crossed the Bay Bridge and started heading north, Sadie got scared and asked him to let her out of the car. He had apparently put his hand on her leg—who knows what he said to her, but how lucky she was, how lucky we all were, that he pulled off the freeway and let her out. When I think about what could have happened to her . . . I cried with relief when she called. But the relief would turn out to be short-lived.

16

At War with Herself

WHEN WE RETURNED TO PORTLAND AFTER THANKSGIVING, IT QUICKLY became clear that nothing had changed. Sadie wasn't "better"; rather, she was even more obsessed with her street friends. She avoided looking straight into our eyes and appeared to tell us only what she thought we wanted to hear. She didn't act apologetic for trying to run away from Pacifica and ruining Thanksgiving. Her detachment from us was so palpable that we decided we needed to prepare for the worst. What would we do if she returned to the streets? We honestly thought she would be dead soon if she went back out there. We began making more calls and doing more Internet searches. What options did we have if we couldn't keep her safe ourselves?

We looked at boarding schools and residential treatment programs for struggling teens—programs that, at the time, typically cost $5,000 to $10,000 per month. When you buy a car, you generally do your research. What are the safety ratings, gas mileage, zero-to-sixty acceleration rate? How well does it hold its value? In other words, what do you get for your money and how does that compare with other vehicles? But how should parents evaluate adolescent treatment centers whose websites all make them sound like the solution to all their child's problems? We all know that such claims don't make it so. And we knew from Sadie's short experience at Northwest Behavioral that outcomes may be far different than advertised.

We also found no statistically valid studies that proved the purported benefits of therapeutic wilderness treatment programs and residential treatment centers. There were websites that rated the various programs but no studies that assessed long-term program outcomes. Some programs take a tough-love or boot-camp approach; others are more traditionally therapeutic. Regardless, you essentially relinquish your parental duties for a period of time by turning your child over to the program—most of which don't allow you to talk or communicate in any other way with your teen for the first month.

Despite all of my confusion about the options available to us, I still did not reach out to family and friend for ideas and support. In our experience, or perhaps only in our imagination, parents who had not experienced the impact mental health disorders have on a child's behavior did not or could not understand and might think all we needed to do was improve our parenting skills and approach. In hindsight, I suppose I didn't really give our friends the chance to prove they understood and could support us.

Frustrated with the lack of reputable ratings for the programs, we again looked for someone who could guide us. A therapist told us about two women, PhDs with extensive backgrounds working with at-risk youth, who were educational consultants for a company called Educational Connections. They specialized in matching troubled youth with a treatment center that would best meet their individual needs for educational and therapeutic options. For a couple thousand dollars, the women would interview the youth, the parents, and select friends, review any psychiatric reports, and make recommendations. And they were located in Portland. Their website explained:

> We know and understand, through first-hand knowledge, the options that are available to parents with struggling teens. We have visited and assessed therapeutic wilderness

programs, emotional growth schools, therapeutic boarding schools, drug and alcohol programs, residential treatment centers and psychiatric facilities throughout the country. We are also familiar with schools and programs for adolescents with learning differences as well as a variety of summer programs and options for struggling teens.

We just could not send our fourteen-year-old daughter someplace based on website advertisements. The thought of doing that made me feel sick. A couple thousand dollars seemed like a small price to pay for someone knowledgeable to help us navigate the various programs to determine which would be best for Sadie.

Needless to say, late that fall we hired the consultants. They interviewed us, Sadie, and some of our friends, reviewed her treatment records, and recommended a therapeutic wilderness program, Second Nature, in Utah. We were relieved to have "expert" advice, and though we still hoped Sadie would pull through without our having to send her away again, every day we watched her slip further and further from us.

However, if things were bad enough that we would send her away, how would we even get her there, given that she would be unlikely to cooperate? Oh, but the learning goes on! It turns out there are actually transport services that, for a fee, will escort/strong-arm your child to a treatment program. Who would have known? So we made arrangements with one such service, getting all the paperwork in place so if it came to that, to a realization that we had to take Sadie against her will to Second Nature, we would have a means of getting her there. I think we knew she wasn't going to miraculously return to what most people would term "normal" life without some sort of intervention. With these backup arrangements in place, we focused on trying again to get Sadie to "see the light"—to start behaving and living the life most teens live.

I was supposed to go to a black-tie awards event the following week in Washington, DC, for work. Yes, Dennis and I still both functioned at our jobs during this period, though I don't know how. I optimistically purchased a beautiful gown for the event, but two days before I was supposed to fly out, Sadie disappeared. The routine began again: we called the police to tell them she was missing; the police came to our house to gather information and obtain a picture of her; they put out a missing-child bulletin. And I canceled my trip. I just couldn't go out of town when I didn't know where my daughter was. But I had to explain to my boss—who, fortunately, was understanding—some of what was going on. One more time, we searched for her in homeless youth centers and under bridges. Dennis and I spent days walking the streets, showing youth a picture of Sadie, asking, "Have you seen her?"

We were completely out of our element and comfort zone speaking with kids who looked to be part of the street culture. Even though I know most of them are harmless, we felt as if we were scratching at the door of another world. Most people just quickly walk by the small groups of tough-acting, cigarette-smoking youth dressed in dirty, ratty clothes, some with dreadlocks or bright orange hair, perhaps sitting on the sidewalk with a guitar or a pit bull and holding a handwritten cardboard sign that says NEED MONEY FOR THE BUS or NEED MONEY FOR FOOD. To find Sadie, we braved this world, with no luck. Mostly, we got "Don't know her" or "Haven't seen her." A few said they had seen her around but didn't know where she was now.

According to a 2013 National Conference of State Legislators article on homeless and runaway youth, the National Runaway Switchboard estimates that "on any given night in the United States, there are approximately 1.3 million youth living unsupervised on the streets, in abandoned buildings or with friends or strangers." And Portland has more than its share. These youth are at high risk for physical abuse and substance abuse and for dropping out of school, and are at greater risk of severe anxiety and depression, suicide, poor health, and low self-esteem. Some come out of the foster care system, others from abusive or homeless families. Some have been kicked out of their homes because of behavioral problems, sexual orientation, or poverty. It was hard to reconcile the Sadie we thought we had raised with the Sadie who joined this sector of society.

A couple of days later, we received a call from the police saying they had seen someone who looked like Sadie. So we met the police and followed the leads, and we found her, dirty, beaten up, swollen eye—it looked like she had an outbreak of poison oak on her face. Wasn't she supposed to be having slumber parties, giggling with friends, going to theater practice? We got her home, but we felt like she wasn't really our daughter. She had turned into someone else—someone we hardly recognized. We could see that all she wanted was to get away from us, from her home, back to her street friends. It was as if she were brainwashed and no longer acknowledged us as her family, no longer acknowledged the life we had together. Why else would she have wanted to return to the street life after she had been physically attacked, when she had a comfortable and loving home? We couldn't fathom. Was it related to depression? Bipolar illness? Why, when she had such a great childhood, had things come to this?

She took a long bath and got into clean clothes but still seemed distant. While she was in the bath, I found a duffel bag under her bed, filled with clean clothes that she must have just packed—clearly, she was planning to run again after we went to bed. I was heartbroken things had come to this, but it was time to launch an intervention.

With extreme trepidation, Dennis called Second Nature to be sure they still had an opening, and then he called the transport team. I wasn't strong enough to make the calls. I remember this period as one of the most horrible times of my life. The transport team came after dark; they had told us to let them in but then to stay in the back bedroom. They went into Sadie's room and told her they were taking her to a wilderness treatment center. She started screaming, "Who are you? Mom, Dad, help me! Let me go! Mom, where are you? *Help me!*"

How could we do this to our fourteen-year-old daughter? Dennis had to restrain me. Tears streaming down our cheeks, we waited silently in the dark, not responding to her cries for help. Once we heard the door shut and the screams becoming muffled as they took her away, I collapsed on the floor.

To this day, I don't know if we made the right choice sending Sadie away, but I know we thought life on the streets would destroy her. It had already turned our beautiful, bright, capable child into an oppositional, wild, obsessed person who was making terrible (if not life-threatening) choices. Looking at Sadie's journal writing in which she reflected on this time only confirms to me that we needed to do what we did.

> by the time i was let out it was late november. my obsession with my friends had not diminished. in my mind i saw them as my only escape. these people never judged. i didn't have to perform for them or win their acceptance. in other words, they weren't my mother. once i was let out, i went into an immediate tailspin. i ran away twice. the second time for 4 days. i was so out of control i didn't know what to do with myself. needless to say, i needed more than a 2-week stay at a psych ward. my parents decided for me. when i finally was brought home, i was immediately escorted by 2 ppl to my old psych ward. from there i was escorted to a wilderness program in the rocky mountains. i stayed there for 3 months in the dead of winter trying to sort everything out in my head. who was in the right? i constantly was at war with myself in my mind as two conflicting voices (Kate's and my parents) vied for attention and loyalty. in the end, i came out even more confused.

17

―――

Life in the Wilderness

SECOND NATURE'S PROGRAM IN UTAH WAS HIGHLY RATED BY OUR educational consultants, who had experience with many of the wilderness treatment programs across the country and in fact had met with and in some cases interviewed key professional staff running the programs. The consultants also believed, based on their experience, that wilderness intervention was necessary for youth who were out of control. Being in the wilderness without distractions gives people time to think about their life. It forces them to face the natural consequences of their behavior and to work as a team with the other youth in the program. Second Nature features a clinically driven treatment model and claims to have the most clinically sophisticated teams in the country. Its website states:

> Second Nature utilizes a therapeutic wilderness model: primitive living, ceremony, metaphor, and affinity for the beauty and spirituality of nature. This model lends itself well to natural and logical consequences, rather than contrived, verbal, didactic therapy models. The child is removed from his/her comfort zone and immersed in a new culture, where therapists provide a small universe of lessons mirroring the larger universe in which the child lives.

Shelter building, backpacking, simple daily chores, group cooperation, relationship skills, and problem solving are taught "in the moment." In spite of the often-resistant response to therapy, the adolescent is engaged in a safe, practical, life-changing lesson. The staff and therapists move between traditional models of therapy and assessment to symbolic lessons, bypassing defensiveness. In some instances, your child's therapist may utilize a walkabout for your child. A walkabout is a guided, intensive therapeutic intervention used to interrupt or reward patterns for particular behaviors. Interdependence and high levels of engagement in therapy, unique in adolescent treatment, are facilitated through leverage inherent in wilderness living. Students often resistant to outpatient therapy models at home respond to the program with openness, honesty, accountability, and insight.

As promising as it sounded, filling out the required Interstate Compact on the Placement of Children request form was heart-wrenching. We were giving up our daughter (albeit temporarily) to someone else in another state. To me, it meant we were admitting failure, that we did not know how to parent our own child. Desperate means for desperate parents. We were scared, torn, grasping at whatever might help, in disbelief that our lives had come to this.

We relied heavily on the education consultants because, while states often regulate publicly funded programs, a number do not license or otherwise regulate certain types of private programs, even though many wilderness and residential treatment programs are privately owned and operated. According to the Federal General Office of Accountability, there also are no federal oversight laws—including reporting requirements—pertaining specifically to private residential programs, referral services, educational consultants, or transportation services, with one limited exception. The US Department of Health

and Human Services oversees psychiatric residential treatment facilities (PRTFs) receiving Medicaid funds.

At least Second Nature was not a boot camp, but I know it was
an extremely difficult place to be. Really, no fourteen-year-old
should have to go through something so physically and emotionally
challenging. These wilderness programs tear people down and strip
them to their rawest emotions in order to rebuild them. Often, as
was the case with Second Nature, teens in the program cannot
communicate with their parents for the first month—only with the
counselors.

After the transport service delivered her, Sadie spent three
months backpacking and camping in the dead of winter with a
group of teens and counselors at Second Nature. December in Utah
is very cold and desolate. Sadie had to spend three days alone in the
wilderness, and I can only imagine how frightening that must have
been at first—although what she wrote to us about those days was
how difficult it was to be "without books and writing materials,"
which were important to her as both an escape and a coping mecha-
nism. After her solo adventure, she and the other teens in her cohort
had to start and cook over a fire each day; they slept in sleeping bags
inside plastic tube tents on top of the snow and had to dig latrines
in the cold, hard ground. After the first month, we had weekly calls
with Sadie's wilderness therapist to monitor progress and understand what was going on.

The therapists and psychiatrist at Second Nature highly recommended that we take Sadie off all her medications. They claimed
that many youth in the program arrived on medications they didn't
really need to be on, and convinced us that Second Nature was a safe
place to try eliminating Sadie's medications while providing her
with the necessary therapy and support. In some respects, this was
exactly what we wanted to hear—that maybe Sadie would be okay,
maybe she did not need to be on medication that, for all we knew,
was scrambling her brain. Maybe a few months in the wilderness

would allow her, and us, to return to normal. So we agreed to Second Nature's recommendation.

A month into the program, the teens each had to write an impact letter to their parents that described what impact their behavior had on their family. In turn, the parents each had to write an impact letter to their child explaining the impact the child's behavior had on their lives.

Sadie's impact letter was full of admissions of things she had done over the years that she knew were wrong, and statements of taking accountability for those things. She admitted to lying, cutting, and taking out her emotions on us, skipping school, letting herself get manipulated by her street friends. Needless to say, the letter was long.

I am sure Dennis's and my impact letters to her were harsh for her to read, but in some ways it felt good to be able to tell her in writing that we loved her but how difficult she had made our lives. We were able to be up front and honest, knowing she had counselors there, as well as lots of time in the wilderness, to help her process what we said and to think about the impact of her behavior on both herself and our whole family. I thought the whole concept was very helpful and perhaps gave Sadie the wake-up call she needed.

After that first month, we could write other letters to each other, which we did regularly. I can only imagine how comforting it was to my daughter, away from her parents and living in a tough environment, to hear, "Sadie—you have mail." So we wrote often and sent pictures and comics to lift her spirits. On our end, receiving a letter from Sadie was the highlight of our day. When I got home from work and saw one, I would well up with tears—we missed her so much. I still have all those letters and can see the progress Sadie was making—the improvement in her attitude and self-esteem each week.

Initially, Sadie also wrote letters to her street friends, had them faxed to us, and asked us to send them on to the recipients. We did not send them. Rather, we hoped her stay at Second Nature would break what we thought were very unhealthy relationships with those kids. Besides, we didn't know where they lived or even their last names. And none of those "friends" contacted us to see how Sadie was doing. In the letters to them, she wrote, "I miss you guys so much it's unreal." She told them that the counselors at Second Nature wouldn't let her talk about her street friends. She told them that the counselors said talking about them was "glorifying unsafe decisions."

But she also wrote heartwarming letters to us, such as one she sent to us the second month:

> I miss you guys so much, it's unbearable. I'm realizing how much I
> actually put you through and it really hurts. I can feel your love all the
> way out here and I'm sending you guys all my love back with this letter.
> I think about you every day and all the stuff we used to do together.
> Remember when we used to gather around the piano and sing
> Christmas songs? And sparring with Papa? And dancing? All I want
> to do right now is be home with you guys.

We knew she loved us, and her letters showed that, but she also thought she loved the street people. She sent us a poem she wrote that showed how conflicted she was:

Love and Hate—to the Street People

> I hate you for what you've done to me,
> making me lose myself in the streets.
> I give you everything I have
> for empty promises in return.

> Yet I love you.

You accepted me for who I am,
let me make my own mistakes.
You loved me.

No, I hate you.
How could you accept me for me
when I don't know who I am anymore?

And I love you still.
You gave me a sense of happiness,
I felt strong when I was around you,
always in control.

But I hate you so.
You didn't let me make mistakes,
You let me crash and burn.

I hate you and I love you.
But above all I'm confused.
How could I believe you were true
when all you did was fake?

Over the next couple of months, Sadie's therapist told us she thought Sadie's bipolar diagnosis was wrong. She said they saw no signs of her being bipolar and thought if she was, they would have detected it over a three-month period. It was another example of the art of diagnosing mental health issues and the conflicting information the "experts" gave us.

Another eye-opener was that staff at Second Nature claimed that close to 50 percent of the program's youth were adopted, when only roughly 2–3 percent of the US youth population are adopted. You can't hear that without thinking that adoption affects kids more deeply than most of us would think. I now realize that the fact that she was given up (or, as Sadie referred to it, "rejected and thrown away") by her birth parents had a significant impact on her self-esteem and her behavior—much more than we realized at the time, as evidenced by one of her letters to us:

> *The counselors here gave me a book on adoption. I think it explains a lot of the WHY in my life. You always told me I was adopted because I was special. At about ten, I started to wonder what I would have to do to stop being special and what would happen if I did. A particular phrase from the book caught my attention. It said that eventually a child realizes that in order to be accepted by one family they have to realize that they were given up by another. That really hit me hard because I realized that that was exactly how it happened for me. I realized that I had always felt a sense of loss for the parents I never knew. That loss showed up as me being mortally afraid of being abandoned. I started testing you guys to see if you would abandon me too. It never really got through to me (until now) that you never would abandon me. When I got to Portland, the street kids accepted me. I finally felt loved. I realize now that I would have done, and did, anything they asked to keep that acceptance. They were so like how I imagined Nannette [her birth mother] to be that I felt accepted by her, as if she were there with them. I now realize how foolish I have been. I mistook the conditional for the unconditional love, love for manipulation. I was looking for them to fill the hole left by being abandoned so young. I now realize the hole will always be there. I will just have to live with it.*

Clearly, given how many of the youth in the program had been adopted, Sadie was not the only adopted child who struggled with the knowledge that she had been "given up" by her birth parents. Dennis and I had always tried to frame the discussion about her adoption positively—that her birth parents were very young and

KAREN MEADOWS

knew they couldn't take care of a child, that they picked us to adopt their child because they thought we could give her the life she deserved, that we desperately wanted her, and on and on. But what we said obviously didn't stop the hurt and rejection she felt. Adoption agencies should help adoptive parents understand the unique issues they may need to address with an adopted child and give or recommend resources that would help them to do so. While some agencies may do this, certainly not all do.

During her time at Second Nature, Sadie frequently sent us poems that she wrote, and took the time to explain the meaning of one of them to us. I only wish she had explained her other poems to us, because I had no idea of the depth of significance behind her work. I have included the poem and her description below.

Mockingbird

A mockingbird sheds a silent tear,
beneath the turbulent blue sky.
A young woman locked in a self-made cage,
a hurt little girl,
grieving alone.
Loving kisses bestowed upon a cold cheek.
Lost love found again.

She explained the poem this way: "All these lines are different parts of me. I am a mockingbird in the sense that I imitate other people and can sing any tune I want to get me out of a tight spot. The next two phrases are the same. They speak of hiding emotions. The young woman is me, and the self-made cage is my need to be accepted. That creates a cage, because in that need, I lock myself up and become a mockingbird. The hurt little girl is again me; I am grieving alone because I am grieving the loss of knowing my birth

– 112 –

parents. I realize now that deep down I never stopped being that hurt little girl. The next line speaks of the interactions between you and me. You would constantly tell me you love me and mean it. I would either not respond or respond with a halfhearted 'yeah, me too.' I really am sorry for this. You now know how much I really love and appreciate you. The lost love found again refers to the street people. The lost love was the love from Nannette and Walter [her birth parents] that I never got to experience. It was found again in my relationship with [the street people]."

Most young people stay one to three months in a wilderness program. Second Nature counselors didn't think Sadie was ready to be discharged until she had been in wilderness almost three months. It was clear from her letters that she really struggled with self-esteem. She talked a lot about how she constantly felt like a failure. She was not going to change those core feelings quickly, although I still don't understand her thinking of herself that way. To me, she was amazing in many ways—a black belt in karate, fluent in French, a vocabulary as good as any college professor's, articulate, a great sense of humor, a beautiful singing voice, and extremely bright. She lived her life with such zeal. Given how much she had going for her, I can think only that her depression was what caused her low self-esteem. What a mean disease.

Over her time in the wilderness, we started to see some of the old Sadie surface. Rather than writing letters to the street kids and asking us to send them, she started describing the scenery, the beautiful vistas, and the local resources available for survival in the wilderness. Sadie was such a sensory/feeling person, it was almost as if being in the wilderness reawakened her senses.

Only three types of trees grow here, pinyon pine, juniper, and mountain mahogany. The juniper is one of my favorite trees. The bark on the juniper is gray and feathery; pine trees drop a lot of needles.

When we put dead pine needles around the fire pit, the needles soak up all the water, leaving our circle nice and spongy. The dirt under the pine is also soft and doesn't have as many surface roots, so it is good for digging latrines and sumps. Sage smells wild and free; it is a bush and grows in the valleys between the hills. You can harvest spindles and fire board from it. The earth is mostly tan, but on the hills, you can see strips of green, red, and orange.

When her counselors thought Sadie was ready to be released, we had to struggle with the question of what next. Should she come home? The counselors at Second Nature spoke with our educational consultants numerous times during Sadie's stay. They believed that she was not ready to come home—that if she did, she would likely regress. After putting her through that challenging three months and spending over $30,000, Dennis and I certainly did not want her to return if she was just going to slip back into her old behaviors. Although we didn't know this at the time, two to three months at a wilderness program is often a prerequisite for longer-term residential treatment programs. Wilderness programs help deescalate participants' emotions and anger, leaving them better able to accept counseling.

18

———

Selecting Residential Treatment— but How?

AFTER MUCH DISCUSSION BETWEEN DENNIS AND ME, THE EDUCA-tional consultants, and Sadie's Second Nature therapist, we agreed that the risk of her regressing if we brought her home now was just too high, and the consequences of that regression too significant, so we reluctantly decided to send her to a longer residential treatment. Our hopes that a few months in the wilderness would turn her around were quashed, as was our vision that she would return to high school and enjoy a normal life.

Our hearts ached to have her back home. Our lives felt empty without her. Every day I saw or did something that I wanted to share with Sadie. I missed her singing show tunes upstairs in her bedroom at the top of her lungs; I missed her laugh, her passion about political issues, and her sarcastic sense of humor. You know that feeling when you look at someone and realize you each know what the other is thinking, and that you're both thinking the same thing? Well, I had that with Sadie—the old Sadie—and I really missed it.

The lesson that life is not fair, that you don't control your des-tiny or your child's, is a hard one. Writing letters back and forth and sending pictures was a poor substitute for having Sadie home, but it looked like that was going to be the best we could do for many more months or even years.

We worked with the Educational Connections consultants to identify the best next steps. We had to quickly learn more than we had ever thought we would need to know about treatment programs. We learned not only that there are different levels of intervention and treatment but also that each treatment program has a unique approach and a unique rehabilitation philosophy. The consultants were so knowledgeable that we would have been paralyzed without them.

Actually, I don't know how any parent could possibly find a way through this maze of programs on their own. What do you do— check the Better Business Bureau? Look at various "troubled teen" programs' websites? Most claim they can successfully treat youth dealing with a wide range of issues, such as:

attention deficit disorders,
anxiety disorders,
major depressive disorder,
bipolar disorder,
identity disorder,
eating disorders,
adoption issues,
attachment issues,
anger issues,
defiance issues,
learning difficulties,
lack of motivation,
low self-esteem,
negative peer relationships,
poor family relationships,
poor social skills,
rebelliousness,

sexually acting out,
substance addiction,
trauma-related issues

They all claim they will turn your child around. The following statements are from a random sampling of program websites:

Parents often come to us in a state of despair and hopelessness, but when they see what we've accomplished with the teens in our program, they become cautiously optimistic. Once their teen progresses in our program, and they begin to see glimpses of the child they remember and love, hope returns. After 12 months at our therapeutic boarding school in Montana, hope turns to deep, heartfelt gratitude, and the immeasurable joy that comes from seeing one's child healthy, confident, and re-engaged with family, school, and life.[2]

Eagle Ranch Academy is a program that helps each student gain the necessary skills and tools to become a productive, happy and successful person.[3]

For almost 20 years we have served thousands of troubled teens and their families, helping them realize their potential and rebuild their lives.[4]

As you read the information on these websites, you start to feel hopeful. You think, *Maybe they can turn my child around, too.* Perhaps you also feel a twinge of caution: *Can these programs really handle youth who are struggling with that wide a variety of issues?* Then, even if you assume the claims are correct, which is the best program for your child? The variety in approaches these programs take is mind-boggling.

To illustrate this point, I have included below a sampling of the approaches these self-acclaimed "successful" programs use, as described on their websites. Some of these programs may in fact be very good, but they are also incredibly expensive and many prey on desperate parents who will spend anything, do anything, to try to help their struggling child. Because, as I stated before, they are not regulated, the vast majority have not been evaluated, and many do not follow up after youth leave the program, so they cannot possibly know whether their program has had a lasting positive impact on a child's life. Yet look at these excerpts:

> The RedCliff treatment protocol recognizes the child and the illness are two distinctly separate components. Each is specifically addressed in the therapeutic process. Our wilderness therapy program helps the student and family understand how a specific cluster of symptoms associated with their diagnosis has impacted the student's developmental progression. RedCliff's therapeutic model disrupts the developmental vacation and reintegrates the student into an age-appropriate developmental progression.[5]

> Arivaca Boys Ranch is a unique program that uses three powerful therapeutic tools to help teen boys get on a right path in life. First, a specialized form of equine therapy. Equine therapy is commonly used to help teens who are struggling, but we take it one step further, we teach the boys to become "horse whisperers." Known as the "Arivaca Way," our therapeutic model teaches boys to understand how their behavior or mood affects their horse, and that helps them become more aware and responsible of their actions and how they affect others. Secondly, we use Arbinger Principles to help provide a foundation for moving behavior from anger to positive motivational action. The principles were devel-

oped by the Arbinger Institute, which is a worldwide leader in training on anger management. And third, we use the working ranch setting for training, responsibility and positive peer influence as a means of helping the teen grow in maturity.[6]

New Haven employs a variety of therapeutic modalities—individual, group, family, talk, experiential, and even equine-assisted—to ensure the highest level of therapeutic traction possible with individual students and their families. Traditional talk therapy has its place, but at New Haven, we know that that place is in a system of relationship-based therapies that engage our students in a variety of ways.[7]

How in the world are parents supposed to sort through this kind of information and figure out which, if any, program will help their child? I remember thinking that the decision of where to send Sadie would have a significant impact on the rest of her life and on us as a family. The right decision, I thought, could turn her life around. It could mean she would return to the happy, funny, passionate person she had been. It could mean she would become the productive, happy, well-adjusted person we knew she could be. The pressure to make a quick decision, the right decision, was enormous. Nothing else in our lives mattered but this decision.

But we still had no idea how to choose, then, and still today. These programs also rely heavily on testimonials—e.g., "as our testimonials indicate"—to imply outcomes. At best, testimonials indicate that a program has helped some individual, at least in the short term. But even if that is true, for how long did it help? And which programs are most effective at helping youth dealing with the same issues your own child is dealing with?

Think about the variables. Did the youth go to a wilderness treatment program first? Which of the "issues" or combination of the issues was the youth struggling with before entering the program—depression, anxiety, addictions, ADHD, eating disorders? Did the youth have a supportive family or an abusive family? Were they on medication and if so, which medication? Were they adopted? How long did the youth stay in the program? Did they go on to a boarding school afterward? Has the program checked to see whether the youth are well adjusted, leading happy, productive lives a year, five years, ten years after discharge? So many questions, yet so little data.

The sad truth is that the outcomes these programs claim, especially long-term outcomes, for the most part have not been verified. In 2004, when we were looking, statistically based studies about specific program outcomes just did not exist. Even today, there are no data to help you understand the odds that any particular program will help your child. The research necessary to verify program outcomes and correlate them with specific characteristics of youth, and then to extrapolate those to the broader population, is expensive and difficult and at the time had just not been done. I remember being stunned, thinking, *Are we supposed to spend enormous amounts of money on something unproven?*

Beyond the lack of outcome data, how are parents supposed to afford this type of treatment? Most health insurance policies will not pay for these programs. And even if parents can somehow find the money, how can they spend what these programs cost without any proof of outcomes? In 2005, when we were looking at programs, costs were typically in the $5,000- to $10,000-per-month range. And while length of stay varies, typically it's anywhere from nine months to two years—likely more than the cost of a high-quality college education.

Yet parents do spend this kind of money if they have it, or can obtain it from a college fund, second mortgage or borrowing from a retirement fund, as we did, because they are so desperate to help their child. Because they are afraid the mistakes their child is making and the behavior they are exhibiting will destroy their lives. Or that they will die on the streets. Because the prospect of doing nothing to help your child is just so frightening.

So, without proof of long-term outcomes, you believe or at least hope that the claims these programs make are true. If nothing else, you think your child will be safe while in the program. But not even that is always true. The Government Accountability Office, in an April 2008 report, described cases at some treatment programs in which ineffective management, abuse, inadequate nourishment, untrained staff, and negligent operating practices resulted in youth deaths.

There has to be a better solution. But we couldn't find one. Parents who send their child to a program like any of these should be demanding that program evaluations be conducted. But how do you do that when you are so desperate that you'll grab at anything that might help your child? This is an area where the scientific community and perhaps even the government should step in and assess how best to channel resources to effective strategies, rather than to whatever program has the best testimonials and marketing.

Interestingly, I spoke with the director of a state adolescent and child psychiatric hospital in the Northwest and asked him if they conducted any evaluations to assess long-term outcomes of their treatment programs. He said no. He wished they did, but they didn't have the money to do so. They tracked many metrics to judge effectiveness—for example, the number of outbursts in a given time period while a patient was there—but they did not have the resources to follow up after discharge. I suspect this is the case with most adolescent psychiatric hospitals like the kind we admitted Sadie to after her suicide attempts. None of those facilities did any follow-up, either.

While I describe these programs cynically, I do think that the therapeutic wilderness treatment program and the residential treatment program helped Sadie—at least in the short term—and, at the very least, kept her alive for a couple of years. If program staff had asked us for a testimonial shortly after her discharge from the treatment facility she attended, we likely would have said we saw much improvement in Sadie and that we had hope again, as did she. The program would likely have called her a success, too. Yet the program never called to find out how Sadie was doing, or to help us understand how to ensure that she did not slip back into old behaviors or how she could effectively reintegrate into "normal" life after her discharge.

If, in fact, these programs are the best way to help troubled teens, a great deal more research and evaluation needs to be done to isolate the elements of the programs that are effective and to link specific disorders with specific treatment elements. I sometimes wonder whether, if these programs were regulated by the government, the companies that run them would be required to conduct independent program evaluations, to statistically assess program outcomes.

Some associations that represent members (treatment programs) do provide program standards or a means of sharing best practices, such as the Outdoor Behavioral Healthcare Industry Council (OBHIC), which has been instrumental in facilitating research to study the efficacy of outdoor treatment. Other industry organizations review and provide accreditation for these programs. Some state that they are accredited by the Joint Commission (JCAHO), for example. But what does that mean? That the facilities are clean? That they adhere to some sort of program standard?

As of 2015, the Federal Trade Commission (FTC), the nation's consumer protection agency, reported:

> No standard definitions exist for specific types of programs. The programs are not regulated by the federal government, and many are not subject to state licensing or monitoring as mental health or educational facilities, either. A 2007 Report to Congress by the Government Accountability Office (GAO) found cases involving serious abuse and neglect at

some of these programs. Many programs advertise on the Internet and through other media, making claims about staff credentials, the level of treatment a participant will receive, program accreditation, education credit transfers, success rates, and endorsements by educational consultants.[8]

The FTC cautions that before you enroll a youngster in a private residential treatment program:

- Check it out online.

- Ask questions.

- Ask for proof or support for claims about staff credentials, program accreditation, and endorsements.

- Do a site visit.

- Get all policies and promises in writing.

According to the FTC, several independent nonprofit organizations, like the Joint Commission on Accreditation of Healthcare Organizations (JACHO), the Council on Accreditation (COA), and the Commission on Accreditation of Rehabilitation Facilities (CARF), accredit mental health programs and providers.

- JCAHO (now called the Joint Commission) accredits and certifies more than twenty thousand health care organizations and programs in the United States, including behavioral health organizations. JCAHO's focus is on performance standards related to safety and quality.

- COA is an international child- and family-service and behavioral health care organization that accredits thirty-eight different service areas, including substance abuse treatment, and more than sixty types of programs. COA accreditation signifies that an organization or program is effectively managing its resources and providing the best possible services to all its stakeholders.

- CARF is an independent, nonprofit accreditor of human-services providers in areas such as behavioral health, child and youth services, and employment and community services. CARF accreditation requires a service provider to commit to quality improvement, focus on the unique needs of each person the provider serves, and monitor the results of services.

These accreditations are important, but they do not address long-term effectiveness of the programs. It is really incredible to think that these treatment programs do not have to do independent evaluations of outcomes. In my field of expertise, energy efficiency, initiatives such as energy-efficiency rebate programs are routinely evaluated. It is common to spend 5–10% percent of program cost on evaluation. How else do you know what is working and what is not? How else do you know how to improve your program? Yet for these mental health treatment programs, parents are spending $5,000 to $10,000 a month without any guarantees of outcomes or any statistical basis for projecting outcomes. Clearly, the cost to evaluate these programs would be high and would result in already extremely expensive programs' being even more costly. Perhaps the variables in individuals, backgrounds, and issues are so great that getting statistically valid results would be difficult. But this work needs to be done.

19

Her Statement Changed Everything

OUR SEARCH FOR A TREATMENT PROGRAM THAT WOULD HELP SADIE was narrowed slightly because, first, we knew she was a runaway risk; second, we believed depression or bipolar disorder was driving her behavior, so we did not think a boot camp–style program would be helpful; and third, she was a bright, creative, independent individual, and we wanted her to be intellectually stimulated. Beyond that, we really didn't know how to sort through the options. But we did our own search, came up with a few programs we thought might be a good fit, then returned to the educational consultants for help. Because they had visited programs, had built an understanding of who Sadie was and what her issues were, and had conferred with the counselors and therapists at Second Nature, they were in a good position to help us.

When we met with them and told them about the programs (based on our Internet searches) that we thought would be best for Sadie, they immediately said, "Oh, no, you don't want to send her to those! They're completely wrong for her and might do more harm than good." So much for our ability to sift through the morass of programs on our own. I was convinced I just did not know enough to be the right parent for Sadie, and I felt so inadequate. I loved her and just wanted her to get better but clearly was not capable of accomplishing that myself. I don't have any way of knowing whether the consultants were correct, but they were certainly more knowledgeable than we were. Even so, they also did not have the benefit of long-term-outcome studies to guide their recommendations.

The consultants came up with a short list of programs they recommended, and before Sadie was discharged, Dennis and I flew to Montana to visit one of the facilities that was classified as an emotional growth school—the program we thought would be the best fit. We really liked the place and thought it would be ideal for Sadie, but, unfortunately, the day before she was to be discharged from Second Nature, she showed a note to another youth that stated she was going to take her life. That note changed everything. No longer was the Montana program sufficient if she was really suicidal; in fact, the Montana program staff stated that, given the note, they no longer believed they were the appropriate placement for Sadie. We argued hard to have her sent there, to the place that seemed like it would provide more of the life she was used to—a more "normal" place—but Sadie's note sealed her fate. So much careful planning was undone by one more upset that required a whirlwind effort to change our plans and strategies.

Rather than an emotional growth school, the consultants recommended a residential treatment program, which would be much more restrictive. Dennis flew to Texas to visit the one they suggested, High Frontier. There, he found out they did not have a bed (which is how these facilities refer to availability), so we turned to our backup: High Frontier's sister program in New Mexico, Rancho Valmora, whose program description on its website was as follows:

Our mission is to provide a positive environment for social learning, teaching care and concern for oneself and others through adherence to the Positive Peer Culture Treatment Model. Positive Peer Culture is the catalyst for systematically promoting social interest as the agent of change for young people experiencing academic, family, emotional, and/or behavioral problems.

"The central position of this model is that young people can develop self-worth, significance, dignity and responsibility only as they become committed to the positive values of helping and caring for others."
—Harry Vorrath, author of *Positive Peer Culture*

Our treatment program is intended for 12–18-year-old males and females who may be experiencing a wide range of emotional, behavioral and educational problems. These problems have reached at a level of acuteness where 24-hour supervision, a structured living environment, special education services and an intensive therapeutic milieu are appropriate.

Even though we hated to send Sadie somewhere we had not visited and where we had not yet met the staff, we liked the positive-peer-culture concept and were again fearful for Sadie's life, given her suicide note, so we reluctantly agreed to send her to Rancho Valmora.

A few days later, we flew to Utah to pick her up and then flew with her directly to New Mexico. We spent a few wonderful—indeed, almost perfect—days as a family together in Santa Fe before we took her to Rancho Valmora. We were all elated to be together again, even if only briefly—we just leaned in to each other. Sadie hadn't enjoyed being with us like that for a long time. We felt like a normal, happy family again. The rest of the world ceased to exist—it was just us, together, feeling blissful—something most people take for granted.

But that time had to end. Moving onward, we proceeded with phase two of life without Sadie. We had to drop her off and leave her again. She was still only fourteen and a freshman in high school, and we knew she would likely need to stay there for twelve to twenty-four months. When we said our goodbyes after we got her settled at Rancho Valmora, it was all I could do to not grab her and run. Couldn't we run off to France, change our names, make a new start? Oh, I knew better, but I did have my fantasies. Even today, I can feel that gut-wrenching pain as I struggle with the conflict between my heart and mind. In my mind, I knew Sadie needed to be there, while my heart just ached—I didn't know how I was going to make it without her for so long. But we just wanted her to be happy again.

20

———

Life in Residential Treatment—
the Good, the Bad, and the Ugly

RANCHO VALMORA WAS SPREAD OUT IN A REMOTE AREA OF THE NEW Mexico high desert, twenty miles from the nearest town. Located on the front range of the Sangre de Cristo Mountains at an elevation of approximately 5,500 feet, it was so far out in the country, off an unused road, that there was really nowhere for someone to escape to. Blue skies were vast and stretched for miles over the area, which receives more than three hundred days of sunshine per year. The entire palette of colors—earth tones everywhere—was different from that of the lush, green Northwest. The air there was so dry, my throat felt parched all the time. So, although Rancho Valmora was considered a secure facility, the location allowed for a more open feel. The campus included an accredited high school, a gym, a horse barn with horses, multiple small dormitories, a dining hall, a recreation room, and many farm-like outbuildings. Hiking trails led to bluffs and a river nearby.

Each person, upon entering Rancho Valmora, was assigned to a cohort of nine youth of the same gender. This cohort went to school, group sessions, and other activities together; its makeup changed only when a member "graduated." Each cohort had its own small, one-story dorm composed of shared bedrooms with a living room. Boys and girls were in separate dorms.

The girls in Sadie's group, all high school freshmen, came from wide-ranging backgrounds. Some were from middle-class, professional families, and others from families in which the youth had been exposed to drug addiction, abuse, or neglect. Other than the Portland street kids, this was Sadie's first deep exposure to young people who came from pretty rough backgrounds. She told me that one evening, when she was reading a book while the other youth were watching TV, they asked her, "Why would you read a book when you can watch TV?" Sadie told me that this was the first time she realized that not all parents valued education like her own parents did. Sometimes I thought it was good for her to witness the diversity of people in the United States; other times I really wished she could have stayed in her safe cocoon and not been exposed at such a young age to the difficulties some people face. Regardless, we could no longer provide that cocoon.

The days were filled with school and homework, just as would be the case for any teenager. The youth also raised goats and pigs, did artwork, worked with horses (animal therapy), and did chores. As for treatment, Sadie had group sessions with her peers after school every day, individual therapy sessions, and weekly family therapy sessions by phone with Dennis and me. The group sessions were hard for Sadie and, I suppose, probably for all the girls. Based on Sadie's reports, the girls called each other out on behavioral problems during these sessions. I'm sure it was meant to be constructive, but Sadie, especially at first, did not find these responses helpful.

We visited her in New Mexico every six to eight weeks. At first, we could visit her only "on campus," but as she progressed through treatment, we were able to be with her off campus. We took trips with her to Santa Fe, Los Alamos (where I was born), Bandelier National Monument, and Las Vegas (where Sadie's grandfather went to college). We always went to what quickly became our favorite restaurant in Santa Fe, La Casa Sena—quite a unique place, where Sadie just came to life. The waiters periodically broke out in Broadway show tunes, jazz numbers, and other songs during dinner, and Sadie always went up to one of them to ask for a special song—sometimes from the musical *Rent*, or "Route 66" (a song she remembered my father and uncle singing boisterously at the piano in my parents' house). What fun we had.

After the first year of the program, we were able to take Sadie on home visits, too. Dennis and I lived for those times. We watched movies, cooked meals, went for walks in the woods, explored Portland—all together as a family. We pretended for just those few days each time that everything was normal. But it wasn't, and each visit eventually had to come to an end. At least we could see the progress Sadie was making, even though leaving her was always hard. As Sadie said in her letter below, "Each parting feels as though I'm being ripped away again." We always smiled her, hugged her, and reminded her that we would be back very soon—stiff upper lip—until we drove off the ranch and the tears started falling. My fantasy was that I would grab her and run off with her somewhere we could be together, but I knew better. Sometimes it's so hard to be the adult.

An excerpt from one of Sadie's "Dear Mom and Papa" letters, sent early in her stay at Rancho Valmora, shows just how hard it was for her:

I don't think I've ever missed you so much. It is almost a physical pain. I know what I need to do, and I remember my promise to you. I feel as if there is something that needs to come out. Maybe tears, but I think I've cried enough to fill the Nile River. Most of all what I miss is someone to hold, so I can be your little girl again and not an adult before my time. I miss so many things, and each parting feels as though I'm being ripped away again. Shoot, now I made myself cry. What am I going to do? Where do I go from here? I'm just so disoriented. One of the things that's making me so sad is waking up here. I guess that's good, though I don't want to become comfortable—I'm fighting through. . . . Don't worry that I'm going to slip back to where I was before. I'm a fighter, remember?

Oh, how painful it is to read that sentence now: "I'm a fighter, remember?" When I first read the letter, I just smiled. Something in that statement made me feel confident that she really was going to make it through. She was our Sadie, after all—our resourceful, passionate, strong girl. What happened that caused her only a few years later to lose that fighting instinct? She was so strong in some ways and yet not strong enough to cope with the hand she was dealt. Not strong enough to overcome the demons in her mind.

After the first several months at Rancho Valmora, we talked with the program's consulting psychiatrist about whether or not Sadie should be on medication. She had been off her meds since she'd started Second Nature, and, given her suicide attempts on different antidepressants, we were not eager to try them again. We really wanted to see whether she could learn to cope with her depression without medication. Perhaps that was an example of my unwillingness to acknowledge or accept that Sadie might have a permanent mental disorder that needed to be treated, yet the psychiatrist seemed flexible, saying we could try either way. So she stayed off.

On the flip side, life for Sadie during those first months at Rancho Valmora was quite a struggle. Her writing that we found years later makes clear how she vacillated between hope and hopelessness, between frustration and success, how isolated she felt. Physical contact was not allowed at Rancho Valmora; I suppose some of the youth there had been abused, so the program erred on the side of caution, but Sadie hated that no-touching rule—she had always been someone who leaned in for a hug, and she loved to snuggle. In pictures of her, she is often leaning in toward the person she is with or holding their hand.

As with Second Nature, Rancho Valmora made her face and question her own behavior and the impact it had on others. How difficult it was for the youth there to do that, and to have others critique everything they did and said. I wished Sadie didn't have to be put through that; I wished she could just have sleepovers with friends, do things most fourteen- and fifteen-year-olds normally do. When she was admitted to the program, she was angry, hopeless, in some kind of internal pain that I cannot imagine, as her journal entries reflect:

I feel like I'm in an endless ocean. I'm in cold ice water, no land is in sight. I can stay afloat for a while. But once in a while my strength fails, and I sink into that frozen world. I hate it there. No hope, emotion, or happiness. Even when I'm in the sunshine I feel cold. I am silent, my soul is slowly suffocating. I want out, by any way possible. But I can't, too much is being hung over my head. Perfection, how can such a thing be asked of this cold corpse? When can the hopeless agony end? I know I need to ask for what I need. Sometimes I sit alone at night wanting something, a hug, support, anything. Why is this happening? God, why don't you love me? Everything happens for a reason? Bullshit!! Sometimes I just want to disappear. I squirm with discomfort knowing this pain will never end. Just help me escape. Let me disappear. What good is life anyway? God sucks. I've been in pain the past 5 years. Just kill me, drive a knife through my heart, at least then you can see the shatters. What kind of help is this? If I try to talk, I get shut down. I want to scream, but no, I can't. Nothing is ever good.

You can't read what she wrote without thinking that she was at rock bottom. In some ways, knowing that she was somewhere that would keep her safe—knowing that for a while, someone else had to take over the responsibility for keeping her alive, when it was just too much responsibility for us—was a relief.

21

Going Back to Serving the Goddess

As her time at Rancho Valmora progressed, Sadie started looking forward to the future; she seemed to have gotten her inner strength back. We could see the positive changes in her over her fifteen months there, and we saw it in her letters to us and in her writing we found after she died. The program did seem to be successful in forcing her to face her behavior and her deep-seated hopelessness. Her writing shows not only how hard that was for her but also her tenacity. The following excerpt from her journal highlights her awareness of her situation and her struggle and, surprisingly, her fear of getting better.

> *Why I pull what I do. I think it's because I'm scared to change. I am trying to think about what Clay [her counselor] said: the truth is simple. I think it is too. And here is the truth: I am fighting a battle between old behaviors and new. I won't just "try" anymore. I will actually do it. I know I consciously make the decision. I actually think about it when I decide to walk away. I know there are times when I just am watching what's coming out of my mouth. I want to get better. I just don't know how. Please help me, somebody please just help me. But I don't want help because that would mean getting better, and I'm scared of that. I'm terrified of having to be healthy. Of not being able to go back. I guess I'll just have to grit my teeth and do it.*

It never occurred to me that Sadie would have been afraid of getting better, but the excerpt below from one of her letters emphasizes precisely that fear, as well as her understanding that she needed to make changes in her life but found it hard to do so.

What am I afraid of? Their criticism? Or maybe hearing that I have problems? Accepting that and quitting being so stubborn? I hate hearing confrontation. I hate hearing everything I did (or am doing) wrong. It seems as if everything I do, there's something wrong with it. But isn't there? I mean, I need to get confronted. I know I do. Why is it so hard? But then again, it's not supposed to be easy. Everybody says I know what I need to do, but I don't. I'm as lost as if I was in the Sahara without a compass. This too shall pass. But how quickly? Have I done anything here? It's been said that I am doing the same things as when I came here, just in more passive ways. What have I accomplished here? Or was this just a big sham? I'm missing something. Just hopping around it and not saying it. I'm terrified. There, I said it. I'm so terrified. I'm hurt and scared. What more can I say? What else can I tell you to make you understand what's going on? That I know what I want, I just don't do it. I know what I need, I just can't find it. I'm blind. I'm so blind it's crazy.

But I choose to be blind rather than face this. What is this, you ask? My mistakes. The big huge mess in my life. I hate looking at it. I hate recognizing it, but I will, I must if I want to come home. That's what is driving me, that is why I try so hard. Right now I don't care what is right or wrong. It just feels good to get it out. I don't know if you recognize me right now, but I'm tired of lying, I'm tired of giving everyone this BS. What is the problem, though? It is that I ignore my problems. I run from them so hard I forget what I'm running from. Then, when I turn around to face it, what am I facing? Nothing. Oh my gosh, I feel a little better. I can't say that everything is all right, but

it's going to be. I have faith in myself. I love you guys very much. I
wanted you guys to see what I'm really thinking and feeling.

As a parent, you have to find the right balance between respecting the privacy of your child and needing to understand enough of what is going on with their life that you know they are safe and healthy. We were fortunate that Sadie wrote to us about her inner feelings at Rancho Valmora, but we (and her therapists) would have benefited from understanding her even deeper thoughts and emotions. Knowing those would have informed her treatment and therapy.

I believe now that as a parent you do need to invade your child's privacy (respectfully and without judgment) just enough to know they are safe and to be able to help them if they are struggling. This is even more important in the digital age of social media, blogging, and online journaling. In 2014, while volunteering on a crisis line headquartered in Portland, I frequently spoke with young people who shared with me feelings that they won't or don't know how to share with their parents. In some cases, they think their parents won't believe them or will just think they are being manipulative. In most cases, I believe struggling youth would be better off if their parents really understood how they are feeling. Knowing what your child is communicating, in personal writing, to others anonymously, or to friends, will help you understand. Dennis and I erred on the side of respecting Sadie's privacy, when, in hindsight, I know that better understanding her inner feelings would have enabled more effective intervention.

At some point during her stay at Rancho Valmora, after months of group and therapy, she seemed to have thrown off the grip of the street kids. We could see her strength and resolve returning. Later, we found this statement in her journal:

I have decided to go back to serving the goddess. It is her that kept me
alive all those times I wanted so badly to die.

I don't know for sure what "goddess" she was referring to or what she meant by "serving the goddess," but I think her statement was a sign of her growing inner strength. Throughout literature, the goddess takes many forms, including Our Lady of Guadalupe, Gaia, and Demeter. Perhaps Sadie believed in a higher power—a universal strength and nurturing force. Perhaps she meant she was going to honor those attributes that are applied to the goddess, to be open to those attributes (or goddess archetypes) in herself. Perhaps, as they say at Find Your Goddess Archetype (www.goddess-power.com), she had decided she was going to discover her true nature—her innate gifts and abilities, recognize where they were best suited in life, and appreciate their strengths, as well as understanding their challenges. Discovering goddess influences within a woman can guide her in creating her own true life story—not a story directed by others. Such understanding and inner access can empower her to make conscious choices that offer her personal meaning and fulfillment. For Sadie, I think this meant she was going to be more true to herself, rather than letting what others thought influence her so much.

In keeping with their efforts to preserve a semblance of normal high school life for the youth at Rancho Valmora, staff there organized a fall prom with youth from a nearby high school. I loved the idea that Sadie was experiencing some of the "normal" parts of high school. The girls in her dorm worked off-site, doing yard cleanup, to earn the money they wanted to get their hair and nails done for prom. We sent Sadie a prom dress. I remember the pictures she sent us of the girls giggling and helping each other with their hair and dresses. Sadie had a date (actually, two) for the event—youth from one of the boys' dorms.

Her pictures from that time show her huge grin, ear to ear, that I loved. She actually looked happy in the photos. It was the first time in a long time. Perhaps, just perhaps, the program was working for her! However, years later, I found a poem that she wrote about that prom night, which demonstrates one of the aspects of Sadie that made it so difficult to help her. If you saw the photos—the huge grin, that laughter—you would think she was doing well, but clearly, underneath that smile, deep inside, she was still hurting. She had merely gained the ability to temporarily get pleasure out of life, or to wall off that part of her that was so desperately unhappy. That ability constantly threw us off—it made us believe (in part because we so wanted to believe) that she was really better. It was yet another example of the many discrepancies between how *I* thought she was doing and how (based on her writing) she was actually feeling.

Prom

Scarred arms,
healing from recent abuse,
wave in abandon,
ball gowns and tuxedos,
 gyrate on the floor,
  to the beat of a bass.
She smiles and laughs.
Be happy for tonight,
forget about your sorrows,
for tomorrow,
the unrelenting sadness,
hopelessness,
depression
will come again.
So be happy for tonight,
for tomorrow carries with it
the threat of
REALITY.

By contrast, the letter below shows the progress Sadie made, as she describes the ups and downs of her day, which sounds much like a "normal" teenage day. Her sense of humor, which had been gone for so long, resurfaced, and her awareness of the things she struggled with and her efforts to work on those things is very clear.

Mama and Papa

Tues. Today has been an up-and-down day. Ups: your package, waking up, the morning, riding tiny bareback (Tiny is a huge horse— his shoulder is taller than I am), and formals. Downs: my peer having problems, getting angry while riding Tiny, taking comments . . . Overall today has been a difficult day. I will elaborate on them so you can have a better understanding of them. First off: your package. My shoe was a very welcome sight. The jewelry and the purse are exquisite. I've already tried my whole outfit on. I felt like a princess in New Mexico. This morning when I woke up I felt in charge and on top of the world. I was quickly disabused of this by my group member. Maybe she was jealous of my halo. During horsemanship I was bareback on a Belgian draft! They are the BIG horses that have hooves twice as big as my face. That was a big ego boost for me. Probably pretty embarrassing for Tiny, seeing as I tied his mane into a ponytail (no pun intended) on the top of his head so he looked like one of these plastic troll dolls. (I'm sure Tiny appreciates that description.) Formals was cool because I was again on top of the world. I was being a "positive peer." Whatever that is. On a more serious note, the lows of the day. My peer has been having problems today but she worked through it and is doing better. I was really stressed, though. I was also having trouble controlling Tiny and got angry. I talked to my peers about that and I am doing better with that too. I also worked through taking problems on. So, overall, a hard roller coaster but a good one. These marks are from my eraser. I was really stressed with everything in my mind earlier today. I took a shower and am calming down.

Wed. morning—today I'm going to make this a good day. I talked to my

roommate last night and we discussed some stuff. I need to go because
Liz wants me to do her eyeliner
Much love,
Your daughter,
Sadie
I ♥ U

At some point during her stay at Rancho Valmora, Sadie's feelings about being adopted surfaced. I don't recall the exact genesis, but I do know that on one of her home visits, she found a phone number for her birth grandmother and called her out of the blue from Rancho Valmora. I am sure she was hoping to talk to her birth mother. Instead, she was told that her birth mother was a drug addict and that Sadie had a half sister whom we didn't know about. Apparently, her birth mother had a second daughter a few years after Sadie was born and decided to keep her but at some point lost custody of her. When Sadie told her birth grandmother that she was in a treatment program, the grandmother told Sadie not to call until she had finished treatment and had gotten her life back under control. The counselors at Rancho Valmora strongly recommended to us and to Sadie that she have no further contact with her birth family—that it was too much for her to deal with at the time.

Were the counselors wrong? Was adoption an underlying cause of Sadie's problems, of her low sense of self-worth? I'm sure they talked to Sadie about her adoption, but should they have addressed it in more depth? Certainly, anecdotal evidence (such as the high percent of youth in these troubled-teen programs who are adopted) suggests that adoption was a factor for her, and research shows that adopted children are more likely than the general population of children to be diagnosed with depression, ADD or ADHD, or a behavioral or conduct disorder.

The question, however, brings up a cause-and-effect issue. Does adoption/abandonment cause mental health issues, or are the mental health issues many adopted kids deal with genetically based, and are young girls with mental health issues more likely to get pregnant, have a baby, and put the baby up for adoption? And why are some children totally okay with being adopted, while others struggle with it for their entire lives? These questions comprise just one more area that needs research, and one more area in which as parents, Dennis and I felt a bit abandoned—the adoption agency never told us how much adoption might impact Sadie, never educated us on ways to deal with the issue if it surfaced. Rather, they told us that it was best to tell Sadie at an early age that she was adopted and that she was lucky her birth mother chose to give her up to a family that could support her, a family that desperately wanted her.

Regardless, I do not think the counselors helped Sadie enough with the adoption issue. Leaving that issue on the table, addressed only partially at the time of her discharge, was like ignoring a dormant but active volcano that would someday blow. But somehow, we all moved around it and, despite our not having thoroughly addressed it, Sadie did continue to improve.

Sometime during the latter part of her stay, she wrote this wonderful poem about fireflies, reminiscing about our days in Madison. While her writing shows the significant improvement in her state of mind, it also illustrates just how difficult it was for her at that young age to be away from home, at a treatment center—such as in the line *Only the cold exterior[s] of houses glare back.* At least at this point, she was remembering her life in a positive light and her mental state seems to have been in a much less painful place—though I cannot read this poem without crying at her statement that someday she will show her own children how to catch fireflies in a jar.

Fireflies

*I remember when, not so long ago it seems, that fireflies held the
mystery of moonlit summer nights and, wet air puffing from our mouths,
we ran after, arms outstretched, old jam jars in our hands to see if we
too could trap the lights that taunted us. And finally, our small bodies
worn out, we would collapse together, a sweaty-limbed pile of mirth.
Thoughts of yesterday and tomorrow left to the wind gently caressing
our mouths as laughter bubbled forth. It was in that instant that
jealousy was forgotten, oblivious to wealth or color or status, those
would be thoughts for another time, a time when fireflies and the sweet
taste of Mother's iced tea were forgotten under files and documents and
the bitterness of dreams thwarted. Where I live now, there are no
winking lights and when I look out my window there are not children
playing. Only the cold exterior[s] of houses glare back at me, as if to
dare me to wish for more. Sometimes I wonder if the world has grown
cold, caught up in fashion and money, racing ahead like dodo birds.
And as these thoughts swirl in my head, I remember laughter and the
shrieking ecstasy of the chase and I know, when I grow old, and the
sun's rays have bleached the mobility from my bones, and all of life has
piled its woes atop me, I will go outside and taste summer night, a taste
that speaks of freedom and laughter and sweating glasses of iced tea.
And I will show my own children the best way to catch 20 in one jar.*

Dennis and I still didn't talk much to our friends about what
was going on with Sadie, particularly not with our new friends and
work colleagues in Portland. We were still naively thinking she
would get better and would be able to return to normal life and be a
happy teenager who would eventually go off to college, establish a
unique career, get married and raise her own family, and, in the end,
do something to make the world a better place.

Sadie's Poetry Journey

Near the end of her stay at Rancho Valmora, Sadie sent us a spiral-bound notebook containing a photo journal of her life. When we read it, and as I read it now, we saw an undeniable transformation toward a positive and hope-filled orientation of life, and we truly thought that the treatment—though it had been extremely challenging for our whole family—had worked magic.

Sadie and Mom (Karen)
Northern Wisconsin, fall 2002

Dreams

A time without knowledge of pain and misery,
Seeming decades away
 Was there really such a time?
 Perhaps once eons away,
 Now will seem like sucha dream,
  As this is

Sadie and Papa (Dennis)
Grand Gulch, Utah, spring 2003

The first day,
  of Happiness,
The first dawn,
  of terror,
Yet thoughts of this,
Was far away this day,
This snapshot of humanity,
Think not of what is,
        to come,
Think not of what has,
    Passed,
Think only of today,
And of how to forget,
    the future

Sadie and Mom
Karate Black Belt Award Day, Madison, WI, Fall of 8th grade, 2003

First Taste

My first taste of sucess,
The first time I found out,
 I can do this,
 Smiles from ear to ear,
 In that hotel lobby,
       I was Queen,
 All sadness forgotten,
 Hopelessness can come later
 For now I'll just bask,
 In my first taste of sucess

Sadie and Papa
Whistler, British Columbia, summer before 9th grade, 2004

The transition,
from bad to worse,
the beginning,
    of an end,
Who would have guessed,
What horrors were in store
Again we face,
    a change
What entity could tell us,
    What is to come

Will it be for naught?

New beginnings,
    have a ring,
        of hope
Old stories are tinged,
    with guilt

Sadie and Mom
Santa Fe, New Mexico, summer before 10th grade, 2005

Nevermore

How **symbolic**
a mother looking,
    towards her child,
the child,
    looking away,
Nevermore,
    Nevermore,
as the raven cried,
Nevermore will this day,
    come again

Sadie and Papa
Backpacking in Mt. Jefferson Wilderness, Oregon
summer before 11th grade, 2006

Memories

Reminiscent,
    of another time,
Yet so,
    similar,
      to now,
What new treasures,
    may we yet uncover?
And what old refuse,
    must we now bury,
      deep,
        deep,
Into the dark recesses,
    of our loving hearts;

Sadie
Second Nature Wilderness Program, Utah, winter 2005

Conquerings

A reconciliation,
    of old anger,
A realazation,
    of fresh hurt,
who shall dare,
    to interrupt,
        this newfound happiness?
And who shall be,
        bold,
And conquer the rest?

Sadie and Mom
Oregon Coast, fall of 9th grade, 2004

Portland

Another time,
Yet the same place,
 how curiously,
     the two coincide,
How Ironic,
    that the same place I once
         considered alien,
             now is my home
   and yet,
      still alien to me

Sadie with her birth parents and adoptive parents
Tacoma, Washington, July 1990

An acorn tree

The root,
    of a mighty oak,
I am only now,
      starting to fell,
Remember now,
    even an oak,
      springs from an acorn,
what is left,
    however,
is to capture it

Sadie, Papa, and Grandma
Central Wisconsin, 7th grade, 2004

The Ending of A Dynasty

Anger,
    of no descent,
unearned,
    unwanted,
        and feared,
a lion,
    who has now been,
            tamed,
I shall now take off,
        this mask,
            of tragedy,
and let comedy,
        this bright-faced,
            angel of mirth,
    rule my heart

Family Reunion
Whistler, British Columbia, 2004

Where Shall I turn?

A congregation,
as one,
It is now,
that I realize,
I am not simply one,
I am a seamless part
of this many,
Where shall I turn,
when I am hungr
They shall be my bread,
where shall I turn,
when I am thirsty?
They shall be my water
And where shall I turn,
when I am weak?
They shall be my strength

Sadie and Papa
Santa Fe, New Mexico, summer before 10th grade, 2005

Sudden Sight

My biggest fan,
    when I am losing,

My staunchest ally,
    when I have none,

My compass,
    when I am lost,

Why is it,
    simply now,
      that I see,
what has been there,
    all along?

Sadie and Mom
Santa Fe, New Mexico, summer before 10th grade, 2005

Mom

Once again,
           united,
   Ecstatic,
     that I am no longer,
            near the end,
I praise,
        whoever is listening,
          That I have my mother back,
            but also my,
               best friend

Sadie, Papa, and Mom
Rancho Valmora, winter of 10th grade, 2005

Family Again

Releif,
    that is all that can,
           be said,
What else,
     can you say,
  to simbolize,
     the resurection,

of a family?

Sadie and Papa
Rancho Valmora, spring of 10th grade, 2006

The start,
    of a long road,
the first step,
    of a thousand miles,
For now,
    I am thankful,
I can rest,
    here for a while

Sunrise
or
Sunset?
The beginning of the new,
Or the end of the old?
Both Are Welcomed

22

Leaving a Chapter of Life

AT RANCHO VALMORA, A YOUTH IS READY FOR DISCHARGE WHEN THE therapists, counselors, and peers in their group all agree on it. The youth has to work with both staff and peers at the Ranch and with their parents to develop a plan for reintegrating back home and a plan for how they will cope when negative feelings threaten to return.

The youth also have to write a petition requesting release that demonstrates what they have learned about themselves and how they are going to cope with their return to "normal" life. After almost fifteen months at Rancho Valmora, during the late spring of her sophomore year, Sadie was told she could write her petition. Our hearts warmed as we read it. We felt relieved and happy and convinced the program had succeeded in helping our daughter return to the person she had once been. Just maybe, she had beaten back the demons she had been facing. Just maybe, life would return to normal for her and us. Just maybe, she would be happy again.

Honors Petition

I have learned that you have to love yourself. And once you do that, you don't have to rely on other people's opinions. Cutting is a vicious cycle: you feel bad, so you cut. Then you feel worse, so you cut some more. My binge-eating disorder is caused by lack of control. When I was younger, my parents regulated what food I could eat. I would go to school and see all the kids take out their Lunchables and fruit roll-ups. I would look at my celery and peanut butter and want what they had. So, whenever I got the chance to eat some of these foods, I would eat as much as I could because I thought I would not get any later. This has continued on into the present, even though I have much more control over what I eat.

In the past, I have been bullied so much, my self-esteem is nonexistent. I began to rely heavily on what other people thought of me to dictate how I feel. For example: if I was talking about something and someone told me to shut up, I would feel horrible about myself. I would cope with this feeling by cutting. I never really cut a lot, but when I did, I wanted to see blood.

All of my illnesses have had big impacts on my life and my family. I love my parents more than anything in the world. It makes me so sad to look back and think about everything I put them through. I am so grateful to them for standing by me and supporting me. My friends were my rock. They grounded me and supported me so much. I'm going to be so sad to leave them after all they have done for me. But I think moving is kind of like leaving a chapter of my life here, and starting over on a fresh new page. I am so proud of myself for overcoming obstacles that I never thought I could get past. I can honestly say that I'm happy with myself and that I'm looking forward to living life as a normal teenage girl. I have realized that I don't need a razor and a super-size bag of chips to make me happy about myself. I feel so free. I think that I have to make sure I can do everything I need to here, before I go into a stressful environment. But I honestly think I'm up to the challenge of being the weird, eccentric drama enthusiast I once was. I finally love myself.

I know that everything will not be perfect when I leave. I will still be teased and maybe even feel like cutting. But I know that I can work through these problems by talking about my feelings and trusting myself. I want to be able to be completely comfortable with myself, to trust myself, and never settle for anything less than I deserve. I'll do this by writing in my journal and talking to my parents and friends. I know that I can get better and stay better. And I am so happy to finally be able to say that I love myself.

—Sadie Ladick, May 2006

Sadie's counselor recommended that we provide wraparound services for Sadie after she was released. As I described earlier, "wraparound services" means individualized, intensive but holistic or community-based services and support that focus on the strengths and needs of the child and involve a team of people—family, professionals, school staff, friends, et cetera. Where do you find that? Well, her counselor recommended that, rather than taking Sadie home, we send her to an emotional-growth boarding high school where she would have access to wraparound services. There, he said, she would experience normal high school but would have continued (although much less intense) therapy to help reinforce what she had learned at Rancho Valmora. Unfortunately, there were no schools like this in the Portland area. The recommended ones were in Utah or Montana—far away from us.

We debated this advice. How could we balance the benefit Sadie would gain from living at a supportive boarding school with the value of her being back home with her family? Didn't love and living together as a family count for something? I just could not imagine her being gone for one or two more years—that would mean she would have lived away from us for her entire high school career.

Who would be influencing her at this critical time in her development, at such a young age? If she went to the boarding school, what
kind of relationship would we have with her? How close would we
be if we could see her only once every month or two during the
school year? After that, she would be going off to college, moving on
with her life as an adult, and would likely never live at home with us
again.

I probed her counselor: "Are you telling us that she cannot be
successful if she comes home? Unless we send her to a boarding
school?" He said that she could be successful coming home but that
her likelihood of success would be higher if we sent her to boarding
school. However, we believed bringing her home to be with family
was best for all, and she desperately wanted to be a family again, so
we decided on that. Were we being selfish? Would this be one of
those "if I had the opportunity to do it over, I would make a different decision" moments? Would a different decision have changed the
outcome? Would she be alive but maybe not very connected to us?

Sadie wrote and sent us two heartwarming poems before she
was discharged. They reinforced to us the importance of family and
being together.

Sadie's Poem About Dennis (Papa) (2004)

Earliest memories,
kindness and warmth,
working so hard on a wall
I don't remember.
Pictures show the love in your eyes,
how badly you must have wanted a child.
Perhaps I yell at you too often,
you work so hard,
large muscles hiding a soft interior,

only the chosen few see
Papa and Pumpkin, the perfect pair,
until now.
Adolescence creeps up on us,
like a lion stalking prey,
and rips us apart.
I don't know how to get back,
maybe I need to remember,
back to the warmth and kindness that suffused our life,
but it can never be the same,
I am not 2,
digging owl holes,
drooling on shirts and laughing
at funny faces,
but neither am I grown.
I still need you
now, when I am trying to find myself,
I need your quiet strength,
knowing you will catch me,
if I fall.
Even when 40,
I will always need to be
your Pumpkin.

Sadie's Poem About Karen (Mom) (2004)

Slim and graceful,
always with a smile on your lips,
laughing forever,
at your attempts to dance,
laughing over countless things,

always expect a smile,
as soon as you open the door.
Loving you,
hating you,
doesn't matter,
we will always laugh together,
quick tempered,
both of us,
exploding,
yelling,
red-faced anger,
then, just as quick,
red-faced laughter
at our stupidity.
Countless memories,
long whining walks,
Thanksgiving,
first crushes,
first day of school,
first breakup,
first day alone at home,
you handle them with so much grace,
it is impossible not to love you.

How could you not believe in the power of family when you read these poems? How could we have thought of sending her away again? We couldn't, or, really, we chose not to. Perhaps it was a fatal choice, but we thought it was right at the time.

23

The Elusive Transition Services

SADIE WAS DOING WELL AND COMING HOME! YAHOO! WE HAD BEATEN the devil, and we had done it without medication. She had been off meds now for a year and a half. We were bursting with excitement. Our beautiful, bright, fun-loving daughter was *back*! She was beside herself with excitement, too—we could just envision her ear-to-ear grin over the phone. Time to close the door on that awful period and restart our lives. Yes, we did have that disquiet, that apprehensiveness, in the back of our minds—*Are we making the right decision bringing her home, instead of sending her to boarding school?*—but our joy at being together as a family again overrode that twinge. *Sadie was coming home!* This time, our tears were those of relief.

Not so fast. The challenges were not over. She was going to have to start a new school in the middle of high school in a town in which she did not have well-established friends. That was a bit daunting, but we were so overjoyed at being able to put those horrible years behind us that we were confident we could make the transition successful. We had started the search while Sadie was still at Rancho Valmora, tackling the big questions. Where should she go to school? How could we help her make new, healthy friends? How could we help her integrate into the Portland community? School first. We researched public and private high schools in the Portland area, met again with the educational consultants for their advice, made calls to the schools that looked most promising, and scheduled site visits for Sadie at our top choices.

Because of her behavior at the start of high school, we had worked with the school district to put her first on a 504 plan to prevent discrimination, then started working on an individualized education plan (IEP). As a result of federal laws that ensure all children have access to free public education (truly one of the wonderful things about living in the United States), kids struggling in school because of a wide variety of "disabilities," such as learning disabilities, emotional disorders, hearing or visual impairment, et cetera, may qualify for support services or special school settings.

The 504 plan, which falls under civil-rights law, is an attempt to remove barriers and allow students with disabilities to participate freely. Like the Americans with Disabilities Act, it seeks to level the playing field so that those students can safely pursue the same opportunities as everyone else. The individualized education program (IEP) plan, which falls under the Individuals with Disabilities Education Act, is concerned with actually providing educational services to children. Parents can work with educators to develop an IEP to help their child succeed in school. The IEP describes the goals set for a child during the school year, as well as any special support needed to help achieve those goals.

At the time, I recall being nervous about putting Sadie on either a 504 or an IEP. Would these plans label her and make her feel like a misfit or abnormal? What were the stigmas associated with these services? Would teachers treat her differently? Would the other kids at school know and tease her about being "special needs"? When I read the list of reasons kids might be struggling, it was clear that many qualify for these services—especially when you consider the number of kids diagnosed with ADHD.

In the late fall of 2004 (her freshman year), we sent Sadie away before we had a chance to finish the IEP with the Portland Public

School District (PPSD). We completed an IEP in the spring of 2005, while she was at Rancho Valmora, and updated it with the PPSD in the spring of 2006, as we were planning for her return to Portland. Thus, we hadn't seen what the impact of having her on an IEP might be when she was back in the normal public- or private-school environment. Well, now we were seeing it. Don't get me wrong—it's great that these programs and services exist, but in times of tight school budgets and increasing class sizes, it can be a burden for schools to take on these kids.

As we embarked on our search for the high school that would be the best fit, it became clear that the IEP put in place that spring had left Sadie "tainted." While an IEP is meant to help a school better provide the services your child needs, it became clear to us that it is also a red flag to a school—perhaps a big red flag—that says TROUBLE or EXTRA WORKLOAD. Sadie was extremely bright and did not have learning disabilities; her struggles had been emotional and related to her depression. Because she was so bright, we wanted her in a school that would challenge her intellectually.

Sadie flew home from Rancho Valmora for a school site–visiting trip. We looked at public schools first. Our neighborhood high school, Lincoln, was the top public high school in Portland with an international baccalaureate (IB) program and was where Sadie had started high school, but it was large (more than two thousand students) and overcrowded and would provide Sadie with minimal and likely insufficient structure. Reject. We looked at a smaller, out-of-district public school, Riverdale, that had more structure and strong academics. We thought it would be a good option, but, after visits and much back-and-forth communication, the school decided that since it had just lost half the funding for its psychologist, it could not take on new students who would need the psychologist's support (as was required because Sadie had an IEP). Cross another one off the list.

We moved on to private schools. We knew it would be hard for

Sadie, as it would be for any teenager, to get dropped into a new high school at the start of junior year, so we worked with the educational consultants to understand the culture of the various private schools. We wanted a culture in which the youth were respectful and accepting of different styles. After much research, we found what we thought would be the perfect fit for Sadie—Oregon Episcopal School (OES)—a private, academic high school in town. Sadie toured there, spent a day in classes, and was interviewed. She loved it. OES was a tough school to get into, so we kept our fingers crossed as we submitted her application and anxiously awaited the letter. The day it came, we tore it open and huge grins crossed our faces—she had been accepted! But wait—OES went on to say that it didn't have space, so she was accepted pending an opening.

Couldn't we get a break after all we had been through? Wasn't it our turn for things to go well? Of course, there is what we wish for, and then there is reality. We were not on the normal path, and were just going to have to struggle through this transition. So we broadened our search and applied at both a small, private arts-and-theater high school that had strong academics and a small, all-girls Catholic high school. Unfortunately, both were downtown and a bit too close to the street culture for our comfort, but our options were limited. We continued the waiting game—would these schools accept her? First came a rejection from the all-girls Catholic school. Although they did not give us a reason, I suspected they were leery of Sadie's background and didn't want to take her on. Fortunately, after interviewing Sadie, the Northwest Academy did accept her. We thought it would be a good choice for Sadie, given her love of music and theater and the school's strong academics. Our collective relief was palpable. Check that off the list. It was a good thing, because the opening for a new student at OES did not happen by the start of the school year.

Next, we had to find wraparound services to support Sadie's transition back home. We knew from our brief effort trying to find wrap around services after Sadie was discharged from Northwest Behavioral Healthcare Services two years earlier that they were not readily available. Still, we were hopeful that things had changed and we would be able to establish some sort of wraparound services. Again however, we were unable to find or figure out how to pull together that sort of coordinated care. It is unbelievable to me today that a residential treatment program would just discharge its participants without providing transition services for them. Did the program (and did we) expect that we could just close a terrible chapter of Sadie's life and everything would just return to normal? Did we not realize Sadie was coming home with experiences and a depth of understanding of herself that her peers at home would not have? That she would come back with the skills to communicate her feelings more effectively but also be back in the real world, where other youth didn't communicate that way? That she would come back feeling positive and full of hope but not "normal," given what she had gone through?

We found therapists, psychiatrists, and a few programs geared toward troubled youth, but we could not find any for youth transitioning from treatment programs. Sadie tried one after-school program, but the youth there were in the place Sadie had been in behaviorally before residential treatment, and she had moved beyond that. We tried several therapists over the summer, but Sadie didn't click with any and didn't want any more therapy; she really resisted going each week. She just wanted to live a normal high school life—not a life dominated by therapy.

Once we knew Sadie was coming home at the beginning of the summer before her junior year, we also spent a good deal of time thinking about how to help her integrate into Portland. What would she do all summer before school started? Fortunately, I ran across an advertisement for the Rose City Rowing Club's summer crew program, which sounded perfect. The club's mission is to "encourage and empower young adults to become capable and confident people within the framework of a nationally competitive, team-oriented rowing program." Sadie had never been much of an athlete, but she did have a good deal of upper-body strength; I had kayaked with her on Lake Superior several years prior and had discovered that she was a natural—I couldn't keep up with her!

She agreed crew would be fun, so we signed her up for the 6:30 a.m. Monday-through-Friday summer practice. Crew gave her a group of teens to interact with and provided the opportunity for her to get fresh air and regular exercise—all important for her mental health. And, as it turned out, rowing was something she loved and was good at.

That first summer she was back was the best we had had in many years and exactly what we had hoped for. She wanted to be around us and was delighted to be home. I call it her "lean-in phase"—holding hands as we walked; leaning against Dennis while sitting on the couch, watching a movie; just enjoying hanging out with us, like she did when she was a much younger child. And she was making good, healthy friends at crew. As for Dennis and me—well, we were so happy to have her back. We were a family again.

24

Don't Put a Label on Me

SADIE TURNED SIXTEEN THAT SUMMER. AND WHILE WE WERE STILL IN a blissful state having her home, seeing her happy again, at least one incident should perhaps have given us pause. The day she turned sixteen, I went into her room to wish her a happy birthday and found her sitting up in her bed, in tears. "What's wrong, Sadie?" I asked.

She told me, "I thought Nannette would at least send me a card to wish me a happy sweet sixteen. I thought she would be thinking about me."

Tears welled up in my eyes. Since her birth grandmother had told Sadie that her birth mother was a drug addict, we had been concerned about Sadie's meeting her. But I told her that morning that if she wanted to, we could try to find her or she could send her a letter through the adoption agency. But Sadie just said, "If she's a drug addict, I don't want to meet her." She didn't want to shatter the nice image she had of her birth mother.

Later, I found the following poem she wrote about Nannette, on August 13, 2006:

Statistics

They call me a statistic,
pregnant at 16.

They take from me my name,
my face, everything that's me,
they turn me into a number,
a precious percentage,
and try to turn me into something
they can try to make sense with.
Looking at my life,
they fall down in shock,
when they see the shit I been
through they can't believe their
eyes, cuz it's crazy,
all the shit I been put through,
by people trying to shove me
into their little boxes. I won't fit,
but
there's one thing I can never get
away from,
the destiny, handed down to me,
from my mother, from her mother.
The one person I
vowed never to become,
I became,
the mother that never showed,
not for me riding my bike down our
cul-de-sac tranquility,
not for my first day of school.
and not for my sweet 16,
though I waited,
for a letter,
a postcard,
a sign

from my ghost of a mother,
and a father so distant,
he can hardly be counted.
Be grateful, I'm told,
you have a new family,
but the ghosts linger on,
taunting me in the voices
of my so-called childhood friends,
Mistake, they whisper.
You aren't wanted, they cry.
Your own parents gave you up, they yell.
I am not a mistake,
and I am not a statistic.
I have my own life, my own soul,
I have all my life to live,
my life,
although I never quite
thought I would want it,
not after all those nights watching
the blood bead up in
red ribbon lines,
on my 11-year-old wrists.
Look close, you can see the scars,
but the ones you can't see
hurt the most,
because they never heal,
and so you all sit there
quietly judging me,
silently laughing at my
naivety
but if anybody is naive it's you and

not me.
How many of you know what it's like
to come home from sixth grade
and cry yourself to sleep,
praying, to whoever
the hell wants to listen, that you
never wake up?
How many of you
know the taste
of the pills
as they slide down your throat
and you hope
that the darkness finally
claims you?
And I can see your surprise,
who would've thought
a white girl with rich parents
would turn out like this?
So don't you try to type me,
put a label on me,
fit me into your perfect box world,
I AM NOT A STATISTIC,
I have my own name,
my own face,
my own soul,
my own heart.
I have all my life to live,
and I'm living it.

I suppose we were naive to think the fact that she was adopted didn't or shouldn't matter. We considered her our child, as good as blood, but for her the trauma of rejection from the people who gave birth to her was real. Regardless, at the time, we thought her sadness on her birthday was a blip on the surface and that she had the resilience to weather that sadness. And life did otherwise seem to take a turn for the better.

25

Peace Out and Save the Whales

THE REST OF THE SUMMER PASSED QUICKLY, AND IN THE FALL, SADIE decided to join the Rose City crew team. Her team of nine girls (they rowed eight-person crew boats with a coxswain) was a tight group, and I can describe the coach only as lifesaving. He loved the sport and mentoring the rowers. He provided structure and discipline but made crew fun for the kids. Rules included no drugs, no drinking, and decent grades at school. Sadie was motivated and proud to be part of a team and continued to be a strong contributor.

Once school and after-school crew practice started in the fall, Sadie completely resisted going to therapy. I'm sure she couldn't figure out what to tell her coach and team members if she didn't show up one day a week, and likely she worried she would fall behind. School, two and a half hours a day of crew practice, homework—life was busy for her.

Late the first month of school, I came home one day to find her frustrated and disappointed. She had been calling local high schools, offering to go speak, to share her experience with depression and help build awareness that suffering youth are not alone and can get help. She thought she could benefit others who were suffering and didn't understand why the people she talked to at the schools said "no, thanks" to her offer. I tried to help her think about how to approach the schools in a way that might be more successful, telling her that cold calling was not the best approach. But careful planning was not Sadie's forte; rather, she used impulsive, though well-intentioned, actions. I tend to be a planner and so got frustrated with her style of tending to reach for the stars without building the steps of the ladder that would help her get there. Then, as was also typical of Sadie, she got busy with school and crew and dropped the idea altogether.

While she struggled to fit in at school, she made good friends and actually had a "best friend" at crew. Ah, the joy of normal life! She was getting tons of exercise, eating healthfully, and doing extremely well academically. On the weekends, the team sometimes met for hikes in the park, and they had out-of-town meets two to three weekends each season. Occasionally, they got together for an evening of fun at our house or for bowling parties. Sadie loved it all and described herself the following way on one of her social media websites that fall:

Bio

I'm an outgoing junior in high school and I'm the biggest people person you'll ever meet. I'm also really open minded. Right now my favorite things are rowing crew at RCRC (GO Rose City!!!), theater, and chatting on AIM w/ tons of awesome pals. If u wanna know more or just wanna chat hit me up @thespian345 or drop a comment on one of my entries.
PEACE OUT AND SAVE THE WHALES.
Sadie

Interests (9):
acting . . . the list goes on, chatting on aim, eating raspberries, kissing in the rain, mountain biking, reading, reading shakespeare, rowing crew, talking to people
pics of me at my races

That bio sounds so like Sadie. It makes me smile I suppose because it also so like a typical teen! While she sounds like an average
teen, she had such insight into herself and her life—insight most
people do not gain until they are much older. She came back from
Rancho Valmora wanting to use her knowledge to help others. She
wrote her version of her life history in an online journaling website

where she could be anonymous. I didn't find it until after she died. Every time I read it, I slide back into that same feeling of inadequacy I felt years ago—it surfaces as an anxiety-driven, sweaty, shaky internal churn of energy. Reading the following, you can see again just how much being adopted impacted her:

July 31, 2006, 9:37 p.m.

I should probably fill u in on what exactly has gone on in my life so far. Of course you'll want to be spared the gory details and i'll try to make this as succinct as possible. Perhaps it would help if i had a timeline for you to better understand my life.

July 3, 1990: I was born to my mother, Nannette (16 years old), and my father, Walter (i don't know anything about him).

July 6, 1990: I was given up to my now-parents, Karen and Dennis. My father never tried to see me again. My mother came to 2 birthdays and then never tried 2 see me again

2000–1: I was in 5th grade and became severely depressed. I covered it up and decided to act happy since i couldn't figure out what was wrong w/ me. I figured if i let it show, my parents would leave me like Nannette did. This would become the recurring theme in my life. "I'll hurt you before you hurt me." I became obsessed with searching for my massive flaw i was convinced had to be hiding somewhere. Otherwise, why would my own mother voluntarily give me up to a stranger? I had always learned that above all, a mother is supposed to love you unconditionally. If I couldn't be loved, couldn't even be bothered to be kept around, then i must have some flaw that made me so horrible. I would spend the next 6 years searching relentlessly for this.

2001–2: In sixth grade it got worse. I was in a private Catholic school called Edgewood. The popular girls (of which I was most assuredly not one) decided that the best way to amuse themselves was to see how long they could torment me before I started to cry. Needless to say I felt alone. During that year I started to cut. It was not an everyday sort of thing, but i did it often enough. It was more to get the pain out than anything else. Be assured that I am not condoning cutting or any other form of self-mutilation. I am not proud of what i did, i cut because i didn't know how else to get out my emotions that i felt. I never let anyone see. Not my parents or my so-called friends. I viewed it as more proof of my undeniable flaw, the reason i was shunted away.

2002–3: During the duration of my 7th grade year, I wore a mask. To anyone who saw me i was happy, healthy (if a bit overweight) and was doing well in school. Inside it felt as though i had shriveled up and died. I talked and laughed and joked, but i was always on the verge of tears. I forgot myself during that time, and i didn't remember who i truly was until several years down the road. Even now when I try to remember that time it all blurs together in my head, like i was a ghost during that year, drifting in and out of my life

Spring 2004: This is when my mask broke. During the spring of my 8th grade year i made multiple suicide attempts, some ending up in hospitalization, more than one was almost fatal. As if by some divine decree, none actually killed me or caused any noticeable damage. Even when I had two seizures from a lethal overdose, i didn't have any liver or brain damage. I consider myself truly touched by an angel to be able to live my life free of consequence from all those horrible mistakes.

Summer 2004: I was sent to a short-term treatment center. During the spring I had visited psych wards to help me stabilize, but none

seemed to work. In order to have some level of safety, all agreed it
would be best for me to go. During that summer, I truly thought i had
changed. I felt happier and even acted like i hadn't in years.
Unfortunately, I was wrong. The following fall was probably the worst
time of my entire life. Once again, i had lied so convincingly and
repeatedly i believed myself.

Fall—winter 2004: I moved from Madison, WI to Portland, OR
during the late summer of my 9th grade year. When i first began
attending Lincoln High i was committed, motivated, and in a very good
position to move up in my class schedule. Unfortunately, it was too
good too be true. I met a girl named Kate, who was involved in the
"street culture" or basically used drugs and ran away. I became very
close to her and also to a man named Adam, who went by Billy for
reasons once told to me but erased by time. Some even thought i was in
love with him. i very certainly thought myself in love. i began to defy
my parents more openly than i ever had before. by mid-october i was
again hospitalized for repeated suicide attempts and self-mutilation.
by the time i was let out it was late november. my obsession with my
friends had not diminished. in my mind i saw them as my only escape.
these people never judged. i didn't have to perform for them or win
their acceptance. in other words, they weren't my mother. once i was
let out, i went into an immediate tailspin. i ran away twice. the second
time for 4 days. during that time i was so out of control i didn't know
what to do with myself. needless to say, i needed more than a 2-week
stay at a psych ward. my parents decided for me. when i finally was
brought home, i was immediately escorted by 2 people to my old psych
ward. from there i was escorted to a wilderness program in the rocky
mountains. i stayed there for 3 months in the dead of winter trying to
sort everything out in my head. who was in the right? i constantly was
at war with myself in my mind as two conflicting voices (Kate's and my

parents) vied for attention and loyalty. in the end, i came out even
more confused.

Spring 2005–summer 2006: During this time i stayed at a
residential treatment center called Rancho Valmora. it was above all
an eye-opening experience. The strangest part about everything was
how I got through it all. The ranch was not a wholesome place or even
all that supportive. They did not allow physical contact, and if you
didn't do what they wanted you to, they wouldn't talk to you or let you
talk to your family. They had rules for everything there. How to think,
how to feel, the best way to live your life, what you should want for
yourself. I remember one time I wanted to go home so bad I told them I
wanted to leave. They sat me down and spent a half and hour telling
me all the shit I was doing wrong with my life and everything they hated
about me. I don't know how it was supposed to do anything to help,
but I decided I needed to get out. I started for the door, but the staff
threw me on the floor, pinned me down, and held me there. I hit my
head and it started bleeding, but they didn't care. I had to have two
girls follow me around for 3 weeks after that. After all, they were only
trying to help. I finally played along and got out in June of 2006.

Summer 2006: This summer i find i am a stranger to my house, my
family and the city. during my absence my parents moved to a new
house in the northwest side of the city and i no longer have any friends
here in portland. i joined a crew team and have a regatta coming up
this weekend. although i try not to spend my life looking back,
sometimes i just have to sit and marvel at how lucky i am to have lived,
while so may others did not.

I hope you now understand where i have come from. i have made it a
point to not share this side of me with very many, since it quite often

leads to misconceptions and jaded views. i feel safer, knowing that this will be shared anonymously and i am hoping that those who read it understand one thing. i do not write this to glorify what i have done, but so a better understanding of the how and why can be shared. if you or someone you know is having trouble, no matter what it is, know that it can be solved. anytime you wish you may contact me through IM or post a comment. i would love to offer any help i can on this or any other subject. perhaps you simply read this because you stumbled upon it. in that case, happy reading. until next time,
Sadie

26

Entering the World of
Youth Social Services

I WISH I COULD SAY THAT WERE FINALLY PAST THE CHAOS IN OUR LIVES and had entered a time of peace and happiness. That we had successfully navigated those incredibly difficult years and our lives had returned to normal. At the time, it felt that way. There were signs that not all was well, but not many. And we were still so hopeful and so glad to have Sadie back, maybe we glossed over some of those signs. While she continued to be happy and had great friends at crew, she didn't connect as well with the kids at NW Academy. We started hearing from the school that when the students were walking in town, Sadie would stop and talk to the homeless and street youth. The behavior kind of freaked out the other kids. While Sadie had been there and understood that most of them were good kids but just troubled, the kids at school had the typical reaction to street people: dirty, dangerous, sick, crazy, et cetera. They didn't understand how or why Sadie thought differently. I think that set Sadie apart. The following short essay that Sadie wrote for a school assignment expresses how different, but also how strong and self-confident, she felt:

I Have Always Been Different

Writing assignment from North West Academy—junior high school year

I've always been different. An outcast, you could say. From the beginning I remember instinctively knowing this. No one would know it to look at me, or through me, as was most often the case. I was quite unremarkable, you could say. A normal girl in a normal school in a normal world. But on the inside I seethed, I yearned to be heard. To let my proverbial hair down. To be noticed.

At my young age it was dangerous to be different, a sin to be separate. I conformed beautifully. How would they know it was me if I let my pen do the talking? And so I wrote. Penned odysseys on bathroom walls, sonnets between the wrinkled bark of my favorite climbing tree. This is how I lived my secret life. A kind of superhero, if you will. I bitingly depicted the cattiness and immaturity of this fragile age. Whimsically depicted the looping flights of swallows. I lived in fear of discovery, yet I craved it. I knew, through a strange type of instinct, they weren't ready for me. I continued my secret life. It was amusing, in a way. These petty girls (and I say girls, not women, they will always be girls to me) could mock me and hurl their verbal spears at me in a desperate attempt to shake off my unaccountable sense of amusement. A middle school Mona Lisa, if you will. Because you see, Mrs. Watson, they can take my property, they can take my friends, they can even take my life. But the power of yearning, wishing, weaving words together, that they can never take.

I harbor much guilt over not having found those wraparound services Rancho Valmora recommended for Sadie, but at the time, she seemed so much better and was so eager to live a normal life. I wanted to give that to her. She had gone through so much to get to this point, and we were thrilled that she was motivated to live life to its fullest and was doing so well at both school and crew.

But, of course, life is not easy. In October of that fall, four months after she returned from Rancho Valmora and just a month and a half after she started her eleventh-grade school year, at only sixteen years of age, Sadie just disappeared one day. It took us totally by surprise. We were frantic. What happened to her? Was it foul play? Did she leave voluntarily? If so, what triggered this? No, no, no. Everything (or so we thought) was going so well! Our hearts sank. We contacted the police and reported her missing, but we found out the police really cannot do much. They can put out a missing-person bulletin, but they do not have the resources to really search for your child. We made flyers and posted them around town. We walked the streets for days, looking for her, showing people her picture, and asking everyone we saw, "Have you seen her?" Was she dead beside some ditch? Where in the world was she? We couldn't sleep; we walked around that whole week in a daze.

Enter the world of youth social services. Let's say your teenage child runs away or leaves your home one night and doesn't return. How do you find her? What help is available to you? How is your child surviving on the street? Why won't those social services programs helping your child help you reconnect?

In many communities, social service organizations provide free clothing, food, and sometimes a bed for homeless or runaway youth. Some of the services are drop-in, no questions asked. Others help youth but for only a limited period unless the teen agrees to work with a caseworker. Some of the more progressive agencies also provide tutoring to help youth get their GED, life-skills and job training, temporary housing, and counseling. These agencies work hard to get the youth off the street, and some work in partnership with businesses such as Ben & Jerry's to set them up with their first job.

This is all good, because the street is a dangerous place. It's too easy for girls there to end up in prostitution, for young people to end up on drugs, and for kids to get caught up in street families. As I've noted, many street youth have had rough lives, parents who were alcoholics or drug addicts, abusive or negligent. Many have been in the foster system, living in multiple homes, with little stability and consistency. For these youth, social services sometimes give them a real chance to turn around their lives. The good agencies provide ongoing support and guidance for the youth as they transition into adulthood.

What's the drawback to these agencies? One of the commitments that many of them make is to maintain confidentiality so that the youth believe they are in a safe place and feel comfortable talking about what is really going on in their lives. To do this, some agencies will not help connect searching parents with their teen—in part to maintain the confidentiality and in part to keep the youth safe from abusive parents.

But let's remember for a moment that not all of these youth come from dysfunctional or abusive families, and not all are in the foster system. Some come from good, loving, and supportive homes. Some are struggling with mental health issues, as was our daughter. How do the social service agencies distinguish between youth who need protection from their families and those who are struggling with mental health issues and need the support of their families? In our experience, they don't. When Sadie left home and we started our search for her, we ran into brick walls over and over again. The youth social service agencies would not tell us whether she was using the services, or even whether she was present or not. In more than one case, we knew she was in the agency's facilities, but they would not let us talk to her or even admit that she was there. Our frustration was boundless. We wanted to help her—she needed our help— yet the most we could do was write a note or letter and ask them to post it inside just in case she was there, just in case she decided to contact us.

Finally, a week after she disappeared, we received a phone call from a youth shelter in Seattle, telling us Sadie was there. On impulse, she had decided to go to Seattle—we think to find her birth mother. Sadie was an incredibly resourceful person—she had figured out how to get bus passes from youth social service organizations to get to Seattle, found shelter and food, and made her way safely from Portland to Seattle. But one evening she couldn't find a shelter and had to spend a very cold night in a doorway (I still cringe at the thought of my sixteen-year-old daughter sleeping there). So, the next night, when she again couldn't find shelter, she walked up to a police officer and told him she was a runaway, knowing that the police would get her a place in a shelter. They did, and the shelter staff called us. As I look back on that kind of behavior—her just running off, totally out of the blue—I wonder if that was an indication that she really was bipolar and had hit a manic phase that caused her to do something so reckless. To this day, I do not understand otherwise why she left.

We drove to Seattle to pick her up. She was embarrassed, ashamed, and quite defiant and at first did not want to speak to us. Eventually, with the help of counselors from the shelter, we talked and she came home with us.

We treated that incident as a blip on the screen, and things returned to "normal" for several months. Sadie went back to school and crew. Then, over winter vacation, we took Sadie and her best friend from Madison, Wisconsin, to Paris, France, and Marrakesh, Morocco, on an amazing trip. Sadie and her friend had fun exploring the markets, negotiating for their purchases, enjoying the sights and wonderful smells from outdoor cooking stalls. One day, they had beautiful mehndi (henna) designs drawn on their hands. The girls did all the communicating in French and loved being the ones we counted on. On our drive into the Atlas Mountains in Morocco, Sadie spoke French to the driver almost the whole way. At one point, she got very quiet, and I asked, "What did he say, Sadie?"

She said, "I told him I thought it was great that the new king had changed the laws allowing women to own property, but he told me he didn't like that law." It totally surprised her that someone would think that way. This was one of the reasons we traveled internationally so much with her—so she would learn things she would never get from books and broaden her mind.

Another troubling incident occurred while we were in Marrakesh. One evening, Sadie went with a woman who worked at the *riad* where we were staying to shop for the ingredients they needed for dinner. The woman came back without Sadie, saying she had just disappeared. She was overwrought, thinking it was her fault. Déjà vu, again. How would Sadie find her way back on the twisted alleys of Marrakesh? How would we even begin to look for her? Fortunately, Sadie ran into a young man who scared her and, unbelievably, found her way back, running all the way. Again, we had no understanding why she would have taken off like that. Even though we told her what she did was dangerous and that we were worried and scared, she wouldn't or couldn't explain herself.

After Morocco, we flew back to Paris and spent New Year's Eve under the Eiffel Tower, watching the fireworks. Bright lights, laughter, people everywhere, flashes of brilliance against the black sky; Sadie, her friend, and I laughing and snapping pictures. The rest of the world ceased to exist for a short time. The trip gave Sadie and her friend the opportunity to reconnect as bosom buddies. We had a couple of rough times during the trip—but hey, traveling can be stressful, so wasn't that to be expected?

27

——

When Will the Roller Coaster
Short-Circuit?

WHEN WE RETURNED FROM OUR VACATION, SADIE WENT BACK TO
her eleventh-grade classes at school and to crew, but things were not
fine. She was still not on any medication, but she was agitated and
defiant, yet she wouldn't talk about what was bothering her, and we
were, accordingly, frustrated and at times infuriated.

Then another nightmare situation happened. The night before
her first-semester finals in January, Sadie disappeared again. This
time didn't make any more sense than the previous ones. Horrific
scenes flashed across my mind: Sadie, raped, beaten up, and left for
dead in a ditch; visions of never finding her or knowing what happened to her; searching relentlessly the rest of my life. Was she
alive? Was she safe? Would we ever find her? Not knowing was the
worst part. I could hear the fear beating in my ears alongside my
pulse; I felt the fear like a ball in my stomach; the rest of the world
kept spinning, but we stood still.

But we had to act. Again, we printed missing-person posters
and put them up all over town. We hit the streets with her picture,
asking if anyone had seen her. We were experts at that routine. After
a week of searching for her, we decided to hire a missing-persons
detective—it seemed like the only way we had a chance of finding
her, but even that meant spending a lot of money and having little

certainty that we would succeed. Luckily, before we signed a contract with the detective, we received a phone call from the National Runaway Safeline (NRS), formerly the National Runaway Switchboard. NRS staff said, "Sadie contacted us. She isn't ready to talk directly to you but wanted you to know she is safe. You can leave a message with us for her, and if she calls back, we will give her your message." I was at a conference for work and had walked into the hallway to take the call. I collapsed on the ground right there in the hall, the fear and stress of the last week melting off me. She was alive and okay. "Tell her we love her and want her to come home," I said.

The NRS crisis hotline is an essential service that every runaway should know about. It's available twenty-four hours a day throughout the United States and its territories, including Puerto Rico, the US Virgin Islands, and Guam. If you are a runaway or homeless, you can call 1-800-RUNAWAY (1-800-786-2929) and talk confidentially with crisis-line workers, who can help you find local assistance from social service agencies and organizations (such as a safe place to sleep, food, medical assistance, or counseling). They can help you work through problems with your parents. If you don't want to contact your parents directly but want to send them a message, the Safeline will deliver it. In essence, you can have a conversation with your parents through the crisis-line worker. This service was a lifesaver for us and for Sadie.

A more detailed overview of the Safeline is included in the resources section at the end of this book. You can also find more information on the Safeline website: www.1800runaway.org/faq/#.

Over the next couple of weeks, we communicated with Sadie through the Safeline and I learned more about runaways than I had ever thought I would need to know. Most of us don't realize just how many youth run away each year. The Office of Juvenile Justice and Delinquency Prevention estimated that 1.6 million youth ran away in 2002 in the United States. The Research Triangle Institute studied runaway youth in 1995 and estimated that 2.8 million youth in the United States had a runaway experience during the previous year.[9] Many may be running away from violence or abuse, but for others, like Sadie, running could have been a reaction to a shift to a manic phase of bipolar illness. Even though staff at Second Nature told us she was not bipolar, perhaps she really was, or perhaps the illness surfaced as she got older. I will never know for sure, but I just can't explain it any other way.

As it turned out, as is the case with many runaways, Sadie had engaged in incredibly risky behavior. She had hitchhiked from Portland to Los Angeles (my heart stops just thinking about her out there, standing along the side of the freeway with her thumb out). She walked the streets in LA and eventually got picked up by the police. They found her late at night, hanging out on the streets with a couple of young people who were high on drugs. The police said Sadie was clean, but she was in a very dangerous part of town late at night. She apparently felt unsafe and saw a couple of policeman so went up to them and told them that she was a runaway, assuming that they would have to find her a safe place to sleep. The officers did, but not the way Sadie had hoped—according to her, they were mean, didn't believe anything she said, and, rather than just taking her to a youth shelter, they logged her into the California social services system. They put her in a foster home for the night and as-signed her a court-appointed special advocate (CASA worker) for abused and neglected children in the court system.

About three weeks after Sadie had left, we received a call from the assigned CASA volunteer. "Your daughter is in a foster home in Los Angeles. I am calling to let you know she is safe. You will be given a court date so a judge, with my input, can determine whether Sadie should stay in a foster home."

What? I remember the feeling of disbelief, the thought *This can-not be happening!* I could feel my world spinning in front of my eyes. *This has to stop! My daughter being taken from me? Put in a foster home? For what purpose? How in the world could some CASA volunteer who doesn't know Sadie or us be in a position to influence Sadie's fate, to decide what is best for her?* She went on to say, "It would be best if you come to the court hearing but you don't have to." I remember thinking, *Oh, sure, I'll just be a no-show and let you and the California court determine her fate! Are you serious? This is surreal.*

We were then thrown into the morass of the California social service system, a system designed to protect abused and neglected children but, in our case, one that seemed bent on keeping our daughter from a loving, safe home. So, there we were, our daughter taken from us while we were assumed guilty of abuse and neglect.

The CASA worker kept probing: "Do you hit Sadie? Was there sexual abuse?" *Oh my God! What a nightmare!* Trying hard to keep my voice calm, even though I was shaking with a combination of fear and anger, I said, "We don't abuse our daughter; we love her and give her a great home. She should be in her own home, not a foster home. She needs us."

"The judge will determine that," the CASA worker said, with a note of disdain, acting as if she were Sadie's protector. She didn't give us an opportunity to share Sadie's treatment records, which would have clarified the situation.

I understand how this all must have looked from the outside. Most parents cannot imagine why we couldn't stop Sadie from running or why she would have run in the first place. Even I would have thought no young girl would run away and put herself in such a dangerous situation unless something bad was going on at home. If I couldn't explain why Sadie ran, how could someone on the outside not have been suspicious? We were in a trap—there didn't seem to be any way to help the CASA worker understand that we were not the bad guys. While most youth from healthy families would not do what Sadie did, rates of mood disorders, suicide attempts, conduct disorders, and post-traumatic stress disorder are higher among homeless youth than they are among the general adolescent population.[10]

According to the National Center for Children in Poverty, estimates for rates of serious mental health disorders among homeless youth range from 19 to 50 percent. That means some (perhaps a significant portion) of these runaway youth may come from good, rather than abusive, families. Yet the system doesn't seem designed to make this distinction and certainly isn't helpful for parents who are trying to do the right thing.

Of course we flew to Los Angeles for the court hearing to determine our daughter's fate and to ask for her release, but my memories of that time are vague, as I couldn't imagine being in this situation, even though we were. How did we get from being normal, "good" parents to fighting for custody of our daughter? Nothing in our lives had prepared us for it.

When we arrived at the courthouse, we were told to go upstairs to the waiting room, where we met the attorney who was supposed to represent us during the hearing. We were not allowed to see Sadie. The room was large, crowded, and noisy, with tables and chairs spread around it and banks of chairs lined up against the rather stark, unadorned off-white walls. There were many parents waiting or meeting with their court-appointed representatives, some ignoring young children running wild, others cussing and yelling, "Shut up!" at their kids.

We sat down at one of the small tables with the attorney. She asked us to give her a brief background of Sadie's history, which we did. She told us it would look good that we had both flown down from Portland for the hearing—that lots of parents didn't even bother showing up. *Are you kidding?* Clearly, even she felt like our case was not the norm. After we gave her some background and our side of the story, she told us to wait until we were called in for the hearing. We still were not allowed to talk to Sadie.

During the hearing, we sat at the back of the courtroom, as we were told. We were not allowed to speak. Sadie sat up at the front, on the opposite side of the courtroom, with her CASA volunteer. It was the first time we had seen her since she had run. She kept glancing at us but couldn't let herself make eye contact—she looked dejected and ashamed. It was all I could do not to run across the courtroom to hug her. The judge allowed the CASA volunteer and our attorney to speak, then asked Sadie a few questions that I don't recall. But I do remember we were not allowed to defend ourselves by telling our side of the story, and the judge lecturing us about the mistakes we made—telling us we had put Sadie in the wrong school, given her needs, as if he, having just met her, knew better than we did. I wanted to shout at him, *You don't know anything about Sadie! How dare you judge us?* But I was afraid we would lose her to the system if I did that, so Dennis and I both kept our mouths shut and quietly took in the jabs. I have never felt so humiliated, so marginalized, so disempowered as I did that day.

Fortunately, the judge finally decided to release Sadie to us so we could take her home. We paid the fees, filled out more paperwork, cried more tears of relief—where do all the tears come from? Won't they ever run out? I recall Sadie once writing that she had cried enough tears to fill up the Nile River. That was how I felt. Our life's roller coaster stopped to let the California social service and court people off and to let us back on. But which way would it go next? Up or down? As Sadie once said, "When will the roller coaster short-circuit?"

We never got Sadie to talk about why she ran off and what she did during those three long weeks. She either was not able to articulate why or didn't want to. She did tell us she used homeless shelters and got food at various social service agencies—she had clearly used her keen resourcefulness to survive on the streets. I will never understand why she ran. Perhaps her reasoning is buried in one of her poems. One thing I know: if I ever had to be dropped off in some other place in this world and I could take one person with me, it would be Sadie. She could find her way anywhere.

Back at home, we went to NW Academy to see if they would let Sadie take her first-semester finals late and let her come back to school to finish her junior year. They told us that Sadie had to present her case to a panel of teachers and administrators. Sadie asked me to go with her for moral support. She apologized to the panel, said she knew what she had done was wrong, and asked for another chance—though she did not explain to them why she ran, either. Poor Sadie—again in front of a panel of adults judging her. Then we were excused to wait in the hall while the panelists debated Sadie's fate. I wanted to tell them she was struggling with depression, that we needed to work together to support her. That punishing her would not help, and in fact that not allowing her to take the exams, when she knew the material would impact her ability to get into college, would be a major, life-changing consequence. I wanted to beg them to give her another chance. But I didn't. I let Sadie do the talking. She would not have wanted me to tell them about her depression.

Eventually, the principal called us back into the room; Sadie looked so innocent and so nervous. The principal said the panel had decided what she had done was deliberate and wrong and that she had to face the consequences, so she was not allowed to make up the finals. The principal said Sadie would not flunk out, because she had A's going into finals, but then dropped the real bomb: the school didn't really want Sadie anymore, so they told her she would be put on probation and might not be invited back the next year. Sadie looked humiliated.

Perhaps they felt unable to trust that Sadie wouldn't run again, or they were worried that other parents might think Sadie was a bad influence, or they truly believed that over the long run, the consequences would help Sadie. I don't know, but I often think about Hillary Clinton's book *It Takes a Village* (to raise a child). I felt like we needed everyone to work together to support Sadie, to get her back on track—instead, it seemed as if everyone just looked at her as troubled and wanted her to go somewhere else. There was one exception, however. One of Sadie's teachers did tell Sadie that she herself had run from school when she was Sadie's age—and that it did impact her ability to get in the college she wanted. She went on to tell Sadie, "You can get past this. I did. I eventually got into a college and got my teaching credential and am now doing something I love." I loved that she tried to share this life lesson with Sadie, that she was telling Sadie she could get past it. I just wish more adults in Sadie's life had willingly provided that kind of encouragement.

The school's decision was just another blow to Sadie's self-esteem and confidence. At the time, I agreed that she needed to face her actions and live with the consequences, whatever they might be, but in hindsight, I know I should have defended her; I should have understood that she wasn't purposely making bad choices but rather that her mental illness was affecting her judgment and she needed me to step in.

28

The Only Time My Brain Is Still

THAT OUTCOME AT SCHOOL, I THINK, PUSHED SADIE INTO HER NEXT phase—what I call her "black phase." Black gone wild. Everything gone black. Black lips, black clothes, black eye shadow, chains hanging from her clothes. If you had seen her during that time, you would never have let your own teen hang out with her. Her appearance turned her into someone people would cross the street to avoid. Anyone who saw her on the street and didn't know her would have thought she was a dirty, cigarette-smoking, deviant, "bad kid"—likely destined for prison. It was so self-destructive—dressing the way she did was almost like asking for people to reject her.

She also started listening to the Insane Clown Posse (ICP), an American hip-hop duo from Detroit, Michigan, whose fans are known as Juggalos. From Wikipedia: "The songs of Insane Clown Posse center thematically on the mythology of the Dark Carnival, a metaphoric limbo in which the lives of the dead are judged by one of several entities. The Dark Carnival is elaborated through a series of stories called Joker's Cards, each of which offers a specific lesson designed to change the 'evil ways' of listeners before 'the end consumes us all.'"

Was it the death theme that entranced Sadie? It seemed cultlike to me, and just one more indicator that all was not well with her.

We tried to get Sadie to go back to high school to finish eleventh grade, but that meant going to a different high school, since NW Academy didn't want her back. We enrolled her in another public high school, but she wouldn't go to class. We would drop her off at school, and she would wait until we left and take the bus back downtown and then come home in the evenings. Over the next few months, she was away from home more and more. I didn't know how she spent her time, but we couldn't seem to convince her to stay in school. I know she was smoking marijuana some, and I suspected she was experimenting with stronger drugs, but I don't think alcohol was an issue for her. Perhaps the drugs were a form of self-medication for her.

Despite the black, I really hoped Sadie would and could return to crew—it had been so good for her and had boosted her self-confidence so much. One day a month or so after she returned from Los Angeles, we were downtown, looking out a window to the river, and I said, "Sadie, why don't you go back to crew, since you loved it so much?"

She replied, "Mom, leaving crew was the biggest mistake I ever made. It's the only place I can ever remember my mind being still. While my crew team is rowing down the river, my mind stops racing. It is so peaceful." She told me she would go back if the coach would have her. Rose City was having its annual crew-team evening event—awards, slide shows of the year's events, dinner. I called the coach, who said yes, Sadie was welcome to come back. Victory! She would of course have to follow team rules—no drugs, no alcohol—and would have to return to school or be homeschooled, but I thought crew was important enough to her that she would comply with the rules. Again, I can say only wonderful things about that coach. He really cared about the kids and knew the positive impact crew could have on their lives. He was more than willing to take Sadie back, and she wanted to go back.

The evening of the event, we all headed to the venue. Everyone was excited, and her teammates were thrilled to see her back; they all talked and laughed together about their shared experiences and whatever teens talk about. Dennis and I were chatting with the parents when, out of the blue, Sadie came running up to me in tears. "Mom, Sally's parents told me to stay away from their daughter—that I was a bad influence. They won't let me sit with my team. How can I be on the team if I can't be near one of my teammates?"

I told her, "Those parents do not have the right to tell you that you can't sit with your team."

"But, Mom, if I stay, they'll make their daughter leave the team. I can't do that to a teammate."

My heart just broke. Dennis ran to tell the coach what was happening, and he reiterated that Sadie was welcome on the team. He and Dennis tried to find the parents. We desperately wanted to reverse the damage, but Sadie ran out of the event in tears before the coach could talk to her, and we couldn't find the girl's parents. We were furious with them: *How dare they say that to our daughter! How dare they interfere with something that might help Sadie get back on track! Bigoted, selfish, insensitive, narrow-minded people* . . . Oh, I had lots of words to describe them.

Before Sadie's fall into the streets, if I had seen a young person dressed the way she was now dressing, I might also have thought, *Deviant, trouble, druggie.* Who wouldn't at least initially think those things upon seeing someone so purposely dressed to shock, dressed so goth? But I would at least have tried to get to know that person without judging, especially when they were participating in something healthy. Besides, that night Sadie had dressed in a more conventional fashion. She wasn't even dressed in black; she just looked like one of the crew. Even if those parents had seen her earlier, dressed in black, or had heard rumors about her running away, why couldn't they instead have banded together with us to help Sadie? I get that they were afraid Sadie would lead their precious daughter astray, but weren't their actions purely selfish? I now know I should have asked for their support, rather than expecting it. Regardless, this episode resulted in one more door being closed.

29

———

Back on the Roller Coaster

THE NEXT YEAR AND A HALF OF SADIE'S LIFE WAS A TOTAL ROLLER coaster. I struggle even to write about it—it is such a blur of upswings and downturns, a pattern of Sadie doing extremely well for four to six weeks, followed by rapid descents into bizarre, risky, unhealthy, and unpredictable behavior and actions. The good times were *very* good. Each led us to renewed hope—maybe this time would be different. Maybe she would stick with what she was involved in. The descents were abrupt, however; she would just drop out of whatever she was thriving at and take off in search of something else.

During this time, she met a young man and started spending more and more time with him. Initially he seemed nice enough, but he was several years older than Sadie, wasn't in school, and didn't have a steady job, all of which made us very uncomfortable. We also suspected he was dealing marijuana. Despite our disapproval, Sadie stayed with him for several days at a time and eventually moved with him into a large, dilapidated house where a number of others lived. The residents had sectioned off several rooms by hanging old bedspreads so that more people could live there and share in the rent. The place looked like a hippie commune and was a dump. Dennis fixed the broken stairs, and we installed smoke detectors and carbon monoxide monitors, trying to make it a little safer, but we felt helpless to really change her environment.

Though Sadie was too young to be living away from home, let alone with her boyfriend, smoking pot, often unkempt—we knew if we laid down the law, she would just leave. What were we supposed to do—chain her to her bed? At least she called us frequently and typically showed up at home once a week for a night, before she took off again the next day, back to the other house. I felt like my life was on hold between those calls and visits.

The psychiatrist she was seeing told us it was quite unusual for someone living the life she lived to stay so closely in contact with her parents. In his mind, that meant there was hope. Yet she was still defiant, difficult to talk to, difficult to be around. When we tried to talk to her about her life, we typically got "leave me alone" or "quit trying to run my life." At times, it was just so hard to maintain our calm around her. While she was not taking any medications for depression or mood disorders during that time, her psychiatrist prescribed Klonopin for anxiety (yes, a medication for yet another diagnosis), but he stopped prescribing it when we thought she might be experimenting with recreational drugs. The two don't mix, and we did not like her having bottles of pills when she was living such an unstable life.

During that time, she made many choices that we thought just made her life harder and resulted in people and society shunning her, thinking she was a bad apple and a bad influence: putting her hair in dreadlocks, adopting a pit bull puppy, dressing sloppily, hanging outside the mainstream. I remember telling Sadie that having a dog would make it difficult to find places to live, difficult to use public transportation. A dog costs money—for food, vet bills, dog obedience training, et cetera, and she didn't have a job to pay for these things. I get that dogs provide unconditional love and perhaps that was what she was looking for, but why a pit bull? Why not a breed with a friendlier reputation? Sadie would tell me, "Pit bulls are really bred to fight other dogs, not attack people, Mom," and I have to admit, her puppy (which she named Guya) was really sweet and loving.

But a pit bull to me was just one more thing that would make Sadie's life more difficult and, more important, one of those things she did that set her apart and often resulted in people looking at her with suspicion, people thinking she was part of the counterculture, people staying away from her or wanting their kids to stay away from her. Why did she do these things when they just made her life harder?

Dennis and I talked about instigating the tough-love concept—telling her she was not welcome back home until she cleaned up her act—but in our hearts we knew she was struggling with demons she couldn't completely control. Kicking her out would have severed all contact—we thought we were better off with her wanting to call us and see us once a week or so. At least that way, we thought, we might be able to have some influence over her. It's probably not the choice some parents would make, but that is one decision I do not regret. In fact, I don't think I could have lived with myself if we had kicked her out and she had died being estranged from us. So we endured the roller coaster—trying to support and encourage the upswings and trying to survive the downward spirals. Trying each time to help her recover from them.

After the crew incident and later that spring, Sadie decided to take the GED and aced it, scoring in the top 2 percent of graduating high school seniors. She even got offers of scholarship money because of her high scores. She had taken the PSAT the prior fall and received an unsolicited application package from Yale because her scores on that were so high. In our minds, she was so bright that if it had not been for her mental illness, she would have been destined for a top-notch college—somehow, her brilliance made it all that much more difficult for us to accept her path. At least after receiving her GED she decided to start college at Portland State University

(PSU). She was seventeen, younger than most of the students, and it wasn't Yale or Stanford, but it was something and we were thrilled.

During the summer before she started college, Sadie seemed to be doing better again and was definitely more pleasant to be around. She spent more time at home, enjoyed listening to Stephen Colbert and doing what teens do on social media; she seemed more focused on her future. I came home one day and saw her working on the computer. When I asked her what she was doing, she told me, "Applying for jobs!" Yahoo! We thought perhaps she had decided she was tired of the kind of life she had been living and was ready to more forward in a more positive direction. She told me she was completing an online application and survey for a job at Fred Meyer, a grocery store chain in the Northwest. I asked her what kinds of questions were on the survey, and she showed me the question she had just answered—something like "How often do you get into trouble?" She had to choose "all the time," "frequently," "rarely," or "never."

I asked, "What did you answer?"

She said, "Mom, you told me always to tell the truth on a job application, so I answered 'frequently.'"

What could I say? I *had* told her always to be honest, but I thought that would doom her in this case. How wrong I was—she actually got a call to come in for an interview and was hired.

A summer job—we were all happy about that. Sadie seemed proud to be going to work and getting a paycheck. She would put on her black slacks and Fred Meyer shirt and head off to work each day on the bus. Unfortunately, at the end of her probation period, I got a call from Sadie, who was in tears. "Mom, my boss said I talked too much at work, so they're letting me go! Why? I did all the work they asked me to do. Why don't they want me?" My heart broke for her. I suggested she call her boss and ask him if he would give her more feedback, but she wouldn't do it.

Soon after that, we turned our attention to college. She signed up for Environmental Philosophy and Arabic, in addition to the standard freshman classes. Even though she was close enough to live at home, she really wanted to stay in the dorms. We supported that and agreed to pay for her housing, and Sadie went online to the college match system to find roommates, and we joined them shopping at IKEA to outfit their dorm room. We had good times together that summer getting her ready, thinking, *Maybe she'll find her niche and be happy in college.*

Sadie loved the first week of orientation. She was in her element, running from dorm room to dorm room, meeting people, talking, laughing. Life was not quite as exciting for her once classes started, but she seemed to enjoy them nonetheless. She even invited me to attend one of her classes, Environmental Philosophy, with her. Watching her there was fun—she was very engaged and a strong participant in the class discussions.

That fall of 2007, I was diagnosed with breast cancer. I discussed my treatment options with Dennis and Sadie; a lumpectomy, followed by daily radiation and five years of a cancer drug, tamoxifen, seemed like a no-brainer if I wanted to survive. Those treatments raised my survival odds to 85 percent. Less certain were the benefits of chemotherapy, which, my oncologist told me, could increase my odds of survival by another three percent, but the real benefits of which were uncertain for my cancer, based on tumor testing.

I decided not to do the chemotherapy, but Sadie tried desperately to convince me to reconsider. She told me, "I would rather have a bald mother than a dead mother." The day after we had that discussion, Sadie came home with her head shaved. She told me she did it so I could do the chemo and would not have to go through hair loss alone. It was very Sadie to do something impulsive yet loving like that. Even though I know she did it with the best of intentions and out of love, it felt a bit manipulative, since I had already arrived at the decision that I was not going to do chemo. I remember hugging her but also thinking, *Oh, Sadie, why did you do this before you knew what I decided?* Her act made me feel pressured to do the chemo even though I didn't want to. I didn't think she should have to go around with a bald head when I didn't have one, but I held firm on my decision. So now she was in college with a bald head—not easy, I'm sure, since it was another "something" that made her stand out as different.

Then, partway through her first quarter, she stopped going to classes. No amount of talking to her worked—telling her we expected her to stick out the quarter, given that we had paid the dorm and fall quarter fees and could not get the money back; telling her she needed to stick with something she had started. She went back to living with her boyfriend. I struggled then and struggle now to understand why she dropped out. I can only think again that she was bipolar and that these upswings and downswings in her life were related to bouts of mania and depression. What else explains the wild ride we were all on? Perhaps she really needed to be on medication, but we were still leery of it, and at that time, she was not willing to go to therapy.

30

The Activist and Running Wolf

THE WEEK OF THANKSGIVING, AFTER SHE DROPPED OUT OF COLLEGE, Sadie just took off again. Somehow (I don't want to know how), she got a ride to Eureka, California, and eventually ended up in Berkeley. My recollection of that time is vague—perhaps I have blocked the memories because of the pain and anguish I felt not knowing, once again, where my seventeen-year-old daughter was. What I do remember is that she called us a couple of days after she left to tell us she was tree-sitting in Berkeley with others to protest the construction of a major recreation center on the UC Berkeley campus. Apparently, the center was to be built on an ancient Native American burial site and construction was going to require the cutting of a beautiful grove of trees.

There was quite a diverse mix of protesters—students, environmentalists, old ladies, and Native Americans. Protestors had built a series of platforms in the trees with pulley systems between them. Some of the protesters lived on the platforms so contractors could not cut the trees, thus stopping construction. The pulley systems allowed them to haul up food and haul out waste. Sadie was thrilled to be part of the action and told us she was living up in the trees with the other protesters. I actually thought it was probably a lot of fun being up in the trees with other people who had a similar goal, at least she was staying in touch with us, and we believed she was relatively safe there—at least, safer than she was hanging out on the streets of Portland.

Thanksgiving night, the ringing phone woke us. It was the Berkeley police. Sadie had been arrested, along with a fellow tree-sitter named Running Wolf and a couple of others, for passing food up to the tree-sitters. Apparently, she and Running Wolf had come down from the trees to go buy food. When they returned, they were standing outside the wire fence the police had constructed to cordon off the protestors and were loading food into baskets that could be hoisted up to the platforms. What they were doing was, by a recent court order, illegal, so they got arrested and taken down to the precinct.

My first reaction was to let Sadie spend the night in jail so she had to face the consequences of her civil disobedience. But the police officer told me, "Ma'am, you don't want to do that. You daughter is under eighteen, so we can't send her to jail. We would have to send her to juvenile hall, and since juvie is so crowed, the youth in there are mostly hardcore—murderers, rapists. You don't want your daughter there."

So there I was, in Portland, Oregon, over five hundred miles from Berkeley, and it was the middle of the night on Thanksgiving. How was I supposed to pick her up? Fortunately, I had a brother living south of San Francisco, so I called him at one in the morning and he graciously agreed to make the hour drive to Berkeley to pick her up, take her home for the night, and put her on a plane to Portland the next day. Life was just never dull with Sadie around.

Sadie returned and decided to try PSU one more time. Reluctantly, we agreed to pay tuition for winter quarter, but what happened was almost an exact repeat of the fall quarter. She again started strong, and her professors said she was a delight to have in class, but within about six weeks, she had dropped out of her classes. She couldn't stay in the dorm once she was no longer enrolled, but, rather than coming back home, she couch-surfed for a while and eventually moved into a rental house.

Late that winter, Dennis and I decided to take a sun trip to the Florida Keys and asked Sadie to come with us. We hoped a change of scenery and being together would be like old family times. She told us she would come only if her boyfriend could join us. Since we thought he was dealing marijuana and didn't think he was good for Sadie, we certainly were not going to pay for him to join us on a vacation. Sadie, still overweight at that time, had this vision of everyone in bikinis on a beach—she didn't feel good enough about her body to do that but told me she could manage it if her boyfriend was there, because he was okay with her weight. Still, we told her it was a family trip and we were not going to pay for him to come. Even though we did not plan to sunbathe on the beach, she refused to go. It seemed like everything we tried to convince her of failed.

When I think about that whole spring, I see a big, blank, black nothing—just a period of time during which we felt like we lost our daughter and were at a total loss for how to parent. At least she had moved out of the dump she had been living in and had rented a room with her boyfriend in a house in which a very nice family lived. The mother of this family sort of took Sadie under her wing, which made me feel a lot better about her living situation. I have always been grateful for the love and support that family gave Sadie.

I don't really know how she supported herself during this time. I think she bartered a lot: things she had bought on our international trips, her clothes, her camping gear. And she was very connected with Portland free assistance—for example, the Portland hippie church that gave out bags of Trader Joe's groceries at the end of each Sunday service. We didn't give her money during this time, and she never asked for any. We kept telling her we would support her if she was going to school and would help her if she had a job but would not support her if she was doing neither. However, we did always tell her that she would have free room and board if she lived at home.

31

The Importance of Connection

DURING THAT YEAR AND A HALF AFTER SADIE DROPPED OUT OF HIGH school, we kept scheduling weekly appointments with her psychiatrist, Dr. M., but she showed up only off and on. The psychiatrist had come highly recommended by one of the academic private high schools in the Portland area as someone skilled in working with adolescents, and he himself had been adopted, so we thought Sadie might be willing to further address her adoption issues with him, someone who understood. Initially, Sadie went grudgingly to the appointments, though I'm not sure how much she really opened up to him and suspect she spent time trying to outsmart him, not telling him how she really felt.

Over time, she began complaining about the appointments and didn't want to go. I can recall many sessions when we waited for Sadie to show up—sitting there anxiously on the soft couch in Dr. M.'s office, updating him on the latest saga in our lives and Sadie's. His office, a converted house less than a mile from our home, had a big, south-facing window that fronted the street, so he kept the venetian blinds closed for privacy. I remember him periodically peeking out the blinds while we were talking, hoping to see Sadie walking up the stairs to the front door.

We kept these appointments as long as we could, but the way our insurance worked, if Sadie was a no-show, even if we showed up, insurance wouldn't cover the cost, and the psychiatrist understandably had a minimum twenty-four-hour advance-cancellation policy. We couldn't afford to keep paying for appointments she never showed up for, so eventually we stopped going. I know her psychiatrist cared, but at one point he told us, "Maybe Sadie just has to hit rock bottom before she will turn her life around." Little did we know, she would hit rock bottom and not survive it.

We really tried to get her to restart the sessions—eventually she told me she would meet with a psychiatrist if she could see somebody different. We had already been through several therapists, and Dennis and I felt like Dr. M. had really gotten to know Sadie. We thought her asking to see someone different was manipulative. It meant we would have to start all over with someone new—explaining what was going on, explaining her treatment history, giving the new person time to get to know Sadie. We thought she was trying to avoid the psychiatrist's getting "inside" her thoughts and feelings. I know money should be no object when it comes to your child, but the reality is that professional help costs a lot, and while we were fortunate to have good health insurance, we still had a co-pay. Starting over, with a new psychiatrist, not only would have set Sadie's progress back to ground zero but would have been costly, and we certainly did not have an endless supply of money.

Now, I wish I had tried to find someone else—someone whom Sadie really connected with—as I realize just how important finding that person is. After Sadie died, I tried four grief therapists and did not connect with the first three. I did not even want to go to my sessions with one of them; I would find myself dreading it—making biting comments (silently to myself) about what kind of chair I had to sit in, about how far apart the therapist would set up her and my chairs. During sessions, I would find myself not sharing my feelings. Perhaps I didn't like her and didn't want to make it easy for her to help me.

But then, when I tried the fourth therapist, I really felt as if we connected; I wanted her help and looked forward to our sessions. Perhaps Sadie was being manipulative in asking for someone new, but if we had found someone she could really open up to, it might have changed the ending of this story.

Based on the reading I have done on therapeutic approaches since Sadie died, I also now think (speaking as a mother, not as an expert), that Dr. M. should have been using cognitive behavioral therapy (CBT) with Sadie, addressing problems in the here and now by targeting negative thoughts and behavior patterns and helping her examine her interpretation of situations. Perhaps he was using some sort of CBT, but it seems like we spent a lot of time in family sessions trying to reach agreements on rules, designing family contracts and reward/punishment systems, and working on improving our communication. Was Sadie in fact bipolar, or was she simply lacking important skills that she needed help developing, such as tolerance for frustration, problem-solving skills, ability to think in a gray space, or something else entirely?

Some schools of thought maintain that all children and adolescents really want to do the best they can, really want to do the "right" and responsible thing, but that some are lacking in the development of critical skills. Rather than understanding that behavior as resulting from a deficit in some critical skill area, parents and therapists often think their child is just being manipulative, stubborn, defiant, or out of control. As a result, and as happened in our case, professionals work with parents to improve their consistency and discipline. Some therapists encourage parents to do this through setting and clarifying rules (such as "be home by 10:00 p.m."), parent-child contracts, point systems, rewards and punishments. Yet if your child is lacking some of the skills needed to deal well with the demands placed on them, you are setting them up for failure with this approach.

The Explosive Child, by Ross Green, is a great book that describes this concept and that is worth reading even if your child is older. When I read it after Sadie died, many of its teachings resonated with me—first and foremost, the idea that kids want to do well but may have gaps in the critical skills they need to be successful in life. Just as some kids need help with math skills, some kids and even young adults may need help developing other life skills. Doesn't it make sense that not all skills come naturally to every child? That some kids need help developing certain skills? Even at work, we identify competencies needed for an individual to be successful in a specific job: adaptability, ability to deal with ambiguity, problem-solving and strategic-thinking skills, ability to work collaboratively, et cetera. Either we don't hire someone who lacks the competencies needed for a specific job, or we recognize that we need to help that individual develop those competencies. Shouldn't we identify competencies for success in life and help our children build them?

People had high expectations for Sadie because she was so bright and articulate. I do believe Sadie wanted to do well and to meet those expectations, but I think her brain disorder and perhaps some underdeveloped skills interfered with her intentions, such as the ability to think in gray space and, to some extent, problem-solving skills. As a result, people (including us) often thought she wasn't trying or she was being manipulative or was making "bad" decisions, and in turn, she felt like a failure. But you don't feel like a failure unless you care.

During those tumultuous months after she dropped out of PSU, we saw some positive signs. One day that spring, Sadie told me, "Mom, I realize now that when people smoke pot, they just sit around and do nothing." That was one of those "yahoo" moments when I remember thinking, *Sadie is always one to learn by doing, by trying—not by being told. And here she's figured out that doing drugs is just a waste of time. Isn't that a good realization to come to?* She wouldn't be tempted, I thought, in the future, when she had decided it would be a waste of her life to do drugs. *Perhaps she's finally ready to turn her life around.* And the roller coaster began climbing up again.

I did talk to her that spring about whether she should try depression medication again, and she told me, "But, Mom, I tried three times to commit suicide on depression medications before. Can you guarantee the medication won't make me suicidal again?" Of course I couldn't make that promise, and, like Sadie, I had that same concern—it did seem risky—so I felt at a loss for an adequate answer to her question. And at that time, none of the psychiatrists and therapists since the ones she'd seen in middle school had suggested she was bipolar, so if we had started depression medication again and she was actually bipolar, she might have tried to take her life again. Even if she wasn't bipolar, the medication might have caused her to have suicidal thoughts. We decided it was just too big a risk.

However, we didn't feel as if we had a good alternative, either. There was likely an expert somewhere who could have done a better job figuring out what kind of medication would help Sadie, but it's hard to know what kind of expert you're looking for when you don't have a solid diagnosis. Regardless, we should have searched for the nation's expert in dealing with the type of behaviors Sadie was exhibiting. We should have at least considered enrolling her in clinical trials for new treatments and explored alternatives such as brain imaging or even something as extreme as electroconvulsive therapy (ECT). We should have focused on the fact that Sadie was very unhappy and that the status quo was not working—something needed to change. But, looking back, I am not sure I would have taken the risk on cutting-edge treatments unless I had known her eventual fate, which of course I could not have.

32

Reaching for the Stars

EARLY THAT LAST SPRING, AFTER HER TWO ABORTED ATTEMPTS AT PSU and months of what appeared to us to be just hanging out (and still renting a room with her boyfriend in the same family's house), Sadie decided she wanted to go to cooking school. She explored options and decided on the Cordon Bleu cooking school located right in Portland. We were willing to pay for the schooling—she was still only seventeen, so we were happy she wanted to do something productive. Classes started in June. Again, we helped her get outfitted. These were small gestures, but for me it was fun being able to go shopping with Sadie—in part because she was so excited but also because she was fun to be with.

After we purchased her required uniforms, she came downstairs later that day dressed in her full garb: black-and-white-checkered pants, heavy black shoes, white chef jacket, and classic, floppy toque. She had an apron on and a small white towel slung over her shoulders. With a big grin on her face, she announced, "I'm going to cook you dinner!" Such enthusiasm was contagious. Of course, she hadn't done much cooking in the past, other than her favorite French dishes, like crêpes and Niçoise salad, but that didn't stop her.

She would come home some days to do her homework and to practice her knife techniques—cutting a potato into the shape of a football or slicing carrots into thin, even, julienned sticks—and was always proud when she was successful. Those were days that again brought us hope. She was happy, engaged, and full of the Sadie spirit we loved.

Another time, she came home from class and said she had applied and been invited to interview for a part-time job cooking for the priests at the Grotto, an internationally renowned Catholic shrine and botanical garden, while the nuns went to Italy for six weeks. The interview went well, and she got the job. I asked her what kind of questions the priest who interviewed her asked.

"Well," she said, "he asked me if I believed in God."

Knowing she was not, in that phase of her life, a religious person, I asked her, "How did you answer that question, Sadie?"

"Oh, I just told him I was too young to make up my mind about something as important as that." She told me the priest said if she had answered yes, he would have been suspicious about her honesty, but he said he was impressed that she told the truth. Sadie could exude such confidence and was so articulate that she could talk her way into anything.

She had to cook dinner six nights a week for six priests, serve the meal, and clean up—by herself. She was given a budget and access to a freezer with some food, and they told her they wanted her to purchase the vegetables fresh from the store each day. Sadie didn't have a car, and the Grotto was over ten miles from our house. That meant she had to take a bus to the store, buy the vegetables, and take another bus to the Grotto.

The first night, she cooked crêpes for dinner, but the priests told her they were meat-and-potatoes kind of people. The second night, she was cooking soup when one priest told her they ate soup only for lunch, not dinner. Frustrated, she finally called her Wisconsin grandmother, who had worked with priests. She gave Sadie some recipes, which she tried, and finally the priests loved what she cooked. *Oh, Sadie,* I remember thinking, *why get yourself into some-*

thing so difficult, and something you have to do alone? But I do know one reason she took the job—she told me she thought her grandmother would be proud of her for getting a job cooking for priests. That showed me how much Sadie really did want to succeed.

During her good times, Sadie always seemed to have to reach for the stars. The problem is that when you reach for the stars without putting up the ladder, you often fall. And you have to be okay with falling sometimes. But when she fell, she fell hard. She ended up quitting the job after several weeks—it was just too overwhelming for her—but that made her feel like a failure. To me, it was just another example of her reaching for the stars without taking the time to prepare for the journey. After she quit the job at the Grotto, the roller coaster began a sharp descent.

33

—

Life in the Fast Lane

ONE MORE TIME, SADIE TRANSITIONED RAPIDLY FROM BEING MOTI-vated, engaged, and seemingly happy to engaging in behavior that we just did not understand. Just six weeks into cooking school, she told us she was taking a leave of absence so she could go to the annual Rainbow Gathering in Utah. The Rainbow Gathering and associated Rainbow Family are described on the website as follows:

> Some say we're the largest non-organization of non-members in the world. We have no leaders, and no organization. To be honest, the Rainbow Family means different things to different people. I think it's safe to say we're into intentional community building, non-violence, and alternative lifestyles. We also believe that Peace and Love are a great thing, and there isn't enough of that in this world. Many of our traditions are based on Native American traditions, and we have a strong orientation to take care of the Earth. We gather in the National Forests yearly to pray for peace on this planet.

So, Sadie had decided to head off to pray for peace. Somehow, she convinced the woman who owned the house where she and her boyfriend were living to drive her and a couple of other people to Utah. Unfortunately, the day she decided to head to the gathering was her eighteenth birthday and also my mother's birthday. My folks, brother, and aunt had traveled to Portland for a joint celebration. Why would she have picked that particular evening to leave?

I remember looking out the window as I was putting the finishing touches on dinner, and there she was with a backpack on, staring in, almost as if she were outside a fishbowl, gazing in at everyone. I remember thinking that she had sort of a dead look in her eyes, almost no emotion. Her affect was flat. She was locked into a path. I ran out and said, "Sadie, what are you doing?" She told me she and her friends were heading out. I couldn't convince her to stay for her own birthday dinner. I burst into tears.

Later, my mother told me she looked out the window and she and Sadie locked eyes for a moment. Sadie looked at her without smiling and turned away. In hindsight, I think Sadie was ashamed—she didn't want to sit at the table and have her grandparents ask her about her life. She felt like a disappointment and didn't understand that we did not think of her that way. Sure, we were disappointed that she had dropped out of yet another endeavor, but that didn't make her a failure in our eyes—only in hers.

She left that July night for Utah. Five days later, we got a call from her—she was having a great time and had decided that when her housemates left to drive back to Portland, she would stay longer. But a couple of days after that, she called and said she needed a ride home. Did we use tough love and tell her that she had to figure out how to get home, since she had chosen to stay, rather than driving home with her housemates? Tough love for an eighteen-year-old girl? If we had said no, I have no doubt she would have tried to hitchhike home, and what mother wants her daughter hitchhiking?

We decided to purchase her a Greyhound bus ticket but then found out she had taken her pit bull with her and the bus driver wouldn't let her on the bus with the dog. She even tried telling the bus driver that Guya was a service dog in training—no go. Some woman she had met at the gathering gave Sadie a place to sleep for the night, and Dennis got in the car and drove all night to pick her up in Utah and bring her home.

I suppose some people reading this will think we were enabling bad decisions, bad behavior. This was one of the many times Dennis and I had a discussion—do we apply tough love or not?—but we always came back to the thought that she was struggling with demons in her mind, and we wanted her to know that we were her rock, that we would always be a safe haven for her, that we would always be there for her. And I just couldn't live with myself if we left her there and she was abused or killed while hitchhiking.

While I think our intuition was correct about Sadie's fighting demons, her behavior often confused us because it didn't fit with our preconceived notions of depression. After Sadie died, I read an article on the myths of teenage depression that was published in a magazine called *Esperanza*, and I saw many signs that Sadie was experiencing depression in the way a teenager might, based on statements in the article:

> When depression enters the mix of garden-variety adolescent self-absorption and moodiness, it's as misunderstood as the teenagers themselves. That confusion creates a breeding ground for myths—myths that prevent kids from receiving help they desperately need.
>
> So, how do you distinguish growing pains from clinical symptoms?
>
> "If it's just sadness, these feelings and moods tend to pass quickly," says Alexandra Barzvi, PhD, clinical director of the Institute for Anxiety and Mood Disorders at New York University's internationally renowned Child Study Center. "If it's truly a depression, it will interfere with everyday activities, including a teen's desire to participate in things they normally love. It can affect their sleep and appe-

tite. They may care less about their appearance, so you'll see that they're less together in terms of hygiene."

"It's often that teenagers express depression not as a typical down-in-the-dumps mood, but a more irritable, oppositional mood," Carol Glod, PhD (a Northeastern University nursing professor and researcher of adolescent depression), counters.

Minus the disorder's hallmark melancholy, it can be tricky for parents to detect depression in their child.

"Many teenagers tell me they don't feel sad. They tell me they feel nothing—that they're without emotions," says Miriam Kaufman, MD, a pediatrician at Toronto's Hospital for Sick Children and author of *Helping Your Teen Overcome Depression: A Guide for Parents* (Key Porter Books, 2000).

"For every sign of depression, the opposite is true. Your appetite can increase; your appetite can decrease. While you find decreased energy in many depressed teenagers, there is certainly a significant minority who become agitated with depression. They're pacing around—they just can't sit still."

These statements, especially the one about how the symptoms a teen exhibits can be the opposite of your preconceived notions of depression, illustrate how hard it is for parents to determine whether a teen acting out is struggling with mental health issues, lacking important skills, or just making deliberately bad decisions. But you can't think that Sadie was just misbehaving when you read her writing. After she died, I found one of Sadie's poems from around this time. It makes me think about how confusing the extreme swings in her behavior were and how hard it was to believe she was suffering only from depression. The poem captures the frenzy she felt in her life—and perhaps, if she was bipolar, indicates how she felt in a manic phase.

Life in the Fast Lane

Some people tell me
I had better die young.
Embittered in the way
only thwarted dreams can make you,
I agree
with the halfhearted promises,
they came a bit too soon,
rescue a bit too late,
and somehow,
I find myself within these same
4 walls,
different colors
and the same design.
Some people tell me
I should slow down some.
But life in the fast lane
is cocaine addictive,
because when life's
Going at 100 mph,
you forget who you are,
a brilliant state of affairs.
I want the flashing lights
of the white and blue cars,
to experience the thrill
of the chase,
so we give them one,
and some people tell me,
I need to focus now,
but no easy task,

when ecstasy is in your blood
and the lights are brighter,
than they never were at midnight.
With the flashlight in my eye,
"no, Officer, I'm not high."
I'm in outer space,
swimming in the starlight and
bathing in the gentle light the moon
will grant me. Love, they say, is ethereal.
Some people say
I should come down to earth,
but why?
When I can make the stars
play hopscotch
and trees jump double-dutch
in my mind.
Some people tell me I should live a little,
but
dying is a bit more fun,
and you,
with your feet grounded
into the current of life,
don't notice me washing away.
Cuz life in the fast lane
is cocaine addictive
and rescue came
a bit too late.

One of Sadie's Portland friends wrote a candle tribute about Sadie after she died that shows how exciting it could be to be around her: "Sadie is my best friend. She taught me that exhilaration of unexpected accomplishments [is] worth the risk of failure."

Somehow, in the heat of the battle, we couldn't seem to stop the roller coaster long enough to sit back and reflect on Sadie's diagnosis the way we have done since her death. Today, I think about it a lot—whether her depression diagnosis was wrong, whether it was right when she was young but then evolved into bipolar illness, or whether it was bipolar illness all along or yet something else. According to Kay Redfield Jamison, an expert in bipolar illness from Johns Hopkins, the most common diagnosing error in adolescent bipolar illness is to assume the child has depression.[11] Is that what happened to us? Was the diagnosis of depression wrong and that error led us down the wrong path—a path that turned out to be catastrophic?

According to the National Institute of Mental Health (NIMH) and the Depression and Bipolar Support Alliance (DBSA), bipolar disorder, also known as manic-depressive illness, is a brain disorder that causes unusual shifts in mood, energy, activity levels, and the ability to carry out daily tasks. Bipolar illness often appears in the late teens or early-adult years and usually lasts a lifetime. It affects approximately 5.7 million adult Americans, or about 2.6 percent of the US adult population. Both genetic and environmental factors are linked to bipolar illness. According to NIMH, some research has suggested that people with certain genes are more likely to develop bipolar disorder than others, and some imaging studies show that the brains of people with bipolar disorder may differ from the brains of healthy people or people with other mental disorders. Interestingly, some 20 percent of adolescents with major depression develop bipolar disorder within five years of the onset of depression. (B. Birmaher, "Childhood and Adolescent Depression: A Review of the Past 10 Years," Part I, 1995).

As I reflect on Sadie's life now, I come to the conclusion that she was bipolar. What else would explain her dramatic swings in behavior? Starting college, starting cooking school, starting her job cooking for the priests, even working at Fred Meyer—she undertook each of these activities with such gusto, such enthusiasm. She once told me that after she started cooking school, she went to the house where she was renting a room, dressed in her full cooking-school uniform, and yelled to her roommates, "You will never have to cook desserts again! I will bring home leftovers from pastry school!" She would be on top of the world for four to six weeks. We would get reports about how well she was doing. We would once again become hopeful. Yet, over and over again, she would eventually fall off the ledge. She would drop out of whatever she had been so passionate about and do something wild and crazy and often quite dangerous.

What else would have caused Sadie, at only sixteen, to take off the night before finals, to just disappear, when, according to her teachers, she was doing extremely well? What would have caused her to do such a risky thing as hitchhiking from Portland to Seattle or LA, taking off in the middle of Marrakesh, or staying alone at the annual Rainbow Gathering, instead of driving back with her friends, when she had no money, a dog to care for, and no other ride home?

Looking at NIMH's list of typical behaviors of people in the manic phase of bipolar illness, I see many behaviors that Sadie exhibited:

- Talking very fast, jumping from one idea to another, having racing thoughts

- Being easily distracted

- Increasing activities, such as taking on new projects

- Being overly restless

- Sleeping little or not being tired

- Having an unrealistic belief in one's abilities

- Behaving impulsively and engaging in pleasurable, high-risk behaviors

Perhaps it was because of bipolar illness that Sadie brought such excitement to our lives. Part of me marveled at and applauded her; part of me loved the fact that she had such passion and was not afraid to do and stand up for what she wanted and what she believed in. Even today, I find it easier to remember the exciting times, the times when she was on top of the world, and to forget the black side of that excitement. But the truth is, it is hard to be bipolar and hard to live with someone who is bipolar. And living with Sadie was very hard. I loved her more than anything, but her illness took a toll on us all.

Suicide rates are higher for people suffering from bipolar illness than for those with any other mental health disorder. Bipolar individuals have higher divorce rates and a harder time holding a steady job. The highs (manic phases) can be exhilarating. People feel on top of the world, as if they can do just about anything. In memoirs I have read, bipolar authors talk about the wild things they would do in their manic phases—like withdrawing all the money in their bank account and spending it on very extravagant things. But these authors also say the transitions from manic to depressive states are brutal.

As for Sadie's diagnosis, we had in some way decided that naming what was "wrong" with her (naming the cause of her behavior) was an art at best, and at worst just a game of darts, so we stopped asking for that information. It had been such a moving target. Perhaps Sadie's original diagnosis of depression was correct, but then her condition evolved into bipolar illness. I understand now that as she got older, I should have taken her again to an independent psychiatrist for an assessment and diagnosis, to have someone fresh do it.

In fact, the diagnosis does matter, because perhaps, as she grew older, her illness changed or manifested in different ways that would have altered her diagnosis. In standard psychiatric circles, the medication follows the diagnosis. Our decision not to try psychiatric medications again was based on our assumption that Sadie's diagnosis was depression, and we didn't want to risk her making another suicide attempt on depression medications.

34

The Emptiness Inside Is Full to Bursting

> Suicidal depression is a state of cold, agitated horror and relentless despair. The things that you most love in life leach away. Everything is an effort, all day and throughout the night. There is no hope, no point, no nothing.
>
> —Kay Redfield Jamison

I UNDERSTAND THAT MANY PEOPLE WHO TAKE THEIR LIVES PROVIDE clues beforehand. Today, I realize that Sadie may have been asking for help in her usual hidden way, through her writing. But there were so many other contradictions that we didn't pick up on the clues, if there even were any. The last Sunday before she died, she left her spiral-bound notebook on the kitchen counter. Normally, she kept her writing private and never left it out for us to see. I did open the notebook, even though I felt guilty reading her private journal. I read only the last thing she had written, likely very recently or perhaps even that very day.

Struggle

I push against forces so deep as to be unknowable, vast, and uncomprehensible.
Is there anyone who yearns as I do?

Fierce and unyielding,
desperation.
All my life it's been suck it up, Sadie,
deal with it, ignore, bottle it up.
And I did. Please believe me, I tried, I found the emptiness inside. I did
what you asked of me so naively, not comprehending, you didn't want
to see, did you?
I'm so full to bursting from relentless years of sucking up and bottling it
all in.
I've tried, can't you see?
I've struggled endlessly with who you told me to be.
And the emptiness inside me is full to bursting with tears, rejections,
broken dreams,
and I might just explode molten yearning.
I'll open my mouth one day,
set free this pressure trapped inside.
Years of subjugation will fly like that volcano
we saw in Costa Rica years ago.
And you, unsuspecting,
will be caught in the outpouring of my sanity.

After reading this, I carefully closed the journal, feeling tears running down my cheeks. She sounded desperate and unhappy. *What can we do to make her happy again?* I asked myself, even as I felt inadequate. Although it was painful to think about, I wondered if there was some truth to her statement *I've struggled endlessly with who you told me to be.* Did we not accept her for who she was but rather try constantly to change her? We so wanted her to achieve the extraordinary potential we knew she possessed. Yet maybe, given her mental health issues, she knew she couldn't ever meet those expectations.

I don't like to think you have to lower your standards and expectations for someone with mental health issues, but you may need to adjust them. Although—and perhaps this goes for everyone—rather than trying to mold your child to be what you think of as successful, you need to help them find their strengths and help them figure out how to best leverage those strengths, even if that results in something unconventional or different from what you expected for your child. Did I really unwittingly contribute to Sadie's feeling of failure?

When Sadie got up later that morning, she and I sat in the sun on the deck, talking. In contrast with her writing, she seemed to be in a good mood. That morning was the best day I had had with her in a very long time. We talked for hours. We talked about my life when I was her age, we talked about some old letters she had found that an old boyfriend of mine who was a poet had written to me, and I remember her being surprised at a side of me she didn't know: "You dated a poet?" I felt like we had shifted from mother-raising-a-daughter mode to the more adult mother-daughter relationship that arrives one day when your child grows up. Sadie even told me that afternoon, "Don't worry, Mom, I *will* go back to college; I'm thinking about applying to Evergreen College in Olympia." I loved that day; I didn't want it to end.

I knew I should talk about what she had written, but I didn't want to bring it up that afternoon and risk spoiling the best day we had had in so long. How stupid of me. I guess I thought I could just bring it up another day. Now I wonder, did she leave the writing on the counter on purpose? Was she asking for help and I . . . I ignored the signals? I cannot think of that decision without doubling over in pain, without thinking that I failed my daughter and she is dead as a result of that failure.

As the day came to a close, so did the good times. I could feel the shift in the air, like when the smell of pine nuts you are toasting suddenly goes from a nice, warm, nutty smell to something slightly acrid and burnt. Sadie asked me if I would pay for her to get her dreadlocks fixed. A friend had done her hair a few days earlier, but it hadn't turned out quite right, so she had been wearing a scarf to cover her head. I told her no, I wouldn't pay for dreadlocks—that was something she had to cover herself. It wasn't about the money, really; rather, it was just another thing Sadie did that I thought made her life more difficult, but I don't think she understood. I think my reaction made her feel alone and, again, like a failure. She didn't even have the money to get her hair fixed and took my refusal to pay as a sign that she was on her own but was not able to be successful. When I told her I wouldn't pay, she told me she had to go. I couldn't convince her to stay for dinner; instead, acting somewhat agitated, she headed out the door. That was the last time I saw her alive.

How did we go from that day to her death just four days later? We didn't see it coming. I was in Monterey at a conference for work that week. I had wanted to bring her but was afraid she would just take off and I would spend the entire time worrying about her or trying to find her. And I knew Dennis was going to be home, so I didn't offer to take her. As usual, I called her every day when I traveled, even though I did not always reach her.

According to Dennis, Sadie had a rough couple of days. Tuesday night, she called him and asked him to pick her up downtown. When he arrived, she was agitated, unkempt, and a bit wild-looking. He started driving her home, but then she saw someone on the street she knew and told him, "Stop the car—I need to get out here." She had him come all the way downtown to pick her up and bring her home but then wanted out of the car? He tried to convince her to go home with him, but she just wouldn't. He let her out but was, understandably, quite angry with her, and she knew it.

The next night, the night before—I now sort everything by "before" and "after"—when I talked to her on the phone, she sounded fine. She remembered I had to give a talk the next day at the conference and said, "Good luck on your presentation, Mom." It felt good that she remembered. I know now that all I was hearing was the outside, the shell part, of Sadie. What was going on inside was not okay. That night she had come home with a friend (someone we hadn't met before) and asked Dennis if her friend could sleep on the futon in the basement for the night, and Dennis had said okay. In the morning, he dropped her friend off downtown on his way to work. When I called the next day to tell Sadie how my talk went, I got her voice mail and thought, *She must have forgotten to charge her phone again.* I kept trying, but all day her phone went immediately to voice mail.

She apparently connected with her friend again that afternoon, and they hung out. He told the police he had been feeling extremely depressed and suicidal and that Sadie spent hours with him talking about why life was worth living, talking him out of taking his life. Eventually they decided to go up into Washington Park, a scenic, four-hundred-acre, wooded, public park in Portland, and took some hallucinogenic mushrooms he had. He said later in the evening Sadie gave him the crystal necklace that she always wore and sang Don McLean's "American Pie" and Johnny Cash's "Hurt," then asked him to go get her some water.

While he was getting water, on a beautiful evening in Washington Park, sitting on the hillside beneath the tall evergreens, all alone in the dark, she wrote a note and took her life. The following is an excerpt from her suicide note:

I had hoped this day would never have to come. I'm sorry for everyone I've hurt. I'm sorry for not being strong enough. I know people say that it will get better. I'm not sure it will, and you see, I just can't stand the pain of one more day. So I ask your forgiveness.

The note continued, but perhaps what best illustrated how she felt and why she took her life was the statement *you see, I just can't stand the pain of one more day.*

35

Shattered

SADIE'S DEATH SHATTERED OUR LIVES. IT CHANGED US FOREVER. IT'S been over eight years, but I think about her and miss her every day and know that I always will. I can laugh and have fun, but joy is not part of my life anymore. To this day, I struggle to understand what Sadie meant by *the pain of one more day*. What pain? What caused the pain? I think of how I felt on my worst days after she died and wonder, *Is that what she described as "the pain of one more day"?* Was it that sense of hopelessness that comes when you believe there is no chance that things will ever get better? I can relate to hopelessness now—now that Sadie is dead. Even though I fantasize about her walking in the front door, yelling, "Mom, I'm home!" the truth is, nothing will ever bring her back. There is nothing I can do to change the outcome of that terrible day. There is no hope. In the years after her death, there were many days when the pain was so overwhelming that I didn't want to live. Maybe that is the pain she felt.

The day I buried my daughter, I also buried a piece of my heart. Your child is not supposed to die before you do. I will miss her until the day that I take my last breath. We lost our purpose in life. We lost our shining star. I am no longer a parent—actually, I am no longer even the same person. My priorities in life have changed. I used to think I controlled my life, but I now believe in randomness.

My work used to be so important to me, and, I suppose, as many of us do, I too often took for granted the good things in my life. But really, nothing matters as much as the important people in your life. Not work, not things—people. I know that Dennis and I will *never* get over Sadie's death. At best, we will learn to live with it. Any happiness that I experience now is short-lived and bittersweet, as I know that she is not here to share it with me.

Not a day goes by when I don't see or experience something I want to share with her. Whenever I see a rainbow, I still have an urge to call Sadie and say, "Look up at the rainbow," like I used to, so that wherever we both were, we knew we were looking at the same beauty. Some days, the blanket of shock still cushions me. It all seems so surreal. *She's not really gone; she's just in the other room.* Other days, the pain rips through me as if it will tear me in two.

I could write an entire book about grief and the grief process, about what it feels like to lose your child, to no longer be a parent, to deal with the guilt that you were unsuccessful in the most important job of your life—in raising your child to be happy and productive—and about how the death of a child changes you. But instead of writing about grief, I want to channel that grief into something positive.

I want the world to take note that we cannot afford to lose people like Sadie. I want society to stand up and say, "This is unacceptable." We lost an amazing young woman, someone extremely bright and talented, articulate, engaging, outgoing, gregarious, and passionate about life. She was destined for big things, our daughter, with her brilliant mind and articulate voice, outgoing nature, sarcastic sense of humor, and enthusiasm for life. I thought perhaps she would end up being an investigative reporter whose beat was the dangerous regions of the world, or a political organizer living constantly on the edge. I really thought she was going to make a positive difference in the world.

But because of her mental illness, she was also intense, impulsive, and often very difficult to be around. She didn't understand the social order of things. She thought deeply about the world and knew so much, yet didn't really understand how to fit into it. Inside, she felt like a failure. She felt hopeless. Yet she kept reaching for the stars.

Perhaps, as the social worker–researcher Brené Brown said, "If you numb yourself to shame and vulnerability, you also numb yourself to connection, joy, and gratitude." Perhaps that is what Sadie did. My brother said she was like an eagle stuck on Earth with her wings constantly clipped, but she needed to soar. She didn't accept societal norms. She didn't understand how to fit in on this planet. This is the person we lost, the person the world lost.

The following shows how her best friend from Madison thought about Sadie:

Some Girls

Some girls smile politely as they walk by
you on the street with their proper goodbyes.

Some girls slide away slowly, step aside
sure not to make any trouble or fuss.

But not our girl with her loud spirit full
of vibrato, with notes both low and high,

with eyes for staring deep into the world
for what it is and how it should be. Isn't

that exactly what she'd say now? I think
about her words and how they knew the way

I once would have missed. I think about
her words and how they echo inside me

when I close my eyes. I think about her
words like the ones I heard her sing

to everyone who met her on the street.

—By Sadie's friend Mia,
written in the early morning when Sadie's words of
encouragement were there to get me on my feet

At a local Youth Center's candlelight memorial for Sadie, a young woman told us a story about her. She said one day four months before, she had been sitting in Pioneer Square, crying. She said she had been taking meth. Sadie (whom she didn't know at the time) came up and sat beside her and said, "It looks like you could use a hug." Sadie did hug her, then spent hours talking with her. When Sadie finally got up to leave, she asked the young woman not to do meth that night, for her. This young woman said she didn't do meth that night and then decided to clean up, and that she had been clean ever since then. Sadie had a lot of compassion for people out on the street. This was just one example of it.

I learned a lesson from Sadie: whenever I see someone on the street, I remember her telling me, "Everyone needs respect, Mom. You don't have to give panhandlers money, but at least look at them and politely say, 'Not today, but have a nice day.'" I have learned how true that old axiom "you can't judge a book by its cover" is. The face someone shows on the outside may be very different from how they feel on the inside. We all need to be careful about judging without understanding. People whom we tend to shy away from because of their outward appearance and behavior may be the people who need us the most.

Perhaps it is best to close with Dennis's tribute to Sadie. Then I ask you to read the epilogue of this book.

Goodbye Sadie

Goodbye Sadie
You had a tender heart too often exposed
Elton John had it right
You were like a candle in the wind
Never knowing who to cling to
when the rain set in

Bye bye my beautiful girl
I know you'd rather we were dancing
Dancing our sorrow away
No matter what fate choose to play

Goodbye Sadie
You had a presence all your own
Jackson Browne had it right
Your dance was your very own
Never wanting to conform to the steps you were shown
And in the end you danced it alone

Bye bye my beautiful girl
I know you'd rather we were dancing
Dancing our sorrow away
No matter what fate choose to play

Goodbye Pumpkin
Your sprit sang
Josh Groban had it right
On that starry starry night
You took your life as lovers often do
But I could of told you Sadie
This world was never meant for one as beautiful as you

Bye bye my beautiful girl.
I know you'd rather we were dancing.
Dancing our sorrow away
No matter what fate choose to play.

Epilogue

THE WORLD CANNOT AFFORD TO LOSE PEOPLE LIKE SADIE. THE PER-
sonal and societal costs are unacceptable. Remember that, according
to information on the website MentalHealth.gov (a one-stop access
to US government information on mental health and mental health
problems), one in five American adults have experienced a mental
health issue, one in ten young people have experienced a period of
major depression, and one in twenty people live with a serious mental
illness, such as schizophrenia, bipolar disorder, or major depression.
That means that some of your family members, neighbors, coworkers,
friends, and people sitting next to you at church or on the soccer
field are suffering from mental illness. But you probably don't know
which ones, because they don't talk about it. At best, perhaps they
whisper about it. Most suffer in silence.

Some of these people do seek help. But, despite the prevalence
of mental illness, diagnosing it is trial and error; we are early in the
learning curve on genetic and environmental causes. Little is known
about the short- and long-term safety and efficacy of current treatments, or which treatments will help specific individuals.

The side effects of many psychiatric medications are unacceptable, too. We don't know how to help those struggling without
dampening the unique creative abilities that some mentally ill people
have. Our mental health system is dysfunctional and suffering from
a shortage of experts, beds, and treatment options.

Many people do not get the help they need. In fact, Mental

Health.gov data indicate that less than 20 percent of children and adolescents with diagnosable mental health problems receive the treatment they need. The ramifications are clear. And think about this: according to the National Alliance on Mental Illness, over 50 percent of students with a mental disorder age fourteen and older drop out of high school. That tells me that public schools trying to reduce their dropout rates need to address mental health issues.

Think about the data on suicide. As MentalHealth.gov reports, suicide is the eleventh leading cause of death in the United States (more common than homicide) and the third leading cause of death for people between the ages of ten and twenty-four. Over 90 percent of those who die by suicide have one or more mental disorders. In 2013, 20 percent of suicides were veterans. Death rates from heart disease, cancer, traffic accidents, and homicides are all declining, but US suicide rates have not decreased over the last several decades. In fact, suicide has proven stubbornly difficult to understand, to predict, and to prevent. It remains a challenge to foresee individual risk, and even once a person screens positive for suicide risk, there are few, if any, strategies to guide matching of individuals with the appropriate intervention.

Consider the costs: the loss of people with so much potential, like our daughter; the lives destroyed due to incarceration and homelessness; the cost of social services and medical systems to care for the mentally ill; and the incalculable personal pain and suffering of individuals, their friends, and their families struggling with mental health issues. NIMH estimates the total cost to be in excess of $300 billion per year,[12] and we can't really put a number on the personal pain and suffering. How much is $300 billion? Well, for comparison, the world population is just over seven billion, so the annual cost of mental illness is roughly forty-two times larger than the world's population. That's a lot of money.

If we are a compassionate society, why are we at best tolerating the lack of answers, the personal and economic costs, and at worst ignoring them? How do we begin to change this? It sounds pretty overwhelming, but it takes one step at a time.

You and I, together, can begin to make a change—just like Susan G. Komen's sister did in the 1980s. She spurred a grassroots movement that increased awareness of breast cancer, which in turn resulted in a significant increase in research funding and, consequently, significantly improved survival rates for breast cancer. We can do the same for mental illness. The problems seem intractable, but—one voice at a time, one research project at a time, one step at a time— we can achieve NIMH's vision of a world in which mental illnesses are prevented and cured.

I know if my daughter were still alive and I were reading this book, I would think, *I need help today. My child needs effective treatment now. I don't have the energy to think beyond today.* I understand the urgency parents dealing with their child's mental health issues feel, because I lived that. I know we struggled with just getting Sadie and ourselves through each day. We were reacting to what seemed like one crisis after another. We weren't thinking about how to improve the mental health system. We weren't thinking about funding research for the future. I talked to people every week on the crisis hotline where I volunteered—people who were struggling just to get through the day. I understand how hard it is to lift your head above the fray.

So let's talk about what you can do today, before I ask you to think about the future. I have spent a lot of time over the years since Sadie died thinking about what we did that helped her, what I wish I had done differently, what resources and advice might help others, and what advice others dealing with similar issues could have given me that would have helped and potentially changed the outcome of our story. So I am going to share my thoughts—parent to parent, and parent to adolescent and young adult. Know that I am not an expert; I am not a professional. But I have gone through one of the most devastating experiences anyone can have and have learned through that experience. It would have helped me if someone had shared their thoughts. Perhaps just one of these suggestions or resources may help you today. Then you can lift your head and take a little time to help tackle the big issues.

Advice for Parents, Children, and Young Adults

My Advice, Parent to Parent

- **Accept**. For many parents, their child's mental illness diagnosis or diagnosis of lagging skills is difficult to accept. You want so badly for your child to have a normal, happy life that it is easy on the good days to believe they have overcome the challenges and are okay. It is very hard for most parents to adjust their expectations, but it is so critical to do so. Dennis and I didn't want to believe that our bright and talented daughter might have mental health issues that would stand in the way of her achieving success. Let's be clear: by saying "adjust your expectations," I don't mean you should give up, and I don't mean you should lower your standards, but you may need to alter your expectations to match your child's unique personality and brain function. By accepting, you can focus your energy on solutions.

- **Get educated**. Check out the resources and references listed at the end of this book. Read as much as you can. Encourage your child to get educated—help them find resources that target people their own age. Network; talk to other people dealing with mental health issues. Find out what resources others have found helpful.

- **Identify and build critical life skills**. If your child exhibits "poor decision making," explosive or manipulative behavior, et cetera, remember that kids do well if they can. Rather than assuming that their behavior is "bad," think about skill areas your child may be lacking that cause that behavior (difficulty handling unpredictability or frustration or considering a range of solutions for a problem, engaging in black-and-white thinking, and so on). Then work on a plan to improve those skills. Think about how mental illness might be influencing their behavior. Don't assume a system of rewards and punishments is the solution. Read the book The Explosive Child; it will help you identify lacking skills and give you strategies for building those skills.

- **Take crisis-line training**. It will help you build your skills as a more effective listener and to learn how to defuse anger and to connect with and understand your child and assist them in collaborative problem solving. After Sadie died, I decided to use my experience to help others by volunteering on a crisis hotline. I went through a sixty-hour training that provided listening skills and techniques to help those in crisis. This training may have helped me have more effective conversations with Sadie. It would have given me tools to better be able to defuse her anger and defiance.

- **Call a crisis line if you need to talk to someone anonymously during especially difficult times**.

- **Directly address your child's feeling about adoption (if applicable)**. If your child is adopted, be aware that some (but not all) adopted children struggle with feelings of rejection. If your child's behavior becomes challenging, seek out a therapist who has expertise in adoption issues. Find books your child can read or websites where they can connect with others who have been adopted and can safely express their feelings. Allow your child to explore their feelings about being adopted. It may not be enough just to tell adopted children that their birth parents couldn't take care of them and wanted more for them than they could provide. It may not be enough to tell your adopted child that you love them.

- **Get a good diagnosis and consider requesting a new independent diagnosis (a second opinion) periodically as your child is growing**. Remember that diagnosing brain disorders is still an art and that mental illnesses may evolve as your child grows. Don't assume that the first diagnosis is correct. In our case, Sadie had a bipolar diagnosis in middle school, but early in her high school years we were told no, she was not bipolar. Had we gone in for an independent diagnosis in her later teen years, perhaps we would have heard a different diagnosis and as a result would have pursued a different treatment path.

- **Get connected to any and all the local and national groups listed that may have resources to help you**. Get on the distribution list of NIMH, NAMI, the Brain and Behavior Research Foundation, the JED Foundation, and other organizations that provide support or are doing research, so you get their updates. I did not do a comprehensive search to find these groups while Sadie was alive—I can't explain why not, but I found many organizations after she died that might have been helpful. You never know when someone might have a useful resource or when a new development might help your child. This is also a good way to locate experts whom you may want to contact.

- **Try not to feel shame**. If your child had a physical illness like diabetes, for example, or a broken bone, you would seek out medical help. Do the same if your child is dealing with a mental illness. There is nothing to be ashamed of. If you feel ashamed, your child may pick up on that. Help your child to understand that their particular brain chemistry, circuitry, and biology may be causing their emotional pain, depression, or other mental disorder. These children are not failures, and they have nothing to be ashamed of, either. Let them know that most people struggling can find help and relief from one or a combination of the many available effective medicines, skill-building exercises, and therapy. Help them realize they are not alone. Give them a different way of thinking about mental health.

- **Change the terminology**. Help your child find terminology that does not support the negative stigma that society attaches to the term "mental illness"—terms like "brain disorder" or "brain chemistry imbalance." I used the term "depression," rather than "mental illness," but I think she associated depression with mental illness and thought others would, too. Perhaps talking about brain chemistry would have helped her to feel less ashamed.

- **Empower your child**. Encourage your child to help him or herself as much as possible. Show them the research that indicates diet and exercise and other strategies, like regular sleep, meditation, and yoga, can make a positive difference and explain that those are things under their control. Talk to your child about the dangers of self-medicating with drugs or alcohol—how drugs and alcohol may make their symptoms worse; how, because of the way your child's brain works, drugs and alcohol may have a different impact on your child than they have on others.

- **Find ways to leverage your child's strengths**. Think about what your child can do to leverage their strengths and minimize the negative impact of their vulnerabilities. Help your child strive to be all they can be, to find that niche where the way they think and their unique skills would be an asset.

- **Get the right professional help**. Find a mental health specialist or psychiatrist who, first, provides the right kind of therapy; second, is good at what they do; and third, is someone with whom your child connects and can build a relationship. The type of therapy a mental health professional provides matters. Do your research: What type of therapy has proven most successful in addressing the issues your child faces? Cognitive behavioral therapy? Dialectical behavioral therapy? Neurofeedback? Other? Is the professional you are working with trained in that type of therapy? I also cannot emphasize enough the importance of finding someone your child will talk to, someone your child is comfortable with.

- **Talk about what is going on with trusted friends, relatives, or colleagues (without destroying your child's confidences)**. I know this is hard—you feel so exposed—but you will be surprised at just how many people open up to you about their struggles once they know you are struggling, too. They may be as relieved as you to know they are not alone. Some may already have observed the challenges you are dealing with and are happy you are finally opening up and talking about them. Sure, some people may turn away because they don't know how to deal with mental health challenges, but help may come from totally unexpected places.

- **Try not to be judgmental**. Most of all, listen to your child and try to understand their feelings, rather than focusing on their behaviors. Use language that doesn't come across as judgmental. Ask your child to help you understand what is behind their behavior, but, rather than asking "why" questions, which tend to sound judgmental, ask "how" or "what" questions. Open-ended questions almost demand a response. Realize that some of what you may think of as "bad" behavior or "bad" decision making may be a result of individual brain chemistry or underdeveloped skills in specific areas. Stand beside your child, no matter what, and never give up. Make sure your child knows you are always there but that you need them to take responsibility for things that are within their control. Let your child know that you don't think of them as a failure.

- **Have a discussion about suicide**. Find out whether your child has suicidal thoughts and, if so, whether they have made plans to act on those thoughts. If so, determine whether your child has the means of carrying out that plan. Many people think that if you raise the possibility of suicide, you might be giving your child ideas. However, the training I went through to work on the crisis and suicide-prevention lines indicates that silence and secrecy are the allies of suicide. The best way to identify the possibility of suicide is to ask directly. Open talk and genuine concern about someone's thoughts about suicide are often a source of relief and are key elements in preventing suicide. Help your child or others understand that suicide should never be an option—that it's permanent, that it represents the absence of hope. Suicide destroys not only one's own life but also the lives of one's friends and family. Your child needs to understand that no one is better off with them dead. Make sure your child knows whom they can talk to if they are feeling suicidal. Post the phone numbers for suicide hotlines in your home. You want to build up resiliency to deal with life's challenges.

- **Most of all, do not give up!** New discoveries and developments in the mental health arena are happening every year. Yes, you may feel as if we have no answers yet, but you cannot and should not give up trying. Don't become complacent. Be proactive, always. You and your child just cannot give up, because your lives may literally depend on your perseverance.

- **Take care of yourself and other family members**. Dealing with a child who struggles with mental health issues is hard, very hard, on everyone in a family. But you cannot help your child if you are too stressed and exhausted. It is not selfish to take care of yourself, your other children, and your spouse; it is imperative. You have to support each other.

My Advice as a Parent to Children and Young Adults

According to NIMH, half of all lifetime cases of mental illness begin by age fourteen and three-quarters begin by age twenty-four. The onset of depression, severe anxiety, schizophrenia, bipolar illness can be very frightening. You may have been a happy, well-adjusted child or adolescent; then, suddenly, something changes. Don't ignore how you are feeling. Research is finding that often the earlier you address mental health issues, the better the outcome. Rather than spending your energy trying to hide how you really feel, take action to help yourself. Here are my suggestions:

- **Educate yourself.** Check out the resources and references listed later in this book, a number of which target adolescents and young adults. Read as much as you can.

- **Connect with others who are struggling.** Just look at the statistics in this book, and you will know how many other people are suffering. Many people, particularly young people, do not share the fact that they are struggling with depression, bipolar disorder, or other conditions. Yet many of your peers may be quietly grappling with the same issues you are, but you can't help each other because you don't know. Find a way to broach the subject with trusted friends. Join a reputable blog or chat room—such as the blogs hosted by the Jed Foundation or NAMI. You can remain anonymous on many of these websites. Check out the websites and chat rooms listed in the back of this book.

- **Ask for help.** Young people frequently think their parents won't take their feelings and pain seriously, that their parents are too busy to be bothered with problems or don't have the money for treatment, that they won't understand or may even think you are being manipulative. The reality is that most parents care deeply but may not understand. You have to find a way to communicate how you are feeling, to help them grasp how serious you are, and to ask for help. If you cannot talk to them, write them a letter, show them information from a reputable website, or ask someone on crisis hotline to help you figure out how to broach the subject with your parents. If you can't talk to your parents, talk to a counselor at your school, or a trusted relative or family friend. Just don't suffer in silence.

- **Be open to help.** Help is out there, and you deserve to feel better, to feel happy. Be open to therapy, skill building, and medication recommended by an expert. Medication will not make you a different person. Rather, most medications you may be prescribed are designed to target the specific brain chemistry or circuitry that is contributing to or causing your illness. Using medication is not a crutch—it is no different than using medication to address a physical illness, like diabetes or cancer. Yes, it is true that some medications have unacceptable side effects, but even if you have tried medication in the past unsuccessfully, remember that new medications are continually being developed. Try again! Just remember that right now, finding the right medication is still partially trial and error—if something you have been prescribed isn't working, tell your doctor or psychiatrist, and be open to trying something else. Also remember that it can take weeks before you feel the full effect of a new medication, so give it time. Be in touch with your feelings and the ways in which your body and mind are reacting to the medication. Only you can tell whether it is really helping.

- **Take therapy seriously.** You may have heard the saying "you will get out of it what you put into it." A combination of therapy (for example, to help you have more positive thinking patterns) and medication may be the strategy your psychiatrist or doctor recommends. Be open to sharing and discussing your feelings. This is not a game—show up for your appointments; express your emotions and how you feel on any prescribed medication. A side benefit is that you may learn things about yourself and life in general that others don't learn until they are much older.

- **Empower yourself.** Push yourself to do things that are under your control: exercise, diet, yoga, writing, or whatever works for you. Sadie wrote a lot as a way of dealing with her feelings, but she also found that competitive rowing helped to still her mind. Push yourself to find something that gives you an outlet and some relief.

- **If you have suicidal thoughts or plans, talk to someone**—your parents, a teacher, someone on a suicide hotline, a mental health specialist. Remember that nothing stays the same forever—that no matter how much pain you feel, it can and will get better. You have to believe. Suicide is a dead end and not only cuts short your life but destroys the lives of those who love you—and believe me, there are many more people who care about you than you may think. Above all, believe that you can get past the dark times. There are always other options. Even when the first thing you try fails or the next thing fails, do not give up. Keep trying.

I hope that just maybe, one of these suggestions will make your struggle a little easier. That one of these suggestions will help you get through today. Then perhaps you can direct a little bit of your focus and energy toward helping to find answers for the future.

Call to Action

My hope is that this book and my advice will provide understanding, tools, and resources to help you, your friends, and loved ones who are struggling with mental illness. But we—you and I—need to do more. We have to raise national awareness of the cost to individuals and society of mental illness, and as a nation we have to increase funding for mental health research and services. If we don't, those with mental illness will continue to struggle. The cost will continue to be a drain on our economy. We need to directly address the fact that the scientific and medical communities do not yet know how to prevent or cure mental illness. That there are not enough answers. This chapter is a call to action—a call to take steps as a nation to break the stigmas and adequately fund research and services so we can improve the science behind diagnoses and treatment.

We can look to the past to find examples of changes and improvements resulting from public outcry. Look at what happened with breast cancer. In 1980, Nancy Brinker promised her dying sister she would do everything in her power to end breast cancer forever. That promise became Susan G. Komen for the Cure, which launched a global, grassroots breast cancer movement. In 1982, breast cancer was certainly not a topic of dinner-table conversation—newspapers balked at even printing the words "breast cancer"—but in 2015, the annual Race for the Cure in Portland, Oregon, for example, draws close to thirty thousand people, and people walk all over town wearing the event's pink T-shirts.

Thanks to initiatives like Race for the Cure, Susan G. Komen has invested almost $2 billion toward ending breast cancer in the United States and throughout the world through groundbreaking research, community health outreach, advocacy, and programs in more than fifty countries. Today, in great part because of this work, about 70 percent of women forty years and older receive regular mammograms, the single most effective screening tool to find breast cancer early. And breast cancer survival rates have dramatically increased. In 1980, the five-year survival rate for women diagnosed with early-stage breast cancer was about 74 percent. Today, that number is 98 percent. Early detection and treatment have resulted in a 33 percent decline in breast cancer mortality in the United States.

Can we not do the same thing for mental illness? Can we not achieve a world in which mental illnesses are effectively diagnosed, prevented, and cured? Clearly, mental illnesses are extremely complex and there are limits to what we know; there are no easy answers, and progress will take time. But I believe—and, based on my reading, experts agree—that we can make significant headway if we can break the stigma and start talking about it. If we can ignite the same sort of grassroots movement Nancy Brinker launched. If we can allocate adequate funding to research. Not only can our action create hope for your loved ones and for future generations, but it can also save the lives of people like my daughter.

Sadie's story shouldn't have ended. Nor should we give up on all those people who are still suffering. I ask you to get angry, to say, "This is unacceptable, and we can change it." If we work together, if we speak up, if we push for and prioritize funding for research, we can and we will achieve a world in which mental illness no longer destroys lives.

It is time to make a difference—time to talk about the impact mental health disorders are having on our personal lives and on society as a whole—so that this generation and future generations do not have to live with so much suffering or die prematurely. It is time to turn our suffering and grief into action, on behalf of my daughter, on behalf of your friends, relatives, and veterans who have died by suicide, on behalf of yourself and your children, friends, colleagues, and relatives who are suffering from mental illness, on behalf of those afflicted by mental illness who are currently incarcerated or homeless on the streets.

Can you imagine how much better the world would be if mental illness could be successfully treated or, better yet, prevented? If we could do that without dampening people's creativity? Think about this world: young people and families no longer struggling with ADHD, depression, PTSD. No destitute, mentally ill homeless people on the streets; empty prison cells; families no longer torn apart. And when we are able to effectively treat, cure, or prevent mental illness, we will dramatically reduce the number of suicides. In that future world, my daughter would still be alive and she and many others would be fulfilling their dreams. I don't know why the public outcry occurred for breast cancer but has not yet for mental health, but I do know that we cannot stand by and not try to build this world. We *can* and we *must* strive toward it. Together, we can get there. It will take time, but, as Margaret Mead once said, "Never doubt that a small group of thoughtful, committed citizens can change the world. Indeed, it is the only thing that ever has."

Now is the time to stand up and say, "Enough." With advancing knowledge of genetics, with new technology that is allowing scientists and doctors to see and better understand the brain, and with our ever-increasing understanding of the intersection of behavior, brain, and genetics, we have the foundation to build on. Now is the time to leverage this knowledge and technology; now is the time to strive to make this world a reality.

Do we know what we need to do to achieve this vision?

Yes. First and foremost, we have to break the stigmas associated with mental illness that are interfering with the public's understanding of the magnitude of the problem and the issues that need to be addressed. We will not succeed as long as people struggling with mental illness feel isolated. As someone at my workplace said, "I am afraid that if I tell people about my mental health issues, I will destroy people's perception of me as normal."

We need to have a broad cultural conversation about mental illness in order to change the perception of it from something shameful to a health issue that needs to be treated as one. We need to eliminate the stigma. The National Alliance on Mental Illness (NAMI) states this objective well:

> Stigma erodes confidence that mental disorders are real, treatable health conditions. We have allowed stigma and an unwarranted sense of hopelessness to erect attitudinal, structural, and financial barriers to effective treatment and recovery. It is time to take these barriers down.

On a more personal level, as I have shared, the stigma kept Sadie and Dennis and me from talking about her struggles with others. As a result, Sadie felt alone and eventually hopeless. She told me she put up a shell and showed friends only the outside of that shell; she didn't think they would want to be around her if they knew how she really felt inside it. Because of the stigma, she didn't benefit from being able to talk to others who were also struggling and might have known of strategies that would have helped her.

Second, we have to reform the mental health system. The New Freedom Commission on Mental Health, established in 2002, which examined the need for reform of the mental health care system, concluded that the problems of fragmentation, access, and quality of mental health care were so great that nothing less than transformation would suffice. These findings are consistent with my family's: shortages of qualified adolescent mental health specialists, shortage of beds in treatment centers, and a lack of the wraparound services that Sadie needed when she returned from residential treatment.

Third, we need to fight for public policy changes and increased funding to reform the system and address research needs. A number of national nonprofit and government organizations and medical institutes have developed research strategies. While you and I may not need to know the specifics of these strategies, it is important we know they exist and require adequate funding. So that you are aware of them and can read them if you choose, I have described three prominent strategies below.

1. The National Institute of Mental Health Strategic Plan, released in 2008 and updated in 2014,[13] provides a framework to focus on and accelerate mental health research so that breakthroughs in science can tangibly improve mental health care and the lives of people living with and affected by mental illness. The four objectives of the plan are:

    • Define the mechanisms of complex behaviors.

    • Chart mental illness trajectories to determine when, where, and how to intervene.

    • Strive for prevention and cures.

    • Strengthen the public health impact of NIMH-supported research.

2. The Annenberg Foundation Trust at Sunnylands' Adolescent Mental Health Initiative produced a book in 2005 that included a research agenda and public policy recommendations. The book is titled *Treating and Preventing Adolescent Mental Health Disorders: What We Know and What We Don't Know. A Research Agenda for Improving the Mental Health of Our Youth.* The editors of the book believed that there was a need to provide "a comprehensive evaluation of what we know, and what we

don't know about adolescent mental health, to create a road map for further scientific study and to point the way toward needed changes in social policy."

3. The National Action Alliance for Suicide Prevention's Research Prioritization Task Force released a road map for suicide prevention, titled "A Prioritized Research Agenda for Suicide Prevention: An Action Plan to Save Lives," in 2014.[14] This is the nation's first prioritized research agenda for suicide prevention. According to the report, to reduce suicide we need to know how to target our efforts: to be able to reliably identify who is at risk, how to reach them, and how to deter them from acting on suicidal thoughts. The research agenda's stated goal is to reduce suicides by 20 percent in five years and 40 percent in the next ten (assuming all recommendations are fully implemented). An understanding of how much risk Sadie was at for suicide, and knowledge of and access to effective interventions, might have saved her life. The best thing we can do to ensure others don't end up with the same fate is to fund this research and implement the resulting recommendations.

Are these research agendas perfect? No, of course not, but they provide focus, a guide, which will evolve as we learn more. Many organizations are working on innovative research projects and on research that supports these strategies, such as the Brain and Behavior Research Foundation. The point is, the scientific and medical communities have road maps to help guide their research—they are not starting from ground zero. Obtaining funding to implement these road maps is the challenge.

Is there a solid economic case for achieving this vision?

Yes. As I noted earlier, the National Institute of Mental Health conservatively estimates the total costs associated with serious mental illness, those disorders that are severely debilitating and affect about 6 percent of the adult population, to be in excess of $300 billion per year. The associated costs stem both from direct expenditures on mental health services and treatment and from expenditures and losses related to the disability caused by these disorders. Indirect costs include public expenditures for disability support and lost earnings among people with serious mental illness.[15]

These costs make mental illness the third most costly medical condition, behind heart conditions and trauma and tied with cancer.[16] Mental health care represented 6.2 percent of all medical expenditures in the United States in 2003.[17] And we know that many people with mental health challenges are not currently getting medical help, so the true cost is significantly higher.

If you factor in homelessness and incarceration due to mental health issues, these costs are still greater. According to the US Department of Justice, at the end of 2009, roughly 2.3 million adults in the United States were incarcerated, at a cost of roughly $31,000 per person per year. That equates to over $71 billion a year. According to the Justice Department Survey of Inmates in State and Federal Correctional Facilities (2004) and Survey of Inmates in Local Jails (2002), over half of prison inmates have mental health issues.[18] As for the people on the streets, according to NAMI, an estimated 46 percent of homeless live with severe mental illness, at a huge cost to our social service systems. That means we are spending massive amounts of resources, tax revenue, and charitable donations in the wrong places—on Band-Aids—rather than on addressing the cause.

At a global level, taken together, the direct economic effects of mental illness (such as spending on care) and the indirect effects (such as lost productivity) already cost the global economy around $2.5 trillion a year. By 2030, that amount is projected to increase to around $6 trillion in constant dollars—more than heart disease and more than cancer, diabetes, and respiratory diseases combined.[19]

These numbers are staggering. While no one knows just how much it would cost to achieve the NIMH's laudable vision of a world in which mental illnesses are prevented and cured, how can anyone looking at these expenditures not justify spending the necessary dollars to find answers?

Do we have the technology and knowledge of the brain and genetics to accomplish this?

The scientific community has made significant progress over the last ten to twenty years in its understanding of genetics and the interaction between the brain, behavior, and the environment, and in the development of tools that allow researchers to see inside the brain. And progress is continuing to be made. For example, according to NIMH, ongoing research is providing information on how genetic factors increase or reduce vulnerability to mental illness, and how experiences during infancy, childhood, and adolescence can increase the risk of mental illness or protect against it.[20]

The progress has been extraordinary. It wasn't until the mid-2000s that researchers finished mapping the complete sequence of the human genome, which is similar to having all the pages of a manual needed to make the human body. This work has provided researchers with powerful tools to understand genetic factors in mental health, and now they are starting to identify specific genes that may be linked to the development of some psychiatric disorders. In 2014, an international team of researchers published the results of their large genome study that identified one hundred genes linked to the development of schizophrenia. The findings, published online in the journal *Nature*, could lead to new approaches to treating the disease, which has seen little improvement in drug development in more than sixty years.[21]

Scientists are exploring using a person's genetic code to determine risk for mental health disorders and suicide and to determine how individuals process medication differently. This undertaking allows medical doctors to identify which drugs will work for a given individual and eliminates some or all of the trial and error that now occurs with psychiatric medications. Some psychiatric hospitals today, such as the Mayo Clinic, are doing genetic testing on mental health patients when they are admitted for the first time so that psychiatrists can identify the medications most likely to be effective for those people.

Research to try to identify and characterize biomarkers for mental disorders is also under way. *Webster's New World Medical Dictionary* defines a biomarker as "a biologic feature that can be used to measure the presence or progress of disease or the effects of treatment." Identifying biomarkers can facilitate more accurate prediction of disease risk, course, and therapeutic responses and ultimately can lead to knowledge-based treatment and preventive strategies.

Powerful tools, such as three-dimensional neuroimaging and other imaging technologies—that enable researchers and physicians to see the wiring and functioning of the brain, to discern the outlines of the complex neural circuits that become disordered in mental illness, and to identify the signaling system in a person's brain that may be causing mental illness—are now available as well. The brain-imaging data that are now being collected and compiled eventually may allow scientists to identify the brain function that is causing a specific mental disorder.

Deep-brain stimulation, called transcranial magnetic stimulation (TMS), is a treatment the FDA approved in 2008 to help patients with treatment-resistant depression.It works on glutamate receptors and appears to strengthen neural connections. TMS uses a highly targeted pulsed magnetic field, similar in type and strength to those produced by a magnetic resonance imaging (MRI) machine, to stimulate cortical neurons. Studies have consistently shown TMS to be effective in two-thirds of patients receiving treatment; close to 30 percent achieve a complete remission.[22] TMS appears to have a longer-lasting response than typical treatment with antidepressants. For patients who do improve with TMS, responses tend to be sustained over the course of one year. TMS treatments typically last thirty-seven minutes and are completed daily, five days per week, for five to six weeks.Unlike electroconvulsive therapy (ECT), a procedure in which electric currents pass through the brain, TMS has virtually no side effects and is extremely well tolerated.[23]

Deep-brain stimulation is being used to treat a variety of psychiatric disorders, including Alzheimer's disease, Parkinson's disease, and anxiety disorders, and to help stroke victims regain functioning, though this research is still in its infancy.

Other exciting new research areas in depression include the use of ketamine, an FDA-approved anesthetic. Research suggests that ketamine can provide rapid relief of the signs and symptoms of depression. It works on glutamate receptors and appears to strengthen neural connections. In his October 2014 Director's Blog, Tom Insel, former director of NIMH, stated that

"Recent data suggest that ketamine, given intravenously, might be the most important breakthrough in antidepressant treatment in decades. Three findings are worth noting. First and most important, several studies demonstrate that ketamine reduces depression within six hours, with effects that are equal to or greater than the effects of six weeks of treatment with other antidepressant medications. Second, ketamine's effects have been noted in people with treatment-resistant depression. Most of the studies to date have tested ketamine in people for whom other treatments were not effective, including both medications and psychotherapy. This promises a new option for people with some of the most disabling and chronic forms of depression, whether classified as major depressive disorder or bipolar depression. Third, it appears that one of the earliest effects of the drug is a profound reduction in suicidal thoughts."[24]

Other new treatment approaches, such as neurofeedback, show promise in altering dysfunctional pathways in the brain. Efforts using neurofeedback (performed by a trained clinician with an EEG machine) are under way to help people alter their brain waves (their response) to stimuli—essentially to train their brain to respond differently to triggers.

These developments and enabling technologies are paving the way to new strategies for the diagnosis, treatment, and prevention of mental health disorders. Researchers still need to translate this progress into better diagnoses, therapeutics, and cures, but they have tools and knowledge now that should give us all hope for a better future.

Do we have the means to achieve this vision?

Achieving the vision will take significant funding—more funding than is currently allocated. There needs to be a public outcry to ensure that funding for mental health is prioritized and dramatically increased. Funding will need to come from a variety of sources, including the government, the private sector, and even small, individual contributions from people like you and me.

Will it take time?

Yes. But we cannot and should not sit on the sidelines and wait. Every one of us can help move this agenda forward more quickly by taking steps to eliminate the stigmas associated with mental illness, by sharing our stories, by donating time or money to nonprofits and research organizations, and by writing our senators and congresspeople to request more funding for research and public policy changes to improve the US mental health system. It is too late for Sadie, but it is not too late for the millions of others who are still struggling.

We have a long way to go, but public awareness about mental illness is higher than ever, thanks in part to new initiatives across the United States designed to build awareness and expand research funding. New laws have been put in place in recent years to address suicide prevention and mental health care coverage. Just look at some recent accomplishments:

- **Garrett Lee Smith Memorial Act of 2004:** This suicide prevention bill, signed into law in 2004, was named in honor of former US Senator from Oregon, Gordon Smith's Oregon Senator Smith's son, Garrett, who died at age twenty-one by suicide after battling bipolar disorder and depression. This bill provided $82 million to mental health and suicide prevention programs on college campuses.

- **Mental Health Parity and Addiction Equity Act of 2008:** This act requires insurance groups that offer coverage for mental health or substance use disorders to provide the same level of benefits that they do for general medical treatment. Final rules for implementing the act were issued in late 2013.

- **Affordable Care Act (ACA):** The ACA builds on the Mental Health Parity and Addiction Equity Act of 2008 to extend federal parity protections to sixty-two million Americans. It will provide one of the largest expansions of mental health and substance use disorder coverage in a generation. In July 2014, the US Department of Health and Human Services allocated $54.6 million in ACA funding to support mental health centers and expand behavioral health services across the country.

- **National Conversation on Mental Health:** In June 2013, Barack Obama launched a national conversation on mental health to help change our attitudes about people with mental illnesses and build acceptance and support in our communities, congregations, schools, and families. In 2003, Former President George Bush's New Freedom Commission on Mental Health, which examined the need for reform of the mental health care system, concluded that the problems of fragmentation, access, and quality of mental health care were so great that nothing less than transformation would suffice.

- **OK2TALK:** In 2013, the National Association of Broadcasters (NAB) launched its new OK2TALK campaign, aimed at educating the public and encouraging youth to start a conversation about mental health.

- **Brain Research Through Advancing Innovative Neurotechnologies (BRAIN) Initiative:** In 2013, Barack Obama launched a major public–private sector collaborative designed to advance innovative neurotechnologies and to undertake basic mapping of circuits and neurons of the brain. The BRAIN Initiative calls for a broad approach, involving a $4.5 billion investment over ten years, beginning in fiscal year 2016, to decode the language of the brain by understanding its circuits.

Let's build on these efforts to stop the suffering and economic drain. We can do this! Remember—one step at a time. We are taking baby steps now—let's accelerate to a run. Here is what I ask:

1. **Tell your stories**—not just to people like me, but publicly, because that is what is going to impact research funding and how quickly we can help others struggling.

2.   **Push for and support funding for school screening programs** that might detect mental illness early.

3.   **Support local, state, and national mental health advocacy, education, and research organizations**. Become a member, volunteer your time, donate money, or participate in awareness events, such as walks.

4.   **Get politically active**. Even if you have never done it before, e-mail or write your senators and congresspeople. Tell them that funding for mental health research and services is a priority—that it is an imperative.

Useful Helplines, Blogs, Information Resources, and Policy and Research Institutes

If you, a friend, or someone you love is struggling, check out the resources included in this chapter. But first, are you:

In Crisis and Need Help Immediately?

- Suicide crisis line (Lifeline): call 1-800-273-TALK (8255)

- LGBTQ suicide crisis line: call 1-866-488-7386

- Veteran crisis line: call 1-800-273-8255 or text 838255

- National Runaway Safeline: 1-800-RUNAWAY

Sadie used both national suicide crisis lines and the National Runaway Safeline. I credit the Safeline (formerly the National Runaway Switchboard) with providing a desperately needed way for her to communicate with us when she had taken off, to let us know that she was alive and okay, without divulging her exact location (which she was not ready to do at the time). I credit the suicide crisis lines with saving Sadie's life more than once when she was in middle school. I can't emphasis enough how important it is for anyone struggling with mental health issues or with a devastating life crisis to have the suicide crisis line number on hand.

Not in an Emergency but Could Use Some Help?

You can access many good sources of information and help online, but one of the challenges anyone faces when searching for help on the Internet is how to determine which sources are legitimate and accurate. I have tried to identify the legitimate resources that I think would be most helpful. The list is not comprehensive—there are likely good sources that I have missed, and some resources I have listed may change over time—but this list should provide a good start. I used some of these resources myself during our struggles with Sadie, and found many after her death, in my search for answers to the big question: *Why?* Some of these are resources to which I refer crisis-line callers, and a couple were provided to me by crisis-line callers or friends who are struggling.

For those who do not have access to mental health professionals, I have included a few of the promising new resources that have emerged as a result of technology innovation—help that anyone with a smartphone or Internet service can access. I cannot comment on the legitimacy or effectiveness of these new resources, but the number and type of online, video conferencing, and smartphone resources are rapidly expanding and improving. I expect there will be more and more research studies looking at the effectiveness of these new tools in the near future.

The resources I have included are organized in the categories listed below. Where a resource fits into multiple categories, I list them in each relevant category but describe them in only one.

1. Are you a teenager or young adult seeking help and connection?
2. Want to better understand mental health issues, diagnosis, and treatment approaches?
3. Need help finding a psychiatrist, psychologist, psychiatric nurse therapist, or treatment program? Looking for consumer information about psychiatrists and treatment program ratings or certifications?
4. Want to learn about the latest research? Influence policy? Support research and mental health services?
5. Looking for alternative support approaches?

1. Are you a teenager or young adult seeking help and connection?

This section includes resources that provide general information on mental illnesses, ways to connect with others who may be dealing with issues similar to yours, ways to help a friend who is struggling, and resources specific to youth grappling with self-harm (such as cutting), LGBTQ issues, or bullying.

To help you better understand mental health issues:

- www.nami.org: The National Alliance on Mental Illness (NAMI) is a nationwide, grassroots mental health advocacy organization with state chapters. NAMI offers support, education, awareness, and advocacy; advocates for access to services, treatment, support, and research; and trains grassroots volunteer facilitators who host individual and family support groups in thousands of US communities. Through the toll-free NAMI HelpLine, NAMI provides free referrals, information, and support. Call 1-800-950-NAMI (6264), Monday through Friday, 10:00 a.m. to 6:00 p.m., Eastern Standard Time.

Ways to connect with others dealing with similar issues:

- www.jedfoundation.org: Through a variety of programs, the Jed Foundation works to promote emotional health and prevent suicide among college students. The website includes facts empowering young people to protect their emotional health, support their friends, and become advocates so every American has access to mental health help. ULifeline, found on the website, is an anonymous, confidential resource center where you can be comfortable searching for the information you need regarding emotional health. The site also has information on how you can help a friend who you think may be struggling. You can enter your college name and find out what resources are available on your campus. The Jed Foundation also has a student advisory council that helps guide its efforts.

- www.halfofus.com: Through Half of Us, mtvU and the Jed Foundation aim to initiate a public dialogue to raise awareness about the prevalence of mental health issues and connect students to the appropriate resources. Based on what you are feeling (angry, sad, weird) or what issue you are dealing with (self-image, digital drama, LGTBQ, self-harm, other), you can find facts and recommendations to help you on the website.

- www.StrengthofUs.org: Strength of Us is an online community developed by young adults and the National Alliance on Mental Illness (NAMI). It's designed to inspire young adults impacted by mental health issues to think positive, stay strong, and achieve their goals through peer support and resource sharing. Through this site, you can join a variety of online support groups: depression, relationships, vent this, #thinking positive, and many others.

- www.7cupsoftea.com: Seven Cups of Tea is a marketplace for emotional support. People go to the website or smart phone app when they need somebody to talk to or to vent. You can touch base as much as you like. For users, the site is anonymous, convenient, free, and on-demand. You can select or get matched up with trained active listeners who, according to the site, are kind, compassionate, and nonjudgmental. Each listener has a short profile, a listing of what languages they speak, and a list of issues or mental health categories in which they are comfortable conversing.

In the same way you might rate vendors on eBay or restaurants on Yelp, users rate the listeners. You can look at reviews and ratings for listeners before you select whom you want to talk to. You also have the option of connecting with a therapist for fee-based online therapy or free online counseling. The site uses bridging technology that lets you connect one-on-one with a listener while remaining anonymous. Also available on the site is a series of self-help guides: "Anxiety Guide," "Eating Disorder Guide," "Surviving Breakups Guide," and many more.

According to the website, "7 Cups of Tea" is actually the name of a famous Chinese poem. I have included a translation below. The concept is that each cup you have provides a different level of healing. The 7 Cups of Tea website is meant to be a place where you can sit down and have several cups of tea with a friend.

7 Cups of Tea, by Lu Tong (795–835 CE)

The first cup kisses away my thirst,
and my loneliness is quelled by the second.
The third gives insight worthy of ancient scrolls,
and the fourth exiles my troubles.
My body becomes lighter with the fifth,
and the sixth sends word from immortals.
But the seventh—oh the seventh cup—
if I drink you, a wind will hurry my wings
toward the sacred island.

—Translated by Christopher Nelson

- www.ok2talk.org: The goal of OK2TALK is to create a community for teens and young adults struggling with mental health problems and to encourage them to talk about what they're experiencing by sharing their personal stories of recovery, tragedy, struggle, or hope. Anyone can add their voice by sharing creative content, such as poetry, inspirational quotes, photos, videos, song lyrics, and messages of support, in a safe, moderated space. The website has information in English and Spanish.

- www.reachout.com: ReachOut is managed by the Inspire Foundation and provides youth with a nonthreatening first step to explore how they can help themselves through a tough time via:

  - Expert knowledge based on research and youth-generated content, stories, and other information reviewed by mental health experts.
  - Improving coping skills, self-help, and resilience through numerous platforms, such as text or online forums, where youth can ask questions and receive support.
  - Reducing the stigmas surrounding mental health; showing, through increased knowledge, many of the issues youth deal with and that getting help is okay.
  - Offering connection and space to share opinions and stories and to provide support to each other in a safe and positive environment.

- www.activeminds.org: This student-run mental health awareness, education, and advocacy organization is dedicated to raising awareness about mental health among college students. It serves as the young-adult voice in mental health advocacy on more than one hundred college campuses nationwide. The organization develops and supports student-run chapters on college and university campuses that promote a dialogue around issues of mental health and educate the entire student body about available resources in and around the campus community. The website serves as a clearinghouse of information on college mental health.

- www.bringchange2mind.org: Bring Change 2 Mind is an advocacy group founded by actress Glenn Close, whose sister Jessie has bipolar disorder. The mission of this organization is to eliminate stigmas through widely disseminated public-education materials and programs and by sharing stories of real people. You can read others' stories and share your own on the website, and can take an online pledge to stand up against the stigmatization of mental illness.

Ways to communicate safely with your parents:

- www.1800runaway.org: The National Runaway Safeline is a twenty-four-seven hotline and website for runaways and homeless youth. This service may be helpful to you if you can't talk to your parents about what's going on, if you feel a lot of pressure from your friends, or if school stresses you out. Maybe you want to run away from home, because you think that might be the answer. Maybe you've left home and you want your parents to know you're okay but aren't ready to tell them where you are or don't know how to face them. Or maybe you need a shelter and don't know how to find one in your area. Through NRS's message relay and conference call programs, you can begin lines of communication with your parents without divulging your location to them. You can also post on the NRS bulletin board, send an e-mail, or start a live chat by clicking on the red button at the top of the screen on the web page. The site also includes research findings about runaways. Call 1-800-RUNAWAY (1-800-786-2929).

Help for cutters:

- http://insteadofcutting.tumblr.com/thebutterflyproject: The Butterfly Project's goal is to help people who have a problem with self-injuring (such as cutting) and are surrounded by feelings of hopelessness, as well as for anyone who knows someone who has this problem. The site targets people who want to get help, get better, and live a happier life. The website includes a blog, an "ask" box, and useful hotlines. The concept behind the Butterfly Project is that when you feel like you want to cut, instead take a marker or pen and draw a butterfly on your arm or hand, then name the butterfly after a loved one or someone who really wants you to get better. You try to keep the butterfly alive. Check out the site to read how this works and to see the photos of beautiful butterflies others have designed.

- www.healthyplace.com: HealthyPlace.com is the largest consumer mental health site, providing comprehensive, trusted information on psychological disorders and psychiatric medications from both a consumer and an expert point of view. Check out the post on the website titled "Self Injury, Self Harm Statistics and Facts."

- www.twloha.com: To Write Love on Her Arms is a nonprofit movement dedicated to presenting hope and finding help for people struggling with depression, addiction, self-injury, and suicide. TWLOHA began in Orlando, Florida, in 2006, when founder Jamie Tworkowski wrote a story about a friend who struggled with self-injury and addiction and the five days preceding her entry into treatment. The story, which was entitled, "To Write Love on Her Arms," went viral, and T-shirts were initially printed and sold as a way to pay for that friend's treatment. Since then, TWLOHA has become a nonprofit that serves as a bridge to hope and help for people facing the same issues. If you would like more information about the counseling or treatment resources that are available, check out the Find Help page. Also on the website is an online store that sells merchandise, such as T-shirts. While these sales help finance TWLOHA's work, more broadly, every piece of merchandise also has a much bigger purpose as a conversation-starter that can tie supporters together as a community. TWLOHA offers a number of ways to participate in its mission: through the website's blog, college campus chapters, storyteller campaigns, street teams that help get the word out, and an intern program.

Help with bullying issues:

- www.stopbullying.gov: This stop-bullying website provides information on what bullying is, who is at risk, and how you can prevent, respond to, and report cyber- and other bullying. The site targets kids, teens, parents, and educators and includes links to videos and information on policies, laws, and other resources.

- www.7cupsoftea.com: This website is described above, but note that the site contains a link to a video on bullying and information on how to stop it. Click on "Self-Help Guides" at the top of the page, and scroll down to "Bullying."

Help with LGBTQ issues:

- www.thetrevorproject.org: Founded in 1998 by the creators of the Academy Award–winning short film Trevor, the Trevor Project is the leading US organization providing crisis intervention and suicide prevention services to lesbian, gay, bisexual, transgender, and questioning young people (LGBTQ) ages thirteen to twenty-four. You can text, chat with, or talk to someone on the phone twenty-four-seven. Trevor offers online interactive training for adults to help them learn about LGBTQ youth and the specific risks and challenges they face, as well as online training for young adults, and has a search engine to help users find local resources. To connect with trained help via a free, confidential, secure service phone number, call 1-866-488-7386. The site also provides a social networking site for LGBTQ youth and a support center where they and their allies can find answers to frequently asked questions and explore resources related to sexual orientation, gender identity, and more.

2. Want to understand mental health issues, diagnosis, and treatment approaches better?

A number of good sources of information on mental health issues and suicide are available. I have listed a few of the more comprehensive websites below:

- www.nami.org: As noted above, the National Alliance on Mental Illness (NAMI) is a nationwide, grassroots mental health advocacy organization with state chapters. NAMI offers support, education, awareness, and advocacy;

advocates for access to services, treatment, support, and research; and trains grassroots volunteer facilitators who host individual and family support groups in thousands of US communities. Through the toll-free NAMI HelpLine, NAMI provides free referrals, information, and support. Call 1-800-950-NAMI (6264), Monday through Friday, 10 a.m. to 6 p.m. (EST). You can join NAMI in advocating on behalf of individuals and families affected by mental illness. A list of current legislation impacting mental health is available on the website, along with an easy way to contact your legislative representatives. This website is a great place to learn about current public policy issues and is also an avenue for you to participate in influencing those issues.

NAMI also sponsors public awareness events, such as Mental Illness Awareness Week and annual NAMI walks (similar to Race for the Cure walks), in an effort to combat stigmas, promote awareness, and encourage understanding.

- www.mentalhealth.gov: This site provides one-stop access to a wealth of US government information on mental health and mental health problems, a treatment locator (enter your zip code), resources for veterans, information in Spanish, and links to resources that will help you find health insurance that provides mental health coverage.

- www.afsp.org: The American Foundation for Suicide Prevention (AFSP) is a nonprofit organization dedicated exclusively to understanding and preventing suicide through research, education, and advocacy. AFSP funds a significant amount of research, creates educational programs, advocates for public policy, and supports survivors of suicide loss. It also sponsors annual Out of the Darkness community walks to build awareness. The website contains a lot of good information on suicide—including information on understanding and coping with suicide and the latest research.

AFSP holds annual advocacy forums to bring together suicide-prevention advocates, volunteers, and AFSP staff to network, share the latest research, and provide the public and policymakers with the information and tools they need to be effective advocates in preventing suicide. Participants from around the country share their personal stories and experiences with suicide, engage members of Congress in discussion on important suicide prevention issues, and share AFSP's federal policy priorities.

If you are interested in advocacy, you can become an advocate through AFSP. Advocates educate their state and local leaders and communities about suicide, help to shape laws and policies, and change the way others think and talk about suicide and mental illness. (Click on the "Advocacy and Public Policy" link at the top of the website's home page.)

- www.nlm.nih.gov/medlineplus: The National Institutes of Health (NIH) maintains a website, MedlinePlus, as a source of medical information for the public. Produced by the National Library of Medicine, it offers reliable, up-to-date health information—anytime, anywhere, for free—about diseases, conditions, and wellness issues in language you can understand. You can use MedlinePlus to learn about the latest treatments, look up information on a drug or supplement, find out the meanings of words, or view medical videos or illustrations. You can also get links to the latest medical research on your topic or find out about clinical trials on a disease or condition. MedlinePlus has a wealth of information on mental health and behavior-related topics, and its Suicide Health Topics page includes overviews, current suicide information, and research and reference links.

- www.ibpf.org: The mission of the International Bipolar Foundation is to improve understanding and treatment of bipolar disorder. It's focus in on research, promoting care and erasing the stigma through education. Kay Redfield Jamison, PhD, professor of psychiatry at Johns Hopkins University Medical School, world-renowned authority on mood disorders, and author of numerous books on mood disorders, serves on the Bipolar Foundation's scientific advisory board.

- www.bipolar-foundation.org: As of 2015, Equilibrium: The Bipolar Foundation is in start-up mode. The foundation's goal is to become a worldwide network of people with bipolar disorder; it is unique because of its two-way partnership between those affected and clinician researchers. The website is designed as a place for users to learn more information on bipolar disorder, to share experiences, and to get involved. At the "Choice" and "Medication" links, you can find up-to-the-minute information about medications used for the treatment of bipolar disorder and other associated problems.

- www.dbsalliance.org: The Depression and Bipolar Support Alliance's goal is to provide hope, help, support, and education to improve the lives of people who have mood disorders. The organization is peer directed. The website has a database of support groups (click on the link and enter your location to find a local support group, or access an online support group through the website). Use the website's "Find a Pro" link to identify a professional or facility that others with bipolar disorder have recommended or to recommend a local expert or facility yourself. In 2016, the "Find a Pro" database seems to be sparsely populated but may be worth checking. The site includes an audio and video library and podcasts.

- www.behavioraltech.org: The Linehan Institute provides information on dialectical behavior therapy (DBT), a cognitive behavioral treatment that was originally developed to treat chronically suicidal individuals diagnosed with borderline personality disorder (BPD) and that is now recognized as the gold standard psychological treatment for this population. Research has shown that DBT is effective in treating a wide range of other disorders, such as substance dependence, depression, post-traumatic stress disorder (PTSD), and eating disorders. This website has a link to Behavioral Tech's Clinical Resource Directory (CRD), which lists programs and therapists that have gone through training with Behavioral Tech or the Behavioral Research & Therapy Clinics at the University of Washington.

3. Need help finding a psychiatrist, psychologist, psychiatric nurse therapist, or treatment program? Looking for consumer information about psychiatrists and treatment program ratings or certifications?

If you're looking for a mental health professional in your community, here are some tips and online resources to get you started. If you have a physician whom you trust, that can be a good place to begin. Talk to school counselors, too—they may be able to provide a recommendation. Ask everyone you feel comfortable talking to if they know of anyone good. If you find someone on one of the sites below, you should do your own background check.

- www.samhsa.gov: The Substance Abuse and Mental Health Services Administration (SAMHSA) has a treatment locator, an online source of information for people seeking treatment facilities in the United States or US territories for substance abuse/addiction and/or mental health problems. To access the treatment locator, click on the box that says "Behavioral Health Treatment Locator" in the "Find Help" menu and enter your city or zip code. If you click on the service you are looking for—say, mental health—you can further narrow your search. This is a resource that my crisis line uses frequently to find local help for our callers.

- www.psychologytoday.com: Psychology Today has an online database of psychologists, therapists, counselors, group therapy, and treatment centers in the United States and Canada. The site allows you to search by location and specialty. Information on each specialist includes a bio, qualifications, accepted insurance plans, and client focus. Professionals pay a fee to be listed and provide the content for the database. It's a good starting point, but, as with all the sites, you need to do your own background checking. Enter your zip code or city, and click on the "Find a Therapist" link.

- www.abct.org: The Association for Behavioral & Cognitive Therapies (ABCT) website includes a CBT therapist database. Click on the "Find a CBT Therapist" link and enter your location. This database includes only ABCT members.

- www.aacap.org: Use the American Academy of Child and Adolescent Psychiatry's (AACAP's) "Child and Adolescent Psychiatrist Finder" link on the main page to find a child and adolescent psychiatrist near you. Also included on this website is a series of very informative guides, called "ParentsMedGuide" (for ADHD, bipolar disorder, and depression) and "PhysiciansMedGuide," which were designed to help individuals make informed decisions about childhood and adolescent depression treatment. This site also includes information on clinical trials—what they are, who conducts them, and how to participate.

- http://clinicaltrials.gov: This is a registry-and-results database of publicly and privately supported clinical studies of human participants conducted around the world. Check this site for available clinical trials if you are interested in participating.

- www.healthgrades.com: On this website, you can look up doctors and child and adolescent psychiatrists by location and specialty. The site provides board certifications, education, experience, philosophy, and patient satisfaction ratings and identifies sanctions, board actions, and malpractice claims, if any.

- www.consumer.ftc.gov: The Federal Trade Commission provides consumer information on residential treatment programs for teens and "troubled youth," as well as guidance on what to look for, links to program certifications, and other sources of information for parents. Enter "Residential Treatment Programs for Teens" in the search button.

4. Want to learn about the latest research? Influence policy? Support research and mental health services?

- www.nimh.nih.gov: With a budget of close to $1.5 billion a year, the National Institute of Mental Health (NIMH) is the largest research organization in the world specializing in mental health. The NIMH website includes information on the symptoms, diagnosis, and treatment of mental disorders, as well as on clinical trials and research. NIMH is funding projects for the BRAIN Initiative through competitive grants. You can also find information on recent and upcoming legislative and policy activity related to mental health and resources for science educators. You can subscribe to the "National Institute of Mental Health Weekly Digest Bulletin" (delivered through e-mail) to stay on top of the latest research findings.

- www.bbrfoundation.org: The Brain and Behavior Research Foundation (BBRF) is the largest philanthropic organization dedicated to research across all brain and behavior disorders. Since 1987, the BBRF has awarded over $320 million in grants to scientists around the world that will lead to advances and breakthroughs in brain and behavior disorder scientific research. One hundred percent of all donor contributions for research are invested in grants leading to discoveries in understanding causes and improving treatments of disorders in children and adults, such as depression, schizophrenia, anxiety, autism, bipolar disorder, attention-deficit hyperactivity disorder, post-traumatic stress disorder, and obsessive-compulsive disorder.

  You can sign up to receive the latest research news in the BBRF weekly e-newsletter by clicking on "eNews Signup" in the top-right corner of the website's home page.

- www.afsp.org: American Foundation for Suicide Prevention. See description above.

5. Looking for alternative treatment approaches?

A number of new smartphone applications are designed to provide real-time "coaching" or immediate feedback to a user about their feelings about and reactions to a situation. Buyer beware: these apps haven't been around long enough for us to know just how effective they are, and I have no personal experience with them, but they hold promise—especially for people who won't go to a therapist or don't have access to one. *Psychology Today* published a January 2013 article entitled "Top 10 Mental Health Apps." Below, I have listed a few of the apps that the article identifies, along with an excerpt describing each. Many of these types of apps are meant to be used in conjunction with conventional therapy. See the article at http://psych central.com/blog/archives/2013/01/16/top-10-mental-health-apps/.

- BellyBio: a free application that teaches a deep-breathing technique useful in fighting anxiety and stress.

- Operations Reach Out: This free intervention tool helps people who are having suicidal thoughts to reassess their thinking and get help.

- DBT Diary Card and Skills Coach: Based on dialectical behavior therapy (DBT), developed by psychologist Marsha Lineha, this application is a resource of self-help skills, reminders of the therapy principles, and coaching tools for coping.

- Optimism: Track your moods, keep a journal, and chart your recovery progress with this comprehensive tool for depression, bipolar disorder, and anxiety disorders.

Notes

1. HealthyPlace.com, "Self Injury, Self Harm Statistics and Facts," accessed January 12, 2016, http://www.healthyplace.com/abuse/self-injury/self-injury-self-harm-statistics-and-facts/.

2. Turning Winds Academic Institute, "Success Stories," accessed January 12, 2016, https://www.turningwinds.com/stories/.

3. Eagle Ranch Academy, "Philosophy," accessed January 19, 2016, http://eagleranchacademy.com/philosophy/.

4. Redcliff Ascent, "Who We Are," accessed January 12, 1016, http://www.redcliffascent.com/about-us/.

5. Ibid.

6. Arivaca Boys Ranch home page, accessed January 12, 2016, https://www.linkedin.com/company/arivaca-boys-ranch.

7. New Haven, "Therapy," accessed January 12, 2016, http://www.newhavenrtc.com/relationships/.

8. Federal Trade Commission, "Residential Treatment Programs for Teens," accessed 1/12/16, http://www.consumer.ftc.gov/articles/0185-residential-treatment-programs-teens.

9. National Runaway Safeline, "Frequently Asked Questions," accessed January 10, 2016, http://www.1800runaway.org/about-us/faq/.

10. Substance Abuse and Mental Health Services Administration, "Current Statistics on the Prevalence and Characteristics of People Experiencing Homelessness in the United States," accessed January 10, 2016, http://homeless.samhsa.gov/ResourceFiles/hrc_factsheet.pdf.

11. Ken Krehbiel, "Diagnosis and Treatment of Bipolar Disorder: Author Kay Redfield Jamison Details What Is Known, and What Psychologists Are Still Learning, About Bipolar Illness," *Monitor on Psychology* 31, no. 9 (October 2000), accessed January 10, 2016, http://www.apa.org/monitor/oct00/bipolar.aspx.

12. National Institute of Mental Illness, "Annual Total Direct and Indirect Costs of Serious Mental Illness (2002)," accessed January 10, 2016,
http://www.nimh.nih.gov/health/statistics/cost/index.shtml.

13. National Institute of Mental Health, "National Institute of Mental Health Strategic Plan for Research," accessed January 10, 2016, http://www.nimh.nih.gov/about/strategic-planning-reports /index.shtml.

14. National Alliance for Suicide Prevention, "A Prioritized Research Agenda for Suicide Prevention: An Action Plan to Save Lives," accessed January 10, 2016,
http://actionallianceforsuicideprevention.org/task-force/research-pri oritization.

15. National Institute of Mental Health, "Annual Total Direct and Indirect Costs of Serious Mental Illness (2002)," accessed January 19, 2016,
http://www.nimh.nih.gov/health/statistics/cost/index.shtml.

16. National Institute of Mental Health, "Total Expenditures for the Five Most Costly Medical Conditions (1996 vs. 2006)," accessed January 19, 2016,
http://www.nimh.nih.gov/health/statistics/cost/total-expenditures-f or-the-five-most-costly-medical-conditions-1996-vs-2006.shtml.

17. National Institute of Mental Health, "Mental Health Expenditures as a Percent of All Health Care Expenditures (2003)," accessed January 19, 2016,

http://www.nimh.nih.gov/health/statistics/cost/mental-health-expe
nditures-as-a-percent-of-all-health-care-expenditures-2003.shtml.

18. U.S. Department of Justice, Office of Justice Programs, Bureau
of Justice Statistics, "Study Finds More Than Half of All Prison and
Jail Inmates Have Mental Health Problems," accessed January 19,
2016, http://www.bjs.gov/content/pub/press/mhppjipr.cfm.

19. Thomas R. Insel, Pamela Y. Collins, and Steven E. Hyman,
"Darkness Invisible: The Hidden Global Costs of Mental Illness,"
Foreign Affairs Journal, accessed January 19, 2016,
https://www.foreignaffairs.com/articles/africa/darkness-invisible.

20. National Institute of Mental Health, "The Teen Brain: Still Under Construction," accessed January 19, 2016,
http://www.nimh.nih.gov/health/publications/the-teen-brain-still-u
nder-construction/index.shtml.

21. Veronica Meade-Kelly, "Researchers Shed New Light on
Schizophrenia," *Harvard Gazette*, accessed January 19, 2016,
http://news.harvard.edu/gazette/story/2014/07/researchers-shed-ne
w-light-on-schizophrenia/.

22. Neuronetics, "NeuroStar TMS TherapySystem," accessed January
19, 2016,
https://neurostar.com/hcp/neurostar-tms-therapy/efficacy/.

23. Neuronetics, "NeuroStar TMS Therapy—Help Your Patients
Reach Remission and Stay There," accessed January 19, 2016,
https://neurostar.com/hcp/neurostar-tms-therapy/efficacy/#NIMH.

24. National Institute of Mental Health, "Director's Blog: Ketamine," accessed January 19, 2016,
http://www.nimh.nih.gov/about/director/2014/ketamine.shtml.

Acknowledgments

First I want to acknowledge my daughter Sadie, whose writing and activism inspired me and gave me the courage to write this book. Thank you Sadie, if only in spirit, for your beautiful writing. Without it, this book would not exist. Thank you Sadie for helping me and all other readers better understand how mental illness can make a person feel on the inside.

Thanks to my initial coach David Miller who helped me develop a structure for the book and helped me find my voice. I can still hear his constant reminders – show don't tell! Many thanks to my editor Merridawn Duckler who provided encouragement at those times when I just didn't think I could finish the book. She patiently had me read out loud section after section of the book. It is amazing how you can identify poorly written phrases, repetitious language or discontinuities when you read something out loud! Thank you Heather Guidero for copyediting and your encouraging words.

I am grateful to Annette Armstrong, Austin Meadows, Rick Mehlman, PhD, Patricia Rengel, PhD, Leslie Taylor, PhD, and Vicki Zarrell for their willingness to serve as beta readers. They provided invaluable advice and feedback.

And to my SheWritesPress publishing team - thank you Brooke Warner, Lauren Wise, Annie Tucker and many SheWritesPress authors for the advice, guidance and support that eventually produced this book. I can't imagine how I would ever have been able to produce this on my own! Of course a book doesn't sell well without publicity so thanks to my publicist Eva Zimmerman.

Finally, thanks to my husband and life partner Dennis Ladick for his never ending support and encouragement, for sharing his memories even when painful, for bearing with my tears of grief as I wrote and for his invaluable contributions.

About the Author

After a six-year battle with her teenage daughter's depression and subsequent suicide, Karen Meadows left behind her successful career in the energy industry to immerse herself in mental health issues. She spent years reading about mental illness and reading her daughter's extensive writing. She volunteered on a crisis line and at homeless youth centers, and serves on the Oregon Chapter of the American Foundation for Suicide Prevention Board of Directors. She also serves on the Oregon Health Authority's Children's System Advisory Committee. This committee advises state policies regarding children's mental health. She has an Executive MBA from UW-Madison, an MS in Engineering from UC Boulder, and a BS in Mechanical Engineering from UC Berkeley. Meadows lives with her husband and two cats in Portland, Oregon.